A PLACE OF PLACELESSNESS:
Hekeng People's Heritage

A Place of Placelessness:

Hekeng People's Heritage

Renyu Wang

LEIDEN UNIVERSITY PRESS

Archaelogical Studies Leiden University is published by Leiden University Press, the Netherlands

Series editors: M. E. R. G. N. Jansen and H. Kamermans
Cover design: Joanne Porck
Coverpage image: Renyu Wang
Lay out: Samira Damato
Illustrations: Renyu Wang

ISBN 978 90 8728 273 8
e-ISBN 978 94 0060 279 3
NUR 682

This book is distributed in North America by the University of Chicago Press.

Table of Contents

FOR WANG JIE

Acknowledgements

I am very grateful to all staff of the Heritage Center of Fujian Provincial Museum for their help during the investigations from 2010 to 2014. I would particularly like to acknowledge the help of Director Lou Jianlong, Mr. Zhang Jinde, Mr. Lan Dongyang, Mr. Chen Jianyun and Mr. Chen Yu. Several scholars in Leiden University offered me generous help in the past four years. Profound gratitude goes to Prof. dr. Willem J.H. Willems, Prof. dr. Maarten E. R. G. N. Jansen, Prof. dr. Frank N. Pieke, Prof. dr. Ian Lilley and Dr. Shu-li Wang. The writing of this thesis can be traced back to 2012 when I began to discuss the research proposal with Prof. Willems. Before Professor Willems passed away in late 2014, he kindly found a new supervisor for each of his PhD students, and so Prof. Jansen began to supervise me in late 2014. Professor Jansen was very enthusiastic and took this PhD supervision very seriously. Apart from providing me with the opportunities to come over to Leiden, he invited Prof. dr. Frank N. Pieke, Prof. dr. Ian Lilley and Dr. Shu-li Wang to join in the supervision work with their Sinological, historical and anthropological expertise and cultural heritage perspectives. Prof. Frank Pieke offered me insightful advice on improving the thesis and many useful references. Prof. Ian Lilley patiently marked up the thesis, made stimulating suggestions and even kindly helped with checking the English. Dr. Shuli Wang read through all the versions of the manuscript and made valuable observations. Special mention goes to Dr. Thomas F. King, who enriched my knowledge of cultural resource management and also helped edit the thesis. To Ms. Rosemary Robson, who skillfully and patiently helped me with editing the English. To Professor Wang Xuerong, Ms. Jin Wenxin and Ms. Ge Meng for always encouraging me to proceed with this PhD research. Sincere thanks go to my wife Dr. Chen Xi, who looked after our only son Django when I was not at home. In August this year, just as I was finishing my thesis, my beloved father passed away. I would like to dedicate this book to him.

Wang Renyu, Leiden

Preface

THE RISE OF MASSIVE DEFENSE STRUCTURES IN THE FUJIAN REGION AND THE TULOU BUILDINGS BETWEEN THE MID-SIXTEENTH AND EARLY SEVENTEENTH CENTURY

In the 1950s, Chinese architectural historians became aware of the existence of fortress-like buildings conventionally known as '*tulou*' (literally earthen mansion) inhabited by the local residents in southern Fujian. *Tulou* buildings are impressive rectangular or circular structures, with load-bearing earthen walls up to three to five stories high, each housing up to eighty families (or even more) and resembling a small fortified town. According to Huang Hanmin,[1] there are over 3,000 *tulou* buildings scattered throughout the river valleys in western and southern Fujian and northeastern Guangdong (Zheng, 2012; Wu, 2008). Since the 1950s, architectural historians have been referring to these massive land features 'Hakka *tulou*' (Needham, 1971; Kobayashi, 2013), assuming that they have a unique association with the Hakka people; a perception that is inaccurate. The Minnan and Chaozhou people also erected *tulou* buildings in exactly the same way (Huang, 1987; Wu, 2008). The misapprehension, as Chen Chunsheng (2011) suggests, could have arisen from various researchers' ignorance of the fact that a large number of *tulou* buildings in traditional Minnan and Chaozhou territories had been flattened by the Qing Imperial Court during of the implementation of the Coastal Evacuation (*qian hai*) Policy between 1661 and 1683, creating a depopulated zone to defend against Zheng Chengong's attacks. At that time *tulou* was already an important architectural type that had been very popular since the middle Ming dynasty among the Hakka, Minnan and Chaozhou rural inhabitants, the majority of whom lived in the mountainous area located between southwestern Fujian and northeastern Guangdong, that is, the southwestern peripheral area of the Southeast Coast Economic Macro-region (Skinner,1965) (Fig. 1).

The mid-sixteenth through to the early-seventeenth century AD was the most important period for the formation of the traditional lineage[2] settlements that constructed earthen defense structures in Fujian. By the middle Ming dynasty, the lineage had gradually evolved into a fundamental organizational unit recognized by the government and used in assessing figures for conscription and taxation. Lineage unity and cohesiveness was cemented by the spread of 'inclusive halls' – that is, ancestral halls and temples available for use to all statuses in a lineage (Szonyi, 2002). This unruly period of the change in dynasties was also characterized by the rise of widespread robberies, plundering and massacres by pirates and mountain bandits. Their threats exerted a dramatic effect on rural society throughout the Fujian region. The local gentry in almost every rural area of the province (the Appendix) began to take the lead in organizing local defense. With the government's encouragement, they donated funds and were in the forefront of their communities in the construction of the forts. Importantly, it should be emphasized, as Szonyi (2002) has noted, that local defense primarily meant defense of one's kin. Consequently, it was the agnatic ties among residents of these rural areas that decisively structured defense patterns.

1.http://www.chinanews.com/cul/2011/08-22/3274963.shtml.

2. As a working definition, Roger M. Keesing (1976) gives a good explanation of the terms lineage and clan, 'A *lineage* is a descent group consisting of people patrilineally or matrilineally descended from a known ancestor through a series of links they can trace... A larger descent category...[comprising people] who believe they are descended from a common ancestor but do not know the actual connections is called a *clan*.'

Chen and Zheng (1985) established a complete typology of the earthen fort-like structures widely distributed throughout the rural areas of Fujian. In their typology, fort-like structures can be divided into three primary forms, namely: walled-settlements (*cheng*),[3] walled-dwellings (*bao*) and home-forts (*jiabao*). In the historical records, the local people in Fujian rural areas usually used the term '*cheng*' (city) to describe walled settlements, because in their form they emulated the walled enclosures in the local urban centers, such as towns and county seats. Settlements with various kinds of walled-enclosures are also found in northeastern Guangdong, even extending to the New Territories of Hong Kong, as Freedman (1966), Oxfeld (2010) and Wu (2008) have discussed. Peasants who lived in central Fujian (for example, Datian) and eastern Fujian (for instance, Nantai to the south of the Fuzhou region) (Szonyi, 2002) built huge fortified dwellings, each encompassing a set of courtyard compounds and peasants in the rural areas of south Fujian likewise constructed the *tulou* that strongly resemble them as home-forts. In a nutshell, there was a diversity of earthen domestic defensive systems, but unquestionably the widespread construction of huge fort-like structures of all kinds originated during the social upheavals that began to plague China during the mid-Ming dynasty. Faced with the challenge of the serious threats posed by pirates and bandits and unable to cope with these, the local government loosened its control over the rural areas. Thrown back on their own resources, peasants had to place their complete reliance on their own lineages and construct earthen defense structures in various forms to defend themselves. One of their achievements born of this turbulence is the development of *tulou* architecture.

The influence these earthen structures exerted on the lineage villages in determining the final layout of the settlement varied greatly between areas. Some villages, whose lineage members had built strong walls around the settlements, were eventually transformed into small rural cities. Some even had wide moats. Others only built provisionally used earthen forts, preserving the major part of their original settlements. These developments were not confined to western Fujian (for example, Shanghang county), but are also found in the rural areas of the Mei and Han River Basins in adjacent northeastern Guangdong (Wu, 2008). In central and eastern Fujian, the addition of earthen forts to villages had little impact on settlement patterns. The historical records of the Ming and Qing (the Appendix) state that, although the people who lived in these two areas did have huge forts, they moved into them only when danger was imminent. By contrast, the peasants who lived in the southwestern peripheral area of the Southeast Mega-region eventually chose to live permanently inside their *tulou* buildings. Unlike the settlements in other parts of Fujian and Guangdong, in the small river valleys occupied by the Hakka and Minnan people the earthen defense structures evolved into the dominant dwelling form. The western and southern foothills of the Daimao Mountain became the foci of *tulou* distribution. In terms of administrative units, settlements located in Yongding, Longyan, Nanjing, Pinghe, Hua'an, and Zhangpu on the Fujian side and Raoping and Dabu on the Guangdong side make up the loci of the huge earthen residences. (Fig. 2)

RESEARCH ORIENTATION

The use of *tulou* buildings as a tourist attraction began in the early1990s (Kobayashi, 2013). In 1991, the local government of Yongding county took the first steps toward setting up the *Yongdingxian lüyouju* (Yongding County Bureau of Tourism) to manage *tulou* tourist resource development on county level. In 1993, the *Yongding tulou lüxingshe* (Yongding *Tulou* Travel Agency) was established. Touristic use of such 'old houses' in the Yongding countryside marks a milestone in the history the adaptive re-use of *tulou* buildings. At the beginning of the 1990s, growing numbers of the local Hakka and Minnan people were seeking new ways to make use of their ancestral properties. Later, in the mid-1990s, the publication of essays about tourist

Right: Fig. 1 The Southeastern Coast Economic Macro-region, Hakka distribution and *tulou* distribution (map based on Leong Sow-Theng, *Migration and Ethnicity in Chinese History: Hakkas, Pengmin and Their Neighbors,* Stanford University Press, 1997).

3. Chen Chunsheng (2011) calls it a '*cun zhai*' (lit. village city).

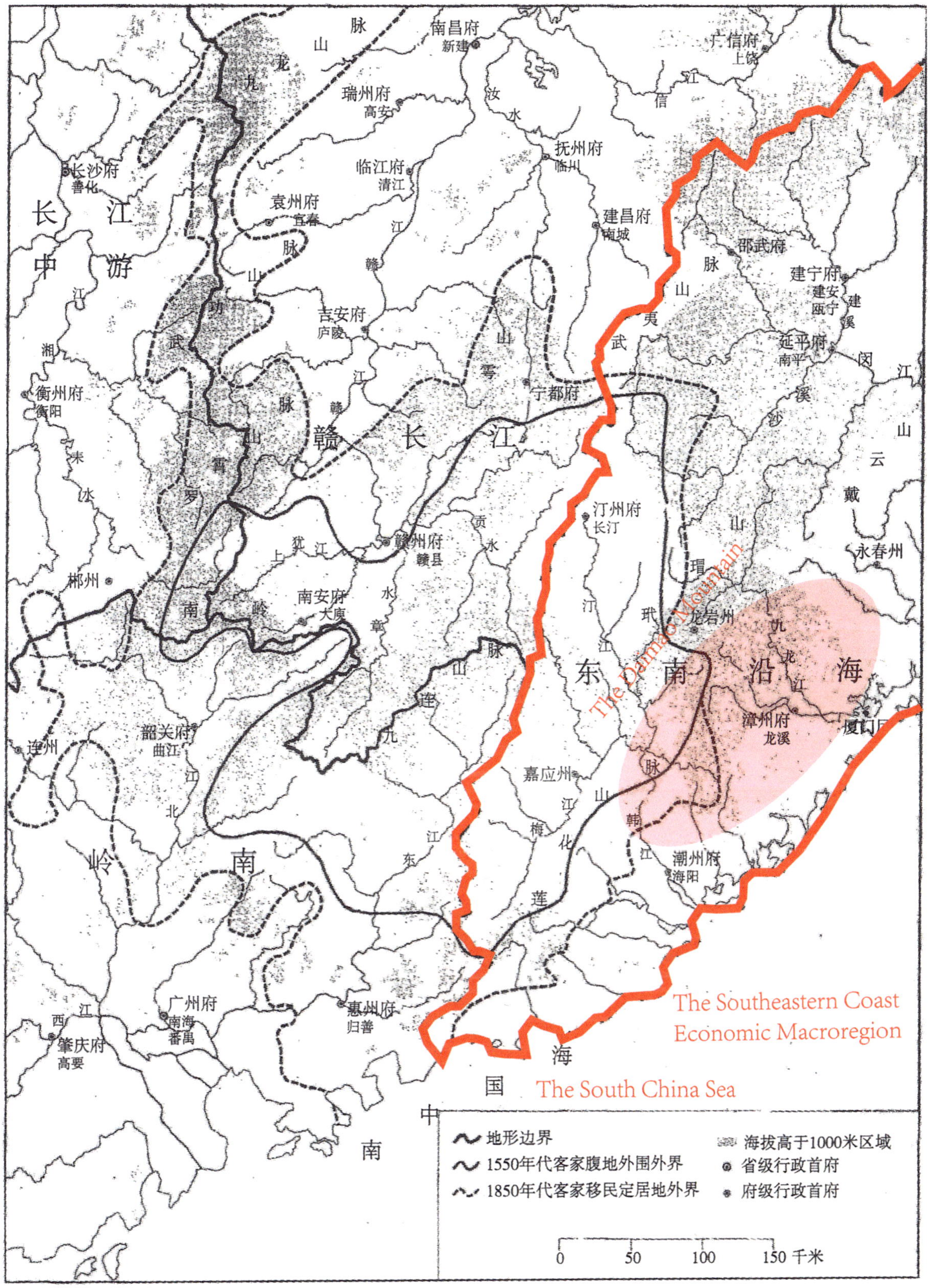
The Danmao Mountain
The Southeastern Coast
Economic Macroregion
The South China Sea
南昌府
新建
广信府
上饶
瑞州府
高安
抚州府
临川
临江府
清江
长沙府
善化
袁州府
宜春
建昌府
南城
邵武府
建宁府
建安
瓯宁
吉安府
庐陵
延平府
南平
衡州府
衡阳
宁都府
汀州府
长汀
赣州府
赣县
永春州
郴州
南安府
大庾
龙岩州
漳州府
龙溪
厦门
韶关府
曲江
连州
嘉应州
潮州府
海阳
广州府
南海
番禺
惠州府
归善
肇庆府
高要
长江中游
赣长江
东南沿海
岭南
南中国海
地形边界
1550年代客家腹地外围外界
1850年代客家移民定居地外界
海拔高于1000米区域
省级行政首府
府级行政首府
0
50
100
150 千米

development increased dramatically.[4] Since 2000, it seems that articles in academic journals about *tulou* preservation and conservation have prevailed over those written solely for exploring their economic value.[5] The preponderance of the former has been even more striking in the 2010s. Significantly, nearly all the regulations governing *tulou* preservation and protection have been made only since the early 2000s. As will be shown in the following chapters, although interest in profit-oriented use and alteration has been stifled in many ways by the officially authorized *tulou* heritage management discourse, spontaneous, non-governmental-based re-planning, development, adaptation and renovation have flourished among the peasants. In short, the active use and re-use of ancestral properties by some rural residents have already challenged the strict regulatory provisions laid down in heritage laws and the procedures set out by specialists with conservation expertise.

Until 2013, architectural heritage experts were appealing for an uncompromising standard for *tulou* preservation. They advocated that the government and people should guarantee that the great historical treasure represented by *tulou* be kept intact and transmitted down to future generations. Realistically, in view of the large number of structures involved and the need of residents to be able to lead their own lives, these wishes seem unattainable. By that time because of these obstacles, some government officials were beginning to be aware of these infeasibilities. Consequently, in 2013 the former director of the *Zhongguo Guojia Wenwujü* (the State Administration of Cultural Heritage, SACH), Li Xiaojie, proposed a new strategy for the preservation of traditional settlement architecture. Li (*China News* reporters, 2014) believed that preservation should be carried out in tandem with utilization. He even suggested the requirement that a specified plan for heritage use be included in any building preservation plan. He argued that these sorts of management plans should take the means of livelihood and the current needs of the local people seriously into consideration. He insisted that this was a sustainable way of going about preservation. His proposal has suggested a possible way to preserve ancestral properties by using them, and is one that this thesis supports wholeheartedly. As will be analyses in this thesis, the preservation of old dwellings is by no means a simple black-and-white affair. It is impossible for heritage authorities on any level to exercise unconditional control over how buildings – like other complex systems – metabolize. In fact, settlements and buildings have never stopped changing. They are in fact living, organic wholes. Any alterations to buildings reflect new demands felt by local residents. Buildings in a rural context, including but not limited to dwellings, survive by changing and adaptation. How the changes come about and to what extent they actually happen are both complex questions. Any possible answer to these matters depends on the stakeholders involved. The decisions made and compromises achieved by stakeholders determine to what extent a settlement or a dwelling can be preserved, restored, presented to the visitors, and/or committed to adaptive use. However, when it comes to the nitty-gritty, are all the stakeholders able to sit at the same table?

Who are the stakeholders in this sort of discourse? In most cases – in theory – local peasants are the main parties with control over and investments in *tulou*. The drawback is that peasants are generally considered to be the most disadvantaged social groups in the country. They are typically beset by three types of problem. The first snag is that, although their ownership via ancestral inheritance is protected by such fundamental laws as the *Property Law*, their right to cultural property is not properly guaranteed by heritage laws. The second stumbling-block is that the attitudes of the heritage authorities and the effect of heritage designation can have a critical impact on their properties. The third obstacle is that they are having to deal with the stress of survival and are in competition with urban centers. These hubs lure away the young and exploit the rural villages in the interests of tourism. At present, one form of competition is revolving around cultural heritage: the local residents 'ancestral' properties,

Right: Fig. 2 The distribution of tulou architecture in southern Fujian and northern Guangdong (map based on Leong Sow-Theng, Migration and Ethnicity in Chinese History: Hakkas, Pengmin and Their Neighbors, Stanford University Press, 1997).

4. According to the CNKI statistics (http://www.cnki.net/).
5. *Ibid.*

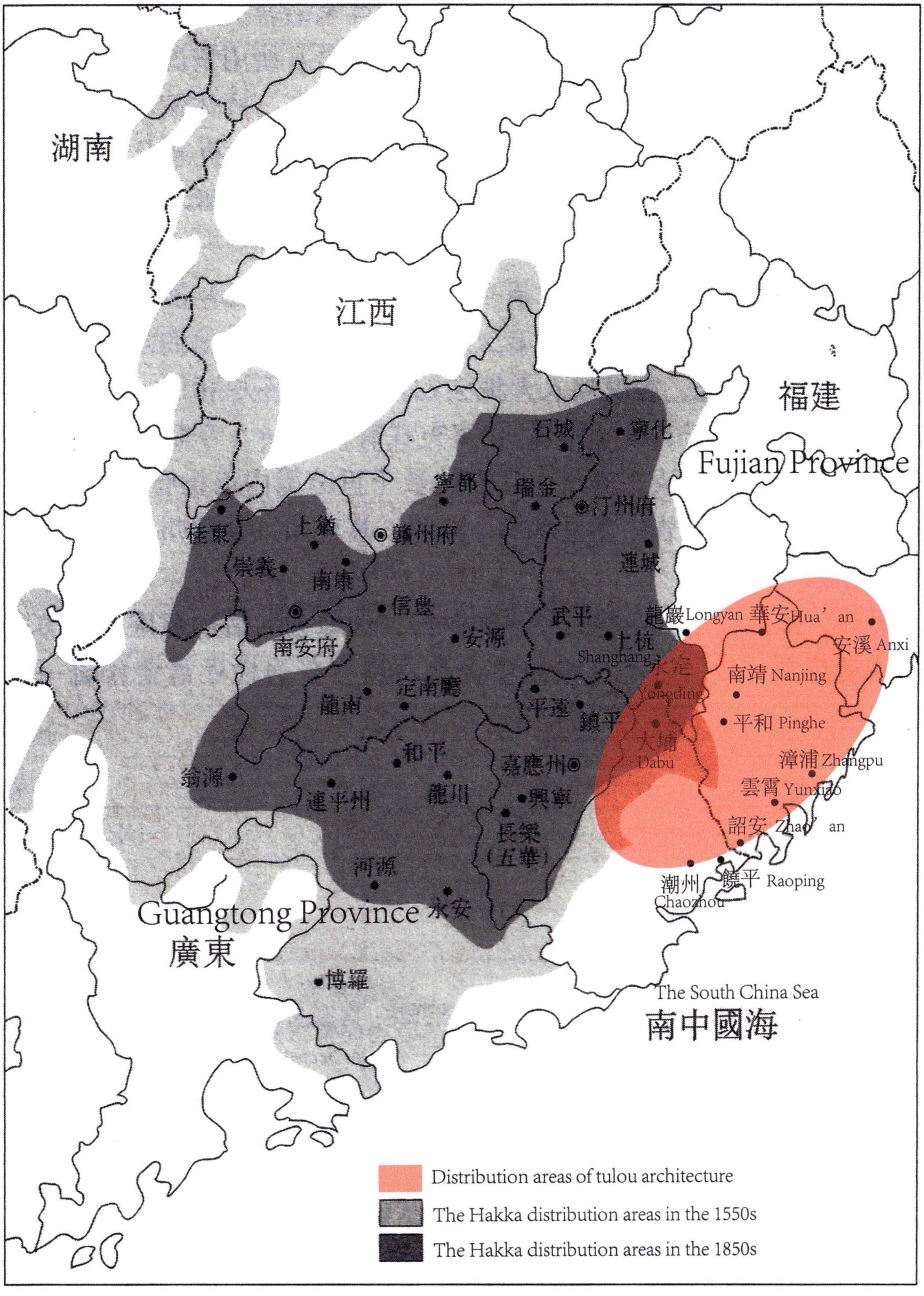
湖南
江西
福建
Fujian Province
石城
寧化
寧都
瑞金
汀州府
桂東
上猶
贛州府
崇義
南康
連城
信豊
南安府
安源
龍巖 Longyan
華安 Hua' an
安溪 Anxi
武平
上杭
Shanghang
永定
Yongding
南靖 Nanjing
定南廳
龍南
平遠
鎮平
平和 Pinghe
大埔
Dabu
和平
嘉應州
漳浦 Zhangpu
翁源
連平州
龍川
興寧
雲霄 Yunxiao
長樂
(五華)
詔安 Zhao' an
河源
潮州
Chaozhou
饒平 Raoping
Guangtong Province
廣東
永安
博羅
The South China Sea
南中國海
Distribution areas of tulou architecture
The Hakka distribution areas in the 1550s
The Hakka distribution areas in the 1850s

'old houses' in particular. As will be elaborated on in later chapters, the peasants form a social group whose continued existence is required by a number of relevant authorities in the outside world. By law, the rural collectives are the masters of their land, but the uses to which rural individuals can put land are restricted and effectively limited by the interests of other stakeholders, notably the state and the local authorities. In practice, citing and paraphrasing the principles and standards of the international heritage regime, on behalf of the Chinese public a local government can require rural residents to preserve their decaying dwellings as they represent a benefit for urbanites with whom they are not personally acquainted. Similarly, tourist attraction development, heavily inclined toward mountain spaces and vistas, might require whole settlements to be preserved unaltered as part of the 'unchanging' scenery. Under these circumstances, any strongly felt local need to redevelop or rebuild is usually ignored.

Issues involving rural heritage, especially the preservation of old houses, have become hot topics of discussion in China in the last decade, inspiring articles in diverse newspapers and magazines as well as in academic journals. Unlike agricultural fields, the patrilocal residences common in the expansive rural areas of China have long been viewed as private property, not only by the peasants themselves but in practice also by the government authorities. This was true even during the Land Reform in the 1950s and the radical era of the Anti-Four Olds campaign in the mid-1960s (Oxfeld, 2010). The essential problem is that *lao fangzi*, literally translated as old houses, are not one solid block. They encompass diverse forms, uses, functions, ownerships and ancestral trusts founded by lineage segments on different ritual levels (Freedman, 1958). On the whole, changes in a settlement's buildings and structures are a reflection of the needs of both individuals and upper-level lineage segments. Illogically, among heritage experts and authorities, changes that have occurred in the past are usually deemed part of a building's history, whereas contemporary alterations in response to the same needs as those felt in the past are regarded as inauthentic and deleterious to the building's integrity, and therefore inacceptable. Conversely, for local residents change is a continuous metabolic process. Consequently it is of the utmost importance to understand the nature of *lao fangzi* as understood by those who live in them.

The most vital point is that these dwellings are an ancestral inheritance the peasants have been bequeathed from their forebears. In precise terms, they are the properties belonging to each household in a lineage village. They stand in contrast to edifices like ancestral halls and temples that are collective properties. Freedman (1958) and Szonyi (2002) have both explored the basic features of ancestral halls and temples. Unquestionably, although it is true that ancestral halls have become more open since the seventeenth century in an endeavor to include as many lineage members as possible, both the ownership of the buildings and the trust that is responsible for each building in the name of the founders are very strictly controlled and managed by only a few individuals or lineage segments in the descent line. In short, lineage members have the right to make offerings in the halls, but ownership remains in the hands of the local gentry families and important donors. The Land Reform in the 1950s did undoubtedly have an effect on the ownership of halls and temples. It seems that since that time, peasants in South China have often preferred to adopt the belief that the ancestral halls and temples should belong to the lineage as a whole. This idea has been gathering growing numbers of adherents since the 1980s, when the Cultural Revolution was officially terminated and the state began to embrace traditional cultural revitalization warmly. Since a large number of ancestral halls and temples were destroyed between 1966 and 1976, the value of the remaining halls and temples have increased for their lineage members who have returned to the observance of their ancestral cults. Unlike residential buildings and structures, that are heritable estates naturally transmitted to descendants, halls and temples cannot be inherited by individuals, and to a large degree they are the public property of the village. Home shrines (*tang*) are similar to halls and temples in terms of ownership. Being on the lowest level of the layered ancestor cult system, they are usually established as part of a household compound. In many cases, home shrines are direct metamorphoses of the old houses once lived in by ancestors. Within three to five generations after the death of these ancestors, their residences could have begun to be used by their descendants as places at which to make offerings to them. Consequently, they are in effect owned by some of the major branches descended from the initial nuclear family (Freedman, 1966). In view of these legal principles, shrines, halls and temples should be thought of as public or collective properties.

The second important point to be pondered is that, apart from private or collective ownership, buildings and structures designated *zhongdian wenwu baohu danwei* (cultural sites under government protection) by the state are in many cases regarded as the property of the country. China's *Cultural Heritage Law*, the *Wenwu Baohufa*, first came into force in 1982. Its fifth clause states: 'Archaeological sites (*gu yizhi*), ancient burials (*gu muzang*) and grottoes/caves are the property of the country as a whole. Designated sites such as important monuments, ancient architectures, stone carvings, wall paintings, representative buildings and other immovable features of the contemporary past (*jinxiandai*) also belong to the country, unless otherwise noted.' In Chinese heritage discourse, important buildings and monuments can be designated the property of the nation and state on three levels, namely: the county level (*xianji*), the provincial level (*shengji*) and the national level (*guojiaji*). At whichever level a site is designated, it is under the strict protection by the government. Clause Six of the *Wenwu Baohufa* states private and collective owners should use a heritage site in full compliance with heritage laws and regulations.

In the twenty-first century, the country's grip on the right to use land has slackened. Under the *Zhonghua Renmin Gongheguo Nongcun Tudi Chengbaofa* (the *Law of Land Contract in Rural Areas of the People's Republic of China*) (2002), peasants can enjoy the right to use the piece of land (*zhaijidi*) on which their own properties are located. In the past, the right to use *zhaijidi* was transferrable only between different individuals or households belonging to the same collective unit (*jiti*). However, in recent years, the right to use *zhaijidi* has been made transferrable from the local residents to outside developers. Although in the first instance old houses are household estates, the transference of *zhaijidi* use rights can have a direct and serious impact on these properties. In rural China, all land is owned by the *jiti*. Consequently, a person's ownership of a house is therefore distinct from the ownership of the land on which the house is built. The dilemma is that whereas, on the one hand old dwellings of historic significance are the cultural heritage of the whole nation (*quan minzu*), on the other, they are privately or collectively owned properties. This double-edged ascription of rights can cause the local people many problems in their daily lives. Heritage discourse highlights the relationship between the local people, such as the Hakka and Minnan people, and the government, the principal focus being on the property right issues.

A third discourse in which the disputed status of an old house can appear is the 'cultural resource' discourse. Old houses are cultural resources. They can sometimes also provide opportunities for making an economic profit, and hence become nodes of tension between different stakeholders. Usually, this rivalry is between the local residents/property owners and outsiders who want to exploit the local tourist resource without giving a second thought to the local people's interests. As this thesis will discuss, in China, development in urban areas is usually based on the exploitation of the rural resources. No doubt this is partly a natural extension of the long-term advantages of and the leading role enjoyed by the urban centers (*xian*) throughout most of the Chinese imperial history. Since the Republican period, the dominance of urban centers has been further reinforced by private capital. Furthermore, capital has quickly become centralized in Chinese urban areas since the 1990s. Urban development needs resources that can only be obtained from the country's vast rural areas – labor, energy, farm produce, mines and so forth. However, rural scenery and landscapes are also resources that urban tourist interests pursue. The overexploitation of rural resources has already caused many social problems.

As discussed earlier, to many of the peasants it seems that what the cultural authorities want from them is a combination of authenticity and integrity of *wenwu* (literally cultural materials), and what the tourism companies want from them is usually picturesque scenery. As private land ownership is not permitted under China's laws, and is so stated in the Constitution, a peasant is unable to use a claim to a small piece of private ownership to obtain fair compensation for any transfer of land-use rights. This disgruntlement lies at the root of many disputes.

The early 1950s to the early 1980s was in effect a very special time period in that collectivism still stood at the core of Chinese socialist ideology. The needs of an individual in this period were largely suppressed. In such a socialist atmosphere, it was everyone's responsibility to serve the country unselfishly and unconditionally. Reward or compensation was a matter about which people felt ashamed to talk openly. Although the Land Quality Improvement Movement (*pingzheng tudi*) led to dramatic landform changes throughout China in the 1960s to 1970s, cultural resources in the form of settlement architecture in South China were less impacted. Despite the Opening Policy and the changes in the land-use right in the 1980s, collectivism still had the rural society in China in an iron grip. The boundary between a person's own property and that of the collective groups was still very blurred. Bewildered by all this uncertainty and confusion, peasants seldom asked for compensation for preserving their own property as cultural sites for the public. They undertook this willing for their country. Another important reason that they failed to pursue any claims is that in the early 1980s any one single individual or household in a village was just as poor as another.

The tide has turned since the late 1980s. A more divided rural society in economic terms has emerged. The differentiation in economic status among local residents has made them more aware of the importance of money. Since the late 1980s, tourism development has extended into China's rural areas. At nearly the same time, control over *wenwu* was asserted by the cultural authorities. In this period of conversion, many changes took place in people' minds. They certainly became more aware of their own personal interests. Making money reemerged as the most essential matter, as it had been over a half century earlier. The peasants no longer unthinkingly followed the path set out by the government in moral and ideological terms. Although the Chinese government still held its grip on all land on behalf of the public, the economic needs of the peasants began to be considered an appropriate topic for discussion. Disputes about land- and property-use between peasants and the *gongjia* (government) became more serious than ever before. The individual responsibility of preserving *wenwu* promulgated by the Chinese cultural authorities in the name of patriotism and collectivism began to be seriously challenged in cultural resource management practice. In many cases, the *xian* government officials began to exercise their prerogative to initiate tourism development projects in collaboration with companies from the outside, without bothering to consult the local people properly. Consequently, it is quite natural that the peasants who have been excluded from the right to share the benefits of development need no convincing that government officials preserve and conserve only for the outsiders and themselves.

Some of the *tulou* buildings in western and southern Fujian have already been designated important heritage sites on the provincial and national levels. As discussed above, *tulou* buildings are undoubtedly personal or household property, and, clearly, fundamental laws, such as the *Property Law*, guarantee the right of personal ownership, even though the country overall is owned by the public. However, *tulou* buildings are also part of cultural heritage and cultural resources. To some extent, cultural heritage preservation can be used as an excuse for stopping the natural architectural metabolization of *tulou* structures. As mentioned above, the legal status of *tulou* rooms is quite different from that of ancestral halls in that they are private dwellings, and they are much more closely implicated in local people's daily life. I shall argue in later chapters that governmental intervention might result in a transfer of land-use rights that can have serious impact on local people's way of life, especially on their means of livelihood. In theory, the use of local people's property for the benefit of the public should only be implemented on a voluntary basis. The fly in the ointment is that compensation issues have not yet been properly regulated under any of the fundamental laws.

The only possible legal document we have been able to find so far in relation to such double-edged property is the *Cultural Heritage Law*, that is considered only a subsidiary law. It regulates what can and cannot be done with properties that have been designated cultural heritage, including some *tulou* buildings, but it does not guarantee satisfactory living conditions for the people who still live inside such listed buildings. The catch is that these conditions can often be achieved only through renovation. The most embarrassing thing is that this law has, in many respects, not been accepted as an integral part of the fundamental laws. As a law it has a comparatively low legal standing overall, but still has enough weight to influence the life of the *tulou* residents. Its influence has increased dramatically since the 2000s with the registration of some *tulou* buildings on the World Heritage List. In the 1990s, people in western and southern Fujian began to use their *tulou* buildings as tourist attractions but in many villages the local people still cannot get their fair share of the benefits from tourism development (Ye, 2006).

Although *tulou* buildings have become a focus of worldwide attention and admiration, many local people have come to associate them with a perceived backwardness of the traditional lifestyle. Some Chinese heritage researchers have concluded that the widespread preservation of these buildings is impossible, simply because they block development and are, in effect, putative symbols of backwardness. Therefore, to preserve as many of the old houses as possible has come to be seen as a metonym for being backward.[6]

In short, the preservation of *tulou* buildings is a very complex question, with answers determined by multiple socio-cultural factors. Most of these factors are to be discovered in the abovementioned three discourses, all of which pose a dilemma for the continued existence of *tulou* architecture. One thing that is certain at present is that the social conditions in *tulou* settlements vary from building to building. Therefore, in terms of preservation, there is no single answer. In some settlements, there might well be a good opportunity to preserve *tulou* for the future, whereas in other settlements, the old houses have had to be demolished to make way for new buildings. It seems to me that we, as heritage practitioners, have become accustomed to highlighting, even overstating, the legitimacy of architectural preservation, while failing to evaluate the case for redevelopment that does have rational purposes even though it irrevocably results in demolition. As professionals, we talk only about the ways to preserve the past rather than about ways to live with the past. Redevelopment is sometimes a kind of taboo subject in *wenwu baohu* (cultural heritage protection) discourses in China.

Taking Hekeng village in south Fujian province as an example, this thesis begins by exploring the factors that might have had important impacts on a 'traditional' Chinese settlement in the South in its evolution from entirely an ordinary peasant occupation toward a place well-known for its *tulou* residences, whose registration as World Heritage site was approved by the World Heritage Committee in 2008. There are three specific questions that I want to try to answer: (1) Who are the Hekeng people? What is the character of their lineage settlements, and how has settlement in the Hekeng area evolved into the way it looks today? (2) How have the *Cultural Heritage Law* and regulations on local, national and international levels influenced the settlement in terms of heritage preservation? (3) How have people both inside and outside the site area used and how do they intend to use Hakka heritage? What roles have these different intentions played in reshaping the built environment? (4) How have the Hekeng people been able to compete with outsiders in their struggle to protect their own cultural heritage rights? On the basis of these analyses, I hope to arrive at some suggestions that will improve the management of *tulou* heritage in the future.

RESEARCH METHODOLOGY

From 2010 to 2013, I participated in a project called 'Cultural Heritage Preservation and Contemporary Chinese Society', funded by the Ford Foundation. In this project I was responsible for investigating the four *tulou* settlements located in the Nanjing rural area. In 2010, I lived in Hekeng village for forty days, and carried out preliminary investigations in Hekeng, Nanou, Taxia and Shiqiao villages. Two colleagues in the Fujian Provincial Museum, Zhang Jinde and Lan Dongyang, helped with the interviews in these settlements. The initial purpose of this research was

6. Personal communication from Wang Xuerong.

to explore ways to protect the cultural heritage in rural South China. However, after the investigation had already commenced, I began to realize that nothing is absolutely destined to be preserved or protected. Preservation can only be sustainable when it is really needed by, or at least has the endorsement of, most stakeholders. In short, nothing can be preserved unconditionally. It is also in the interviews that I was made aware of the three discourses mentioned above, namely: the property discourse, the heritage discourse and the resource discourse.

Important sources of information obtained in 2011 and 2013 include the historical records of Nanjing county, genealogies of the local Zhang surnames, oral history materials, questionnaires and digital interview recordings. I maintained contact with four important informants: Zhang Enhan, Zhang Mintai, Zhang Wenzhu and Zhang Kuncheng. They are the descendants of the major branches (*fang*) of the Hekeng Zhang surname. It is important to note that Enhan, Wenzhu and Kuncheng have each served as head of Hekeng village (*cunzhang*). Enhan had this honor in the 1990s, Kuncheng in the 2000s and Wenzhu in the 2010s. They provided important information on lineage history, kinship relations, the histories of the settlements, sources of livelihood, local industries, oral histories pertaining to the extant buildings and the buildings demolished during the Cultural Revolution, and so forth.

In 2012 to 2013, I began to analyze the materials. I used the data the informants had provided to reconstruct the landscape evolution process. With the information extrapolated from interviews and questionnaires, I undertook a stakeholder analysis to determine how people from different backgrounds understand the peasants' property, what their intentions concerning the use of heritage are, what changes these intentions have introduced to the local society and how such intentions and subsequent practice have influenced their daily lives. I then classified the information about the use of the *tulou* heritage in Hekeng into three categories corresponding to the three discourses, and attempted to determine how, in each context, the local people have interacted with other stakeholders, especially those from the outside the river valley. I was then is a position to answer the four questions outlined above.

CHAPTER ARRANGEMENT

Chapter 1 explores the diffusion of *tulou* buildings and settlements in the Fujian area. Before discussing the three heritage discourses in detail, it is necessary to set the scene by examining the heritage itself and the people living there in some depth. Who are these Hakka people? What is their heritage, and how did it become heritage? It is also essential to state clearly how the local people have linked themselves and their social memories to their built environment. How did they use the built environment and the landscapes? The goal of the chapter is to provide a context into which later discussions on heritage right issues can be put. This context is conceptualized in relation to landscape biography. As Roymans (2009) has argued, 'places and landscapes play an active role in the biographies and genealogies of people, binding persons and generations together, while at the same time creating their own life histories at different time scales through successive social contexts.' Landscapes provide the settings against which real personal and public lives are played out over time. Therefore, a landscape biography can combine communal memory with the evolution of the land surface features. Consequently, it provides a good standpoint from which to view the past of a small society such as that of the Hekeng Valley. A landscape biography offers a narrative about the correlations between the Hekeng landscape evolution and changes in Hekeng society at different critical points in history. This analysis should substantially enrich interpretation of Hakka heritage.

In Chapter 2, I explore *tulou* buildings as private properties. In the past, agnates who were members of the same lineage segment usually raised the construction funds by collecting money from each household in that branch. Although a *tulou* building remains as a whole the collective property of a lineage segment, the rooms inside are the private property of individual single households. In the villages such as Hekeng, Nanou, Taxia and Shiqiao, the local Hakka people usually observe the *fenjia* (household-split) ceremony when the eldest son of the family gets married, at which time when senior members of the family are usually still alive. This is quite different from the situations reported by Freedman (1966), Cohen (1979) and Hugh (1979).

In practice, the private ownership of the household dwelling is actually legitimized by *fenjia* customs. Usually, the eldest son and his wife are given a new room inside the same *tulou* building in which his parents and siblings live. Hence, the ideal is that the nearest relatives in the descent line live together in the same building. At least some of the male descendants of the donors in each generation are able to find a place to live inside the building. This guarantees that the household residences in a *tulou* building can be inherited patrilineally. The special internal arrangement of *tulou* buildings reflects the fact that most of the families in it are stem and joint families. Therefore, a *tulou* is larger than the building compound defined by Hugh (1979). Each one is a small-sized community. In fact, people from the five degrees of mourning relations (*wufu*) can still live in the same building. Purchase and transfer with compensation are both possible, because the rooms are *de facto* personal property. The chapter focuses on the peasants' rights under the fundamental laws governing the use of their own immovable property (*budongchan*) and the violations of such rights under the Heritage Law and relevant regulations on lower administrative levels. To date, compensation for *wenwu* use is still a problem pending in the Chinese legal system. I shall also present some thoughts on this in Chapter 2.

Through a discussion of the Hekeng settlements, Chapter 3 explores the questions of what should be remembered and for whom it should be remembered. The World Heritage (WH) framework is a state-based management regime of a typically European sort (Willems, 2014), intended to protect an important heritage of all humankind. The goal of this international regime is to help each state preserve its own social memories by recourse to systemized procedures. The WH system works as a selection tool, employing the 'Outstanding Universal Value' (OUV) principles, that are based on European values (Smith, 2006). However, the question is: Who is eligible to judge whether the features selected by the World Heritage Commission as WH sites under the OUV rules can or cannot represent the past of a place? Who should have the final say? To what extent can such designation represent the social memories in a place? Logically, the people who are the best qualified to answer such questions are the local people, because they are the heirs to all the architectural properties. The chapter will examine whether and to what extent the past reconstructed using the WH method does reflect the past in local people's minds, or do they have their own ways of commemorating the past? These questions are very important in that they can help us reassess the role the WH system can play in preserving social memories.

The bulk of Chapter 4 is devoted to a discussion of the 'cultural resources' discourse. Since the 2000s, heritage experts in China have become increasingly worried about the disappearance of vernacular buildings in South China. The biggest problem they face is that the reasons for these disappearances are by no means cut and dried. One of the most important stumbling-blocks is that the adaptability of the old buildings to modern use is not straightforward. Without heavy investment, it is virtually impossible for buildings in traditional styles to escape the fate of being totally redeveloped. If their financial status allowed them to do so, understandably most people want to improve their quality of life by constructing completely new small apartments with better sanitary facilities. Redevelopment can usher in a dramatic change in the built environment in only five years or so. What is often overlooked is that the dwellings are highly variable parts of the built environment. The outside world has provided the peasants with various architectural styles to emulate. 'If I cannot make a good use of my old houses (to earn money), why not make it a better place to live in?' one of my informants, from the Jinjiang rural area in southern Fujian, stated pragmatically. In the small village in which he lived, over 90 percent of the *tulou* buildings have already been replaced by brick and reinforced concrete houses. Old houses are disappearing from these villages simply because the local people refuse to use homesteads in traditional ways. They prefer to have their property in the form of a private residential resource rather than as a public cultural resource. In view of this, as said earlier, Li, an official of the Chinese cultural authority, has put forward some constructive proposals. My understanding is that, if a body wants to preserve the built environment, it has to provide the peasants with a compelling reason why it is worth their while to do so. Therefore the corollary is 'to preserve' a building necessarily implies 'to use' it profitably. In some extreme cases, in which the local residents display little affection for their own ancestral properties, the preservation of this cultural resource – if it occurs – has to be based on a deal in which outsiders help the local residents exploit their cultural resources in exchange for their maintenance of the house. However, the waters are muddied as the outsiders, either the government or the tourism companies, might have their own interests in the use of the insiders' properties. Undoubtedly, the maximization of their interests can dramatically lower the strength of the peasants' desire to preserve cultural resources. This chapter will discuss the sustainability of the vernacular built environment by exploring the fundamental rights and duties of both insiders and outsiders in this heritage game.

The last chapter will have an open ending. It is not my purpose to provide conclusive results. Therefore, the chapter will focus on some suggestions for the future, in the hope that they can be of some use in resolving dilemmas in the use and preservation of vernacular buildings and settlements.

1. The Zhang Lineage and their Hekeng *Tulou* Settlements

A full understanding of the history, character and other important qualities embedded in a historical place – referred to here as an 'appropriate site interpretation' – is widely considered to be an essential basis for making the right choices in the heritage management process. So far, however, *tulou* site interpretation in the southern Fujian region has frequently proved rather unsatisfactory. Often it is simplified to nothing more than an architectural interpretation. The people living in such settlements and their formation processes are overlooked.

At some World Heritage attractions, such as Tianluokeng in Yongding county, the site managers have interpreted the *tulou* building arrangement by referring to the record in the *Zhou Li* or the *Rites of the Zhou Dynasty*. Assuredly folklore is one source on which to base site interpretation, but it is the responsibility of its interpreters to provide site visitors with a well-argued analysis on the basis of modern studies drawing on the social sciences. It can be said with certainty that, looking at the majority of *tulou* buildings, the site managers have fallen short of this aspiration. A large part of this failure arises from basic difficulties in understanding the site formation process. Most importantly, the way in which the local people have interacted with their built environment in the past is usually rather confused in both interpretations of the site and in statements about its significance. This creates a huge problem as understanding such interactions is crucial, because they offer clues to the importance of the heritage in the minds of the local inhabitants. It is easy to find an abundance of information about the history of the Hakka people and their 'fortified strongholds' in libraries and on the Worldwide Web. Unquestionably these buildings are of great significance but the present interpretation of these building complexes does not place one single individual building in its real historical and social context. By and large, the existing interpretations focus on the typologies of *tulou* architecture, and fail to take the essential step of inquiring into what place the *tulou* buildings occupy in the actual habitation history of such settlements as Hekeng, that has a history stretching back perhaps more than 500 years. It seems that the local site managers do not feel drawn to undertaking this sort of contextualization work.

Generally, in the eyes of the Hakka people, the *tulou* buildings are just the tried-and-tested dwellings they have known and occupied since childhood. Conversely most site managers are outsiders, as indeed were the architectural historians who carried out the interpretation and documentation leading to their registration on the World Heritage List (WHL). These outsider experts almost unswervingly tend to adhere to the traditional building research methodology developed by early building archeologists during the first half of the twentieth century (Tan, 2008; Lin, 1995). This methodology highlights the importance of style sourcing, a method that involves emphasizing structural comparison and analysis, and overstates the importance of traditional northern Han cultural architecture and its possible influence on the buildings and structures in other parts of China. The upshot is that the socioeconomic processes that can be extrapolated from the settlements are generally left to historians and anthropologists. In their turn, researchers in these fields tend to occupy themselves with such questions as the cultural and economic interactions between different parts of river corridors (Zhou, 2007), the migration routes of the historical refugees from the North (Huang, 2009; Lin, 2010), the dialectical evolution (Guo, 2007; Cai, 2007), the social structure and organization (Zheng, 2012) and so on. Unfortunately, these two kinds of studies, namely: architectural comparisons and socioeconomic process reconstructions, have very few points of intersection. As a result, a fundamental question such as how a settlement has evolved into its present form and appearance – presumably a social-cause-oriented question – is very likely to go unaddressed, essentially ignored by both research fields. This is a serious oversight because surely an inquiry into the settlement formation process should be the core element of both site analyses and of heritage interpretation and management.

When a WHL nomination concerns architecture or, rather, architectural clusters, as in the case of the *tulou* buildings, the assumption seems to be that the buildings and structures are meaningful in themselves. This idea stems from the fact that building specialists have become accustomed to judging the value of their subject from a typological perspective (Huang and Chen, 2012), their focus fixed on structures and their elements, the techniques visible in the structures, similarities between buildings and so forth. This sort of analysis is embedded in the theory of Architectural Diffusionism that has been prevalent in China since the late 1980s (Lin, 1995; Yongding *Tulou* Compilation Group, 1990). However, it is my contention that it is meaningless to talk about how the Ming dynasty *tulou* architecture as a whole might have evolved and diffused from its predecessors in the Tang or Song dynasty in the Central Plains area of China, because comparisons of building styles do not answer the question of why such buildings were constructed there in the first place. As we shall see in the following chapters, the rammed-earth wall building technique is by no means a highly complicated construction method, beyond the competence of the average builder. In fact it was commonly employed to provide the 'basics of life' in terms of shelter and defense for the members of rural societies. Therefore, a Ming dynasty community could have built whatever type of buildings its members thought best, as long as the basic techniques they already possessed or had acquired provided them the expertise to make such constructions. A unique prototype in a faraway land is not always necessary to offer an explanation. The upshot is that a building archaeology whose theory is based on architectural typology and Cultural Diffusionism might have its limits in understanding the rise of huge earthen buildings in the specific settlement context of the hilly region of southern Fujian. When people visit the *tulou* settlements nowadays, all they learn from existing interpretations is that the buildings originated in the North and they are of great historical, scientific and esthetic value. Architectural specialists tend to construct a mega-narrative about the homogeneity of the history of the Hakka buildings. The more intricate questions of how the buildings varied in step with the changes in the settlement landscape and especially with the immediate and long-term needs of local people have often been omitted from *tulou* interpretations. In short, in the existing interpretations the *tulou* as buildings are detached from the history of the local people. By and large, local interpreters state, or restrict themselves to, little more than the date, the architectural and esthetic characteristics, plus some groundless anecdotes fabricated to attract tourists.

Following Rapoport (1969), the buildings and structures could be thought of as having been erected to satisfy the needs of the clansmen who built and lived in them. Usually it is impossible to extrapolate their establishment, use, disuse, relocation and even destruction from the amount of land available to their builders a whole. Despite this postulation, how the ancestors used and managed the limited land resources in a river valley is the core issue that motivated and organized their construction work. In real life, people need to maintain a balance; they have to decide if it is really worthwhile establishing a new *tulou* building at the expense of losing a piece of arable land. Over and above this, the building environment might be influenced by a number of factors such as changes in population size, land supply, industrial forms, subsistence patterns, accessibility to cross-regional trade paths and other environmental and historical elements. As we shall investigate in the following chapters, these superficially invisible socioeconomic factors have all played key roles in shaping the landscape of a Hakka settlement. Axiomatically, any interpretation of the built environment should at least relate it to its social context. Unfortunately, in the available interpretations of the Hakka built environment, discussions of the specific reasons or mechanisms that have affected the evolution of the built environment in its current form are as scarce as hen's teeth.

In an attempt to right this imbalance, this chapter will give an introduction to the Hakka heritage of the Zhang surname in Hekeng village, in an attempt to understand what it is and how it has been formed.

1.1 HEKENG PEOPLE, THE HAKKA NEWCOMERS

The villages mentioned in this dissertation are all situated in the buffer zone area between the central Hakka territories and those of the Minnan local people. These river valley settlements are traditionally famous for their huge earthen fortresses, the *tulou* buildings (Xie, 2007). According to the *Nanjing Gazetteer* by Zheng Fengren published during the Republican period and recompiled in 1994, thirty-nine lineages from twenty-one surnames resident in this hilly area lived first in Ninghua but later pushed on to Yongding, thence to Dabu, before ending up in their present locations. A thorough investigation of the local genealogies collected from the hilly area near Nanjing (Lin, 2010) reveals they commenced their movement into the river valleys in the early years of the Ming dynasty. All these Hakka surname lineages can be more or less regarded as the descendants, or sub-cultural groups, of the late-Tang to Southern-Song period migrants from the North. Among them is the Zhang surname lineage whose members settled down in the valleys of the Shiqiao and Hekeng Rivers near Shuyang township.

The Shiqiao Zhang lineage is named after the lineage's first settlement in the Shiqiao River Valley. The *Shiqiao Zhang Surname Genealogy,*[1] published during the Republican period, reports a piece of traditional oral memory transmitted from the early Ming dynasty, noting that the first-generation founding father, Zhang Niansanlang, was born in Xiaoqing near Dabu township in Guangdong province. Making his way up the Ting River corridor by way of Pingshuikeng,[2] a small river valley, then along the Yongding Stream (a tributary of the Ting River), he finally reached area of the Shiqiao Mountains in 1443 (the eighth year of the Zhengtong reign era of the Ming dynasty) (Fig. 3).

As recorded in the *Genealogy of Kuikeng* compiled in 1824 (the fourth year of the Daoguang reign era of the Qing dynasty), the Zhang surname residents usually described their pre-settlement in this way: 'The Southern-Song dynasty founding ancestor, Zhang Huasun, who first migrated to Shanghang County from the North, had eighteen sons… and they migrated to Fuzhou, Zhangzhou, Longyan, Changting, Shanghang, Ninghua, Wuping, Qingliu, Yongding, Dabu... Zhangpu, Zhangping... Nanjing (the peripheral mountain ranges in which Hekeng is located), Xiaoxi...'. This genealogy tallies very closely with those that can also be widely observed in the lineages with the same surname Zhang in northeastern Guangdong (Szonyi, 2002; Wu 2008). Despite the fact such statements are highly suspect,

1. This part has been incorporated into the updated version of the genealogy published in 1994 by the Zhang Genealogy Compilation Committee. As the population of a lineage grows, newly born lineage members need to be added to the old pedigree every few years. Apart from such additions, because of the growth of a settlement population, some of the lineage members/families have had to choose to leave for other places nearby to settle. They continue to compile pedigrees of their own at new settlements. Consequently, the members of the Zhang surname living in different river valleys have different pedigrees going back to the same apical male ancestor. For that matter, the Shiqiao Zhang as a whole, for example, have a number of pedigrees, including the *Pedigree of Shiqiao*, the *Pedigree of Hekeng*, the *Pedigree of Jiaokeng*, the *Pedigree of Zhuta*, the *Pedigree of Kuikeng* and so forth. Nevertheless, the lineage heads could cooperate to recompile a grand genealogy for the whole Zhang surname at certain important points in the lineage history, primarily based on as many as pedigrees as they can collect from descendants in valley settlements. Theoretically, the interval between two such genealogical recompilations is usually 30 to 50 years (Chen, 2009). The outcome of such a recompilation is double-edged. On the one hand, it can serve as a population census of the whole descent group. It therefore enables a male lineage member to find his position in a much wider network based on kinship relations. On the other hand, some descendant settlements might choose not to continue writing their own pedigree. Instead, they might simply add the names of new members to the recompiled genealogy. This has led to the loss of the branch pedigrees in physical terms, although the information should have been largely preserved in the newly recompiled one. All it is possible to find at present is the recompiled *Zhang Shiqiao Surname Genealogy*, printed in 1994. It contains not only the pedigree of Shiqiao, but also the population of all the other nearby Zhang settlements. It also includes the introduction to the process of pedigree collection when the genealogy of the whole Zhang surname lineage was last recompiled during the Republican period. Information from different periods (as early as the early Ming dynasty) and settlements was gradually deposited and finally formed the grand *Genealogy*. Therefore, the genealogy I use in this thesis is a sort of combination of the Republican period genealogies and the new amendments made prior to the 21st century. Throughout the whole of Fujian province, the earliest genealogical writing can be traced back to the Tianbao reign era of the Tang dynasty (8th century). During the Song dynasty, genealogical writing was regarded by the local Han elites as a very rigorous and prestigious research discipline. However, all such early genealogies have disappeared. We only know about such early writing traditions from the prefaces in the later pedigrees dating from the Ming dynasty and thereafter (Chen, 2009).

2. The character *'keng'* refers to a small stream or brook in southern Fujian dialects.

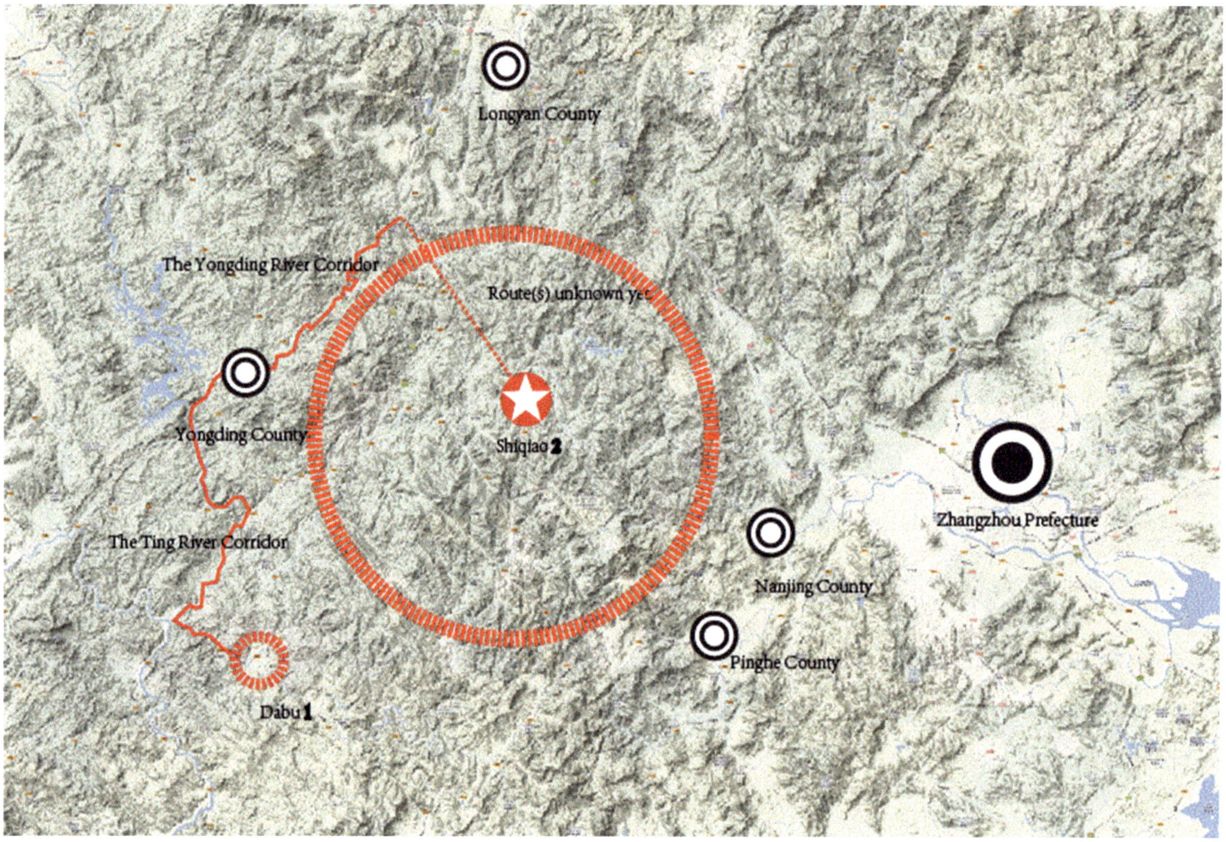

Fig. 3 The migration routes of the Shiqiao Zhang surname ancestors.

keeping an open mind it is still possible to study their early settlement history from the record of interactions between the Hakka and Minnan local people who had settled in this area much earlier.

Prior to the arrival of the Hakka people, the small river valleys in this mountain range area had previously been occupied by other Minnan Fulao surnames, including Wu, Chi, Gao, Cao, Tang, Diao (Lin, 2010), Li, Liu, Huang (Guo, 2007) and so forth. The Shiqiao Zhang lineage provides a good example of the earliest Hakka migrants to this area. Anthropological studies have established that, after their arrival in this mountain area in the early-to-middle Ming period, the Hakka lineages did try to deploy different strategies to become fully integrated into the local Minnan communities (or at the very least to reduce tension). Some of them chose to enter into an uxorilocal marriage relationship with the local Minnan people.[3] One example is Niansanlang, the ancestor in Shiqiao, who married the daughter of a village notable. By contrast, another Zhang lineage that settled in nearby Taxia seems to have chosen not to marry into non-Hakka village lineages. Their recalcitrantly conservative attitude toward the locals inevitably generated tension in this region (Guo, 2007). Eventually, this reached such heights that, in a later period, the Taxia lineage went as far as deciding to break its ties with some of the other Hakka villages because it disapproved of the extent of their assimilation into the local Minnan communities in terms of spoken language and customs.

In their assimilation and dissimulation processes, the Hakka newcomers, as competing opponents, exhibited varying attitudes toward the local Minnan

3. In their book, Wolf and Huang (1980) talk systematically about such *ruzhui* phenomenon in Taiwan.

cultures and communities. Some eventually emerged victorious and conquered the river valley territories previously inhabited by the locals, among them the Huang and Li lineages; some, like the Liu lineages, adapted themselves to the local dialectal and deity worship systems, for instance, the worship of the male Protector and the goddess Mazu, without forswearing their own gods such as the Common Lord. Others like the Shiqiao ancestor, who was made a son-in-law of the locals, were integrated into the kinships systems. Consequently, in his own lifetime he was able to pioneer and manage new land resources in other places such as the valley of the Hekeng River. After a three-generation effort,[4] the Shiqiao Zhang lineage finally rounded off its land acquisition and reclamation and built its first formal settlement— the Qiaoxia settlement in the heart of Hekeng Valley, where its members have continued to live for the next five hundred years.

It is now widely accepted that, although they belong to different *minxi* (folk groups) of the Han nationality from the point of view of history, society, culture and linguistics (Xie, 2011; Nanjing County Government, 1984), for a lengthy period of time the Hakka and Minnan peoples have actually shared many social, cultural and religious traits. It seems feasible to assume that these correspondences stem from the interactions[5] between the two groups since the early years of the Ming dynasty, when the descendants of the late-Southern-Song dynasty migrants moved into the mountainous ranges of southern Fujian (Zhou, 2007). This trend toward amalgamation is particularly reflected in the emergence of the bilingual zone centered on the upper reaches of the Chuanchang Stream, that is straddled by the Hakka and Minnan people. Males in such villages as Taxia and Liwu can speak both the Hakka and Minnan dialects. Even more cogently, the Hakka villagers in Shangban speak only Minnan dialects, indicating a thorough dialectical conversion from Hakka to Minnan during the assimilation era. A frequently mentioned case is the Huang lineage that lived in two linking settlements along the same brook; although sharing an identical descent line, they each chose to speak a different dialect (Guo, 2007).

The close relationship between these two groups of people is also incorporated into religious cults. Although becoming increasingly Minnanized from the Middle Ming dynasty, the Hakka descendants gradually took over not just the whole area but also the subsistence resources, marginalizing the Luo, Hua and other Minnan surnames in their advance. Nevertheless, surprisingly the Hakka intruders assimilated and retained the ancestors of the marginalized as their own religious cults,[6] known as *dizhuzai*, and made offerings to console these male spirits on the fifteenth day of the seventh month in the Lunar Calendar, on *Qiyue ban* or the Ghost Festival, the day for appeasing and placating the dead. One plausible interpretation of this adoption is that this was a way to commemorate the benefits that the Hakka settlers had obtained from the local Minnan people in the early days of contact. In my 2011 heritage investigation, a similar early contact story was also perceptible in the pedigree record of the Zhang lineage in Shiqiao. The male ancestor of this lineage married a girl of local origin whose maiden name was Chen. However, the pedigree only refers to this marriage in passing as follows:

4. Fei (1953) has pointed out that if there were any free land nearby, the family might spread out, and a new concentration that can be construed in terms of a village might be developed within a few generations.

5. Language is one of the most sensitive indicators reflecting *de facto* interchanges between social groups. As Guo (2007) has pointed out, in terms of vocabulary, the Hakka dialect in this region has retained many single words traditionally used by the Minnan people. Moreover, the formation of the bilingual belt in the upper reaches of the Chuanchang Stream is principally ascribed to the Hakka people's active adaptation to local Minnan valley societies. In this respect, the so-called 'bilingual' learning is indeed unidirectional. Turning to religion, large numbers of local religious cults were imported from Minnan society, such as *Fude zhengshen* (the God of Good Fortune and Virtue), *Sanping shizu* (a reincarnation of a Tang dynasty Buddhist monk), *Baosheng dadi* (the Protector), *Guangze zunwang* (the Benefactor) and the goddess Mazu. Their absorption of local religious cults occurred during the Hakka people's adaptation to the local Minnan social conditions. This also represents a unidirectional learning of Minnan beliefs by the Hakka. Even today, such deities, kept either in temples or small shrines at the entrances to or exits of their villages, are still worshipped by the Hakka people.

6. James L. Watson (1987) also mentions that the local people of Hong Kong's New Territories made offering to T'in Hau as well as keeping other local deities in the temple.

> *'...(Zhang) Niansanlang, a blacksmith from Dabu township [in the northeastern part of Guangdong province], worked for the local gentleman Chen Wushilang... after winning the old gentleman's trust, he became Wushilang's son-in-law...'*

We know relatively little about the social structure of Shiqiao prior to this blacksmith's arrival in the valley, but all the versions of the genealogies collected during the Republican period kept by Shiqiao descendants by the local county government begin with this paragraph. What is known as *zhuixu* (or mukoyōshi, its counterpart in Japanese culture) is a very common anthropological feature in southern Fujian. When a family of high social status or with a well-established business has no male heir, this kind of cross-surname adult adoption seems to be a realistic option. In exchange for being legitimized as the family's heir, the adopted son is expected to take the family's surname, or at least allow his first son to take his father-in-law's surname, even though he might still keep his own (Szonyi, 2002). This legitimacy is the price to pay for renouncing one's own or one's first son's paternal surname and taking on the responsibility of caring for the elderly of the (adoptive) family and making them offerings after their death. Consequently, such adoption systems are built on two foundations: a real social need and a religious belief in an afterlife.

Shiqiao village is now a single surname village, meaning that all the males share the same descent and are all surnamed Zhang. Local oral history preserves the tradition that, before the advent of the Zhang lineage, the valley was already inhabited by several other surname families of Minnan origin, among them Xue, Cheng, Luo, Lin and, of course, Chen. The truth, now lost in the mists of time, might be that, although the blacksmith entered into a *zhuixu* relationship with an indigenous Shiqiao family, his descendants never adopted the benefactor's surname, or perhaps they chose to resume their previous surname later, and all other surname lineages of Minnan origin, including the Chens, had in fact been gradually expelled from that river valley by the Hakka people at different periods of time. The days when adoption was prevalent are presented only very briefly and vaguely in the *Shiqiao Zhang Surname Genealogy* and it is impossible to deduce from such texts how accurate the record is. In this instance, there are two possible scenarios: either the tensions between the Zhang lineage and the lineages of other surnames of local origin had already been effaced from the written sources by the time the pedigrees were compiled or the compilers of the pedigrees chose to overlook facts that might have recalled past tensions.

A valid claim to the land and property left by a father-in-law is absolutely essential in that it vitiates any challenges to the newcomers' legitimacy and right to live in this river valley. This supposition explains why the Chens are the only other surname lineage recorded in the genealogy. Be that as it may, the Zhangs, at least as recorded in the *Genealogy*, were probably subjected not just to pressure but also outright hostility from other local Minnan people living in the same river valley and, subsequently, within just three generations, they were forced to seek new land in other valleys. This fragment of memory is recorded in the text below:

> *'...The third-generation ancestor Shiliang, grandson of Niansanlang [still alive at this time], Shiqiao the First, discovered a new valley with a wider aspect and fertile land when herding cattle, and that is Hekeng...'*

In fact, these lines tie in with other contradictory statements, such as:

> *'...about Niansanlang's sons... Shiyin, his eldest son had his eye on land and houses in both Shiqiao and Hekeng; Shiquan, his second son left for Zhuta; and, his youngest son Shihui, with his mother, went back to their hometown in Dabu...'*

These scant but important written records allow us to draw one very brief conclusion. During his own lifetime, the blacksmith who later became Shiqiao the First of the Zhang lineage, had already become aware of the lack of land resources and had begun to take measures to mitigate the resultant pressure. Before the lineage established itself properly, the first three generations had to resort to different strategies to survive various challenges. The solution was either to move back home (Dabu) or to pastures new like Hekeng.

An investigation of genealogies is very important to an interpretation and representation of the heritage of the local communities. Hakka researchers (Guo, 2007; Cai, 2007; Zhang, 2006) now agree that the early days of the life of the Hakka people in this hilly area was largely occupied with making adaptations to the local environmental and social conditions. The problem is that, as the Hakka lineage genealogies, these local histories pass over the accommodation of the Hakka people to the local environment, both natural and social. This lack of information is compounded when, finding no direct source about the early settlement of the Hakka people in written historical literature, planners and local cultural resource managers have tended to underestimate, under-represent or even completely omit the early phases of settlement (namely: the middle Ming dynasty to the early Qing dynasty) in their interpretations and representations of the past. This trend also quite clearly pervades the *Nanjing Tulou Buildings Protection and Management Plan* (Tongji University, 2006) and the *Fujian Tulou Buildings Protection and Management Plan* (Tsinghua University, 2006). The interactions between the two groups of people must inevitably have led to diverse socio-cultural changes, including language, burial patterns,[7] religious cults, marriage patterns and landscape management. Unquestionably, the concrete past of the Hakka is enshrined in these works but, as an integral part of a social process, they are also a product of the long-term fusion and growth of new cultural features in each river valley.

It is axiomatic that a well-designed interpretation of the distant past of the Hakka should begin with a clear explanation of the early acculturation processes between the two folk groups. Pragmatically, if they were to survive and develop into a truly local society, the Hakka had to take on board many aspects of the Minnan people's cultural heritage, both tangible and intangible. In doing so, since the early days of their occupation of this region, the Hakka would have blended local cultural elements with their own. Alongside this inexorable socio-cultural adaptation, the competing or even conflicting relationships between the Zhangs and the lineages of local Minnan surnames were probably the moving force behind population movement to other, unoccupied river valleys such as Hekeng.

1.2 THE 'HAKKA TULOU' AND EARLY HAKKA SETTLEMENTS WITH NO TULOU BUILDINGS

Although people might be impressed by the high incidence of huge castle-like *tulou* in the traditional

7. In comparison to religious and dialectal adaptation, cultural exchanges in burial practices might have been more complicated. In Hekeng and many other similar villages situated in the bilingual belt, early Hakka burials unequivocally dated to the early period of the Ming dynasty are easily distinguishable either inside the settlements or at localities outside yet near the village. Most such burial sites are set out according to the rules of geomancy (*fengshui*). The burial sites of the Minnan locals investigated in 2012 in neighboring Pinghe county (Minnan) are identical in shape to the burial sites of the early Ming dynasty observed in Hekeng (Hakka). Other relevant evidence comes from Malacca, where burial sites of the descendants of the early Ming dynasty sailors led by the Triratna Eunuch Zheng He have been discovered. The earliest extant such burial sites can be dated to the Tianqi reign (1620-1628) on the basis of the epitaphs (Lin, 2006). These burial sites share external features with the Hakka burials distributed in the Nanjing hills. To judge from the historical texts, most of Zheng's sailors were conscripts called up from traditional Minnan regions such as Quanzhou and Zhangzhou, where Zheng built port bases (Wu, 2006). Hence, we can draw the conclusion that long before the Tianqi reign (even in the early Ming dynasty), the Minnan regions had already adopted the same burial patterns as the Hakka. This piece of evidence implies that assimilation in terms of burial behavior did occur in the southern part of Fujian. According to the Ming dynasty writer Ma Huan's book entitled *Yingya Shenglan* (The Overall Survey of the Ocean's Shires), Malacca was the place where the Eunuch set up a base and transshipment station to serve Chinese merchant ships. In this book he wrote, 'After the Ming dynasty royal fleet had arrived in the port, the sailors began to construct a city whose walls were built by erecting wooden stakes [beams are horizontal and in the roof]. There was one drum tower at each gate. Sailors, holding a ring tightly in their hand, patrolled at night to guard the city. A small warehouse was constructed inside the city, to house food, money and supplies. In early summer each year, having moored their ships in this port, Chinese sailors had to wait until the middle of the fifth month for the south wind to go back home. The king of Malacca enjoyed buying wares from sailors and merchants. The local royal court sometimes sent envoys, who traveled to China on Chinese royal ships to pay tribute at the Ming Dynasty royal court.' The palisaded city was indeed constructed under the leadership of the famous Eunuch Zheng He in 1403, i.e., the third year of the Yongle reign. Later, the city gradually waned and fell into ruin. To commemorate Zheng's achievements, Chinese settlers there finally transformed the site into a public cemetery for the local Chinese. (Kong 2000)

Hakka territories, the idea of the 'Hakka *tulou*' (that is, the association of the *tulou* solely with Hakka people) is actually a cultural 'invention' (Hobsbawm and Ranger, 1983) dating from the 1950s (Liu, 1956). Despite the fact that, in his investigation report Huang (1988) has already argued a very strong case that the Minnan people also built a large number of examples of *tulou*-like architecture, he has failed to dispel the notion of the 'Hakka *tulou*'. In terms of sheer numbers of publications, essays about 'Hakka *tulou*' have increased dramatically since the mid-2000s.[8] Unquestionably, this expansion can be traced to some of the local Hakka officials and residents who have propagated the 'Hakka *tulou*' legend in a calculated attempt to attract more tourists and to try to monopolize the reputation of the great *tulou* heritage. In a 1990s tourist pamphlet, local residents of Yongding county formally proposed the hypothesis that the *tulou* buildings had originated in the North and, when they came South, the Hakka people either brought the idea of *tulou* architecture with them or invented it themselves. This publication immediately stirred up disputes about *tulou* origins and the debate that has lasted several decades is still ongoing. Taking up the gauntlet for the South, Zeng (2006) believes that the round *tulou* architecture originated in Zhangzhou, traditionally the territory of Minnan people. Adopting a slightly different tack, Wu (2002) postulates that *tulou* architecture first emerged in northeastern Guangdong province, namely, the Raoping rural area. Since the early 2000s, these have been the three major hypotheses that have dominated the discussion about the origin of *tulou* architecture.

From the standpoint of constructivism, it is easy to conjecture that the first hypothesis – that published by Yongding county – is a reflection of the Hakka genesis narrative that developed during the early Republican period in the 1920s, a critical stage in the formation of Hakka group identity (Tagami, 2013). The theoretical basis of this hypothesis is the five-stage Hakka Exodus story proposed by Luo (1933). Taking up cudgels for a southern development, Zeng's hypothesis implies an indigenous Minnan origin, in such coastal areas as Zhangpu and Pinghe in which there have been concentrations of Minnan people long before the advent of the Hakka people. Wu's hypothesis embraces a northeastern Guangdong origin, as he argues (2006) that the two round buildings he saw in Raoping rural area can be dated even to AD 1402 and 1413, and hence are both earlier than Zeng's observations in southern Fujian. These three competing theories proposed to explain the origin of *tulou* architecture reflect the quite different orientations on the three different sides toward the origins of the *tulou* heritage. One point left unsaid in Wu's hypothesis is that northeastern Guangdong province is believed by many to have been the center of the Hakka population, and therefore this area also shores up the reputation of the Hakka as the inventors of these huge edifices. Similar ideas can also be observed in the first two hypotheses. Echoing what has happened in the Hakka identity creation process since the 1920s, in the past two decades or so the Hakka people living in southwestern Fujian and northeastern Guangdong, in collaboration with Hakka scholars and officials, have fabricated the idea that the *tulou* heritage that is the exclusive property of the Hakka.

The preface to this dissertation has already briefly touched upon the rise of not only *tulou* buildings but also other earthen defense systems in the sixteenth-century Fujian region. It could be speculated that, in a later period, the construction of the *tulou* buildings in this border area provided an opportunity to improve Hakka-Minnan acculturation. However, in any discussion about these earthen buildings the folk divide should not be overstated. Both the Hakka and Minnan people built their own fortresses, each applying the same in-depth knowledge of earth ramming and wood construction techniques. Looking for reasons these buildings were needed, Xie (2007) has pointed out that not only the conflicts between the local residents and pirates could have stimulated the erection of *tulou* buildings in this area, but also the endemic contentions between the Hakka and Minnan folk groups should not be overlooked when seeking for an explanation. That said, we cannot rule out the possibility that the Hakka might have learned about *tulou* construction techniques from the local Minnan residents in the course of their conflicts. Tagami (2013) has stated that intermarriage between the Hakka and the local Minnan people

8. http://epub.cnki.net/kns/brief/default_result.aspx

continued for a very long time; but, in the Hakka identity creation process of the Republican era, the contributions made by the indigenous maternal side were usually stifled. In fact, the more the Hakka blended themselves into the local social groups in biological terms, the more they wanted to expunge local elements from their cultural expressions. In the process, any idiosyncratic characteristics that would have served to differentiate themselves from the local people might have been overstated by the Hakka themselves. However, the Hakka could not erase the identical features exhibited in the eye-catching *tulou* architecture on both sides, so they simply made it 'their own'. Further investigation will very likely show that these fortresses were not built until the middle period of the Ming dynasty. Prior to this date, the sedentary valley societies of the two folk groups, the Minnan and Hakka, might have both pursued similar architectural styles and shared similar settlement arrangements. In other words, the consensus would seem to be that the Hakka had no idea of the concept of *tulou* architecture when they arrived in the area. This leaves us in the position that we cannot even say that the *tulou* is definitely a Hakka building style. The early settlement period of the Hekeng people lasted some fifty to seventy years, from the late-fifteenth century to the mid-sixteenth century. It is known that, during this period, the early Hakka settlers in Hekeng did not build one single *tulou* building; in other words Hekeng was not originally a *tulou* village.

1.3 LIMITATIONS TO TULOU SITE INTERPRETATION

Before offering an interpretation of the Hekeng *tulou* site, several important limitations in this research must be acknowledged. In such settlements as Hekeng, Taxia, Nanou and Shiqiao, there are many ways of gaining a knowledge of the past: reading carved epitaphs and inscriptions, visiting vernacular buildings or attending traditional festival rituals. A local resident's memory about his/her forebears can still be rekindled by the sight of a garden in which his/her great-grandfather, grandfather and father had once worked. Today, the local people still write their own histories in the form of compiling lineage genealogies in more or less the same way as their ancestors did in the past. Therefore, unlike prehistoric or early historical sites, their settlements are obviously more specific, palpable, visible and complete. This might lead people to jump too easily to the conclusion that 'the old ways' and traditions are still alive. Therefore they will expect that more information about the past of such settlements can be obtained by exploring the abovementioned sources of evidence, especially the written sources. However, this is easier said than done as three obstacles stand in the way.

The first stumbling-block is that people might prefer to remember a past that can be used to justify the present (Gathercole, 1994), or, simply, a past that pleases them. New memories might be constructed at the expense of losing those seen as outdated or undesirable, even though the outdated or unwanted memories could actually be indispensible keys to the past. Even within genealogies, not unexpectedly, unwanted social facts will be hushed up and family trees 'improved'; indeed sometimes the history of a lineage might even be rewritten. Memory, as reflected in the Hekeng case, does undoubtedly provide useful information about the location of buildings and the evolution of landscapes, even though it still obliterates or suppresses the tensions between families or individuals within the settlement. Importantly, very little is ever said about female lineage members. Although it proudly recounts the arduous journey of the migration, the difficult days of the early settlement period and the unwearied work of the ancestors, it rarely mentions quarrels, competitions or even outright fights within the Zhang lineage itself. It glosses over the competition with local non-Hakka people in the early settlement period. As in other places, when pedigrees are compiled, the lives of rich families and persons are usually recorded in more detail than those of ordinary families and community members (Chen, 2009). In a nutshell, the people in a lineage have created a history of their own, a narrative of their ancestors' glories and honors, an ideological statement that is morally and mentally acceptable to generations of the lineage mainstream and hence it has been transmitted down to the present. This selectively remembered history (Pieke, 2003) is partly responsible for the paradox noted above. The statement of significance in the WHL nominations of the *tulou* earthen 'castles' almost without exception focuses attention on building techniques, the authenticity of the materials and the structural integrity, tending to sideline the functions of or the reasons for which such massive strongholds were built – despite the fact their very massiveness and apparently defensive character are their most obvious characteristics. Although written records have deleted nearly all relevant information about the context in which a given stronghold was constructed (Xie, 2007), clues about the wars that required their construction can be found, at least in part, in the official documents of the Ming and Qing period prefecture or county governments. It stands to reason that strongholds are built to meet a defensive purpose. However, with the passing of time, in part the enemies of those who built the settlements and the undoubted tensions between the individuals and families involved have grown rather ambiguous in people's memories.

It would seem axiomatic that the construction of such huge buildings would have always been symptomatic of periods of wars, fighting and tensions, and that information about such upheavals has not been allowed to sully serious and reverential lineage pedigrees.[9] As a result, heritage managers are floundering when they try to match the construction of any single *tulou* to known important events in history books. Intra-clan or intra-lineage fighting, although quite a frequent occurrence in the hilly regions of southern Fujian until as late as the 1950s, is usually passed over in silence in local people's genealogies. Taken as a whole, all these factors mean that it is impossible to form a comprehensive view of either the settlement process or the reasons for the construction of *tulou* buildings purely on the basis of written records, and the material remains *per se* obviously do not tell us what they were. The upshot is that the 2007 WHL nomination says little about the formation process that produced any individual settlement, or of the landscapes in which the nominated buildings are located. This leaves the problem that, owing in large part to the deliberate deletion of 'negative' socioeconomic evidence that reflects the 'forgetting principles' of the local people, it even seems impossible to reconstruct the process of landscape development on a settlement scale.

The second hurdle to be overcome is that what is understood as 'official history' might not only be selective, but is sometimes even fabricated. In this chapter, I shall discuss some of the *citang* (ancestral temple or hall) buildings in southern Fujian. In front of such temples, it was usual to erect stone pillars/stele (*shi qigan*) to commemorate the glory that some lineage members had allegedly won as candidates in the imperial examinations. However, a double-check with the official documents of that time issued by the Imperial Court in Beijing suggests that some of the local people, especially the wealthy ones, might have fabricated such significant episodes in their lineage histories. Rural societies, insular as they are, can nonetheless share many values with the wider society. Historical veracity is not something about which local society showed much concern. Therefore, stone pillars, even if real and authentic in a material sense, could well lie about the events that never happened in history at all. This realization requires us to rethink the nature of authenticity, or rather, what we think it might be. However physically authentic a building or an object might be in the eyes of heritage managers, it might or might not be historically truthful. With no trustworthy historical reference – a situation that we experience all the time – what we can expect to know about a settlement might be no more than what the physical evidence itself offers. Under these circumstances, authenticity says little about historical truthfulness. When historical truthfulness is actually replaced by or viewed as no more important than the physical authenticity in heritage interpretation, we are in danger of losing the real significance of the heritage we are to manage. This begs the question of how much can physical evidence in itself contribute to the appropriate interpretation of a Hakka settlement?

The third and last problem to be faced is that the modern land surface area resembles nothing more closely than a patchwork quilt, represented by

9. A pedigree usually contains the following items: (1) paternal lineage origin; (2) the names of male lineage members and their kinship relationships; (3) records of the major male family heads, including name, official rank (if any), virtuous deeds when alive, wife, offspring, contribution to the family and lineage, and tomb location (Chen, 2009).

buildings and structures of different dates. As Roymans has pointed out, 'all landscape transformations necessarily involve a reordering, reuse and representation of the past which gives landscape development an almost non-linear character' (Kolen, 1995; Roymans, 1995). Archaeological sites invariably provide only layered compounds of remains representing different time periods. It is a truism that, on the whole the human occupation process in the hills in southern Fujian consists of multiple periods of habitation. A recent archeological survey of the nearby caves of Longyan has traced the earliest human habitation of the area to prehistoric times,[10] but officially the earliest occupation of the lower reaches of the Jiulong River began in the Yuan dynasty (1271-1368). It can be said with certainty that by that time a small number of local Minnan (*Fulao*) people had already settled in some of the river valleys, such as that of Shangban. However, in 90 percent of the river valleys in the area, no evidence of human habitation has been found prior to the early Ming dynasty (Chen, 2005). Since people might have continued to use the land from the very beginning of the settlement down to the present, it is feasible that much of the evidence of early Ming occupation could have already disappeared or the buildings that now occupy it might be entirely different. For most places along the lower Jiulong River, it is impossible to extrapolate a settlement interpretation framework from the successive occupation layers. Land in southern Fujian is extremely limited, and nearly all landscape uses (for example, agriculture) have been practiced continually on the same land surfaces, destroying evidence of earlier land use. We simply cannot use 'conventional' archaeological approaches to understand the reordering, reconstruction and reuse processes that have regularly occurred only to disappear horizontally. Unlike the 'layered' landscape biographies commonly seen in site-management practices, along the lower Jiulong River a five-hundred-year-long settlement history has been condensed into the same flat spatial dimensions. In interpreting a stratified archaeological site, heavy reliance is placed on the description of each layer and the characterization of the period it represents. Sometimes it is impossible to say no more than a few words about each period.[11] Hence, the details of history can have been reduced, or even replaced, by the number of layers of which we are aware. In abstract terms, it is periodization (not the totality of the real past) that creates a sense of history. In more concrete terms, both villagers and visitors can put their hands on the walls of an earthen fortress, tread the small path on the hill behind an ancestral temple and read an epitaph in front of a late Ming tomb. They might have both experienced precisely the feelings about the landscapes, vivid, specific, invariable and sensory. Although, standing in a *tulou* settlement, we are distinctly aware that all the huge buildings are to some extent antiquities themselves, the flat dimensions of the landscape reveal no clear layers and sequences. This renders archeological site periodization invalid. Through a long-term ongoing process of adaptive transformation or metabolism,[12] they have developed into what they look like today.

10. Since 2010, six prehistoric sites have been discovered in the Longyan mountain ranges, the earliest of which could be dated to the late Palaeolithic Age.

11. An archaeological site can be viewed as an agglomeration of different earth layers. In most cases, it is true that each layer derives from a stable land-use pattern. It is often the case that an archaeological layer has been formed over a long period from the time when the destruction of buildings and structures began to the time when a new land-use pattern commenced. Therefore, how many of the original building and structural remains that can be found in each layer depends primarily on how the later people decided to use the land. On land that has been successively occupied and used, evidence of earlier land-use is not always visible. In particular, even if such remains can be found, they do not always guarantee a good structural reconstruction, not even building foundations. Consequently, we cannot expect more from the layers. In essence, more often than not they show only the evidence of destruction and the impact of later land-use activities.

12. Basically, such processes include a wide range of changes ranging from room content replacement, roof-tile replacement, adornment refinement and substitution, and the complete reconstruction of a building after it has been damaged, abandoned or devastated by fire or for any other reason. However, it should be emphasized that buildings with different functional categories change at different rates. Similarly, different parts of the same architecture can also be substituted at different rates. The thick walls are by far the most durable part of a fortress and might not even change over a four-to-five-hundred-year period, whereas the pottery tiles and wooden parts are usually replaced every few years.

Five to six hundred years is certainly not a very long time period, but it definitely exceeds the time-depth that 'contemporary archaeology' defines (Buchli and Lucas, 2001).[13] With a relatively rare rate of abandonment, the land resources in almost every river valley have been used continuously and successively since the first settlement as early as over five hundred years ago. Although interpreters might hope to discover what really happened to the old *tulou* houses in the past, the very creation of those we can see today probably involved the modification or even destruction of the older ones. Wooden structures and weak-rammed earthen walls are very easy to destroy and dismantle. Construction, repair, restoration, destruction and reconstruction have recurred continuously since the establishment of the *tulou* buildings. Settlements had to renew themselves in order to 'survive'. The old earthen walls of the late Ming dynasty could have been embellished with very recent wooden structures. An ancestral temple could still preserve the form of its original design from the late Ming dynasty, yet have been reconstructed with new bricks. Parts of buildings and structures might remain in use until they can no longer function properly. As a result, more often than not, the now extant 'traditional' settlements are a kind of composites of the old and the recent. Even more importantly, we cannot draw a clear divide between the new and the old. The homological characteristics (changes and replacements recurring at the same locations) of spatial and architectural evolution play an important part in determining the interim form, not only of the architecture but also of the whole landscape. Therefore, at the very least, the process of morphological evolution cannot be reconstructed simply in a linear fashion, and by and large cannot be figured out at all. Quite unlike purely archaeological sites, vernacular settlements, that are still densely inhabited and actively used, usually maintain a balance between the old and the new, to the extent that the entire built environment is able serve the needs of daily life. As we shall explain in the following chapters, this process of the ongoing renewal of the built environment, or 'landscape metabolism', is an essential feature of living heritage. In any attempt to understand landscape history, this ongoing process of dynamic change means that materials as such can provide little, if any, useful information for reconstructing the key changes in a settlement, no matter on which spatial scale it is examined.

13. It focuses on the most recent (20th- and 21st-century) past.

Because of all these factors, living heritage[14] as such never stops changing, nor can it be expected to do so. Living heritage cannot be approached as though it and its products are archaeological sites. Certainly examples of material culture such as *tulou* architecture do provide physical evidence, but not enough, and arranging it along a timeline is not necessarily meaningful. Landscape biography methodology tells a history by using archaeological evidence, especially the concept of layers and assemblages. However, this is not applicable to a settlement context; we therefore need to modify and develop this approach. In short, we need to take up the challenge of building up a narrative about a place with no layers at all. Therefore, what we can rely on are primarily local historical records, including lineage genealogies, oral history materials plus other useful information documented in the Ming and Qing dynasty official records. In a nutshell, we can understand the architecture only by working out land-use patterns.

The purpose of the following interpretation of Hekeng settlement evolution is to answer the question of how Hekeng village has gradually evolved into its current form.

1.4 HOW HAS THE LANDSCAPE EVOLVED INTO ITS PRESENT FORM?

It would be too ambitious to reconstruct each episode of Hekeng settlement history from the extant written and oral evidence, but it is still necessary to pass some important facts that might help us understand the evolution of the built environment in the Hekeng River Valley briefly in review.

14. The term 'living heritage' is usually a term used by cultural resource management practitioners to denote intangible heritage. I am using it here to refer to the traditional built environment of the Hakka settlements.

Fig. 4 The façade of Chaoshui-lou, the first *tulou* building at Qiaoxia.

1.4.1 The Qiaoxia Settlement and the First Camp Shelter in the Mid-Sixteenth Century

The genealogy records that the Zhang lineage established its first settlement in Qiaoxia in the late fifteenth century,[15] occupying the heartland of the Hekeng River Valley. According to local historical records[16] preserved in the Nanjing County Archive Center,[17] the new settlers built their first *tulou* in the late Jiajing reign period, around 1549 to 1553, over half a century later than the foundation of the village. After the establishment of the Chaoshui-lou[18] in the sixteenth century, Hekeng became a settlement with a 'camp shelter', that might have only been used in the event of a bandit raid.

Fei (1953) argues that kinship organization and the need for mutual protection are the two most important factors that rural residents choose to

15. Niansanlang, founding father of the Zhangs, the high ancestor at Shiqiao, settled in Shiqiao in 1443, and hence his grandson, Shiliang, Hekeng the First, might have resettled in Hekeng in the late-15th century.

16. Dating information usually comes from inscribed stones, or in some cases, wooden plaques which were originally hung above the *tulou* main entrances. The year in which the construction of a *tulou* building was finished is said to have been inscribed on such plaques.

17. Also interviews with Zhang Enhan and Zhang Mintai in 2011.

18. It is said that the building caught on fire in 1923 and was later repaired by its residents. Therefore, what we see today is an almost fully restored building dating from the Republican period. The repaired building now has three stories, each with 20 rooms. New rooms have been added to each floor; now it has 67 rooms altogether. In the late-16th century, the Qiaoxia settlement in the Hekeng River Valley presented a typical 'one *tulou,* one settlement' pattern. The second *tulou* building was built in the late Wanli reign or early seventeenth century, but before 1620. Therefore, the Chaoshui-lou might have been in use for at least three-quarters of a century prior to the erection of the second *tulou* building.

Fig. 5 The inside of the Chaoshui-lou, corridors, ancestral shrine (*tang*) and rooms.

live together in villages. Farming communities are easily invaded, and the emphasis on defense is most clearly shown in the way 'farmhouses' are constructed. In the historical records, it would seem that the most serious upheavals in the Nanjing region in the Ming dynasty were caused by attacks either by local brigands or Japanese pirates. They include those that occurred on: (1) the tenth month of the fourteenth year of the Hongwu reign, 1381, in *Taizu Shilu* (The Chronicles of the Ming Dynasty, Taizu Emperor, Vol. 139); (2) the third month of the ninth year of the Xuande reign, 1434, in *Taizu Shilu* (The Chronicles of the Ming Dynasty, Taizu Emperor, Vol.109); the fourteenth year of the Zhengtong reign, 1449, in *Zhangzhou Fuzhi* (Zhangzhou Prefecture Gazetteer); the first year of the Zhengde reign, 1506, in *Zhangzhou Fuzhi*; the eighth year of the Zhengde reign, 1514, in *Zhangzhou Fuzhi*; the twenty-eighth year of the Jiajing reign, 1549, in *Pinghe Xianzhi* (Pinghe County Gazetteer); and the thirty-seventh year of the Jiajing reign, 1558, in *Zhangzou Fuzhi*. Clearly, around the late fifteenth century when the Qiaoxia settlement was established, whole areas of Nanjing county had been frequently threatened. Therefore it seems reasonable to assume that, in the 1550s, nearly seventy years after the establishment of the Qiaoxia settlement, the Hekeng people began to build their own square *tulou* 'castle' to defend themselves against attacks and pillaging from outside the valley. As said earlier, the first *tulou* building in the Hekeng River Valley was most probably established to defend the first lineage settlement in Qiaoxia. However, it is still a matter of speculation whether the local residents had already become accustomed to living inside such a public shelter for very long periods, or even permanently, when the Chaoshui-lou was initially built (Figs 4 and 5).

The first 150 years of Hekeng history appear to have undergone two periods of population growth. In the *Genealogy* (1994), Shiliang plays the leading role in the whole process of the Qiaoxia resettlement. His father and grandfather had moved to the new settlement, and both passed away and were buried in Hekeng. The record also unequivocally states that, soon after Shiliang moved to Hekeng, his elder brother Zongren's son, Foyang, also arrived with his own family members. Even if we make a rather low estimate of the total population of the joint families, such as one couple with one or two children in each nuclear family, three to four people per family, in the first seventy-five years prior to the first *tulou* construction, the population size of the first Hekeng settlement in Qiaoxia can be roughly reckoned at thirty to fifty people. By and large, the rooms on the first floor of a *tulou* building are used for cooking, animal husbandry and so on. The barns and storehouses are usually located on the second floor. Therefore, rooms for purely residential use only account for 30 to 40 percent of the total space inside the Chaoshui-lou. In a normal situation, only twenty to thirty rooms would have been used as residential rooms, just enough to house the members of the Qiaoxia settlement, about fifty people in all, and the structure of the first *tulou*, like that of many other contemporaneous ones in this hilly area, would have presented an equity in room size and arrangement.

This unusual domestic arrangement has prompted researchers to ask an essential question: late Ming dynasty Imperial China was highly commercial and stratified in both social and economic terms, therefore why did the people living here acquiesce in having accepting such equally partitioned spatial arrangements? Basically scholars, such as Huang (2009), believe that social equity, evident in the establishment of lineage trust and the ways the local gentry dealt with the lineage affairs in traditional rural society in general, decisively shaped the inside spatial arrangement of the *tulou* buildings. This interpretation is based on the assumption that an equally divided room arrangement pattern derives from the concept of social equity in general. However, what we know about Hakka rural society directly contradicts such an interpretation. Usually, the lineage had no right to limit the expansion of each family's own real estate and wealth. While it is true that, when newly built, on the whole the Chaoshui-lou would have served the whole lineage as a communal shelter, like most farmhouses, cottages and workshops in the settlement, the ownership of the wooden lodges inside the *tulou* building belonged to individuals and households. They were ordinary household property. It is an established fact that, from the turbulent late Ming dynasty, earthen 'castles' were usually constructed by raising funds among the lineage members throughout the whole Fujian rural region and that the wooden lodges inside the buildings were allocated on the basis of the contribution to the project, in effect the families bought the rooms. Nowadays, although the rooms in a *tulou* building are fairly similar to each other in size, the total number of rooms one household can own is quite a different matter. Richer families can have access to more space in the 'public' shelter than the poorer ones. The ostensible equity visible in the room partitioning might have been a reaction, in part at least, to the external threats. In emergency situations when war raged and raids threatened, social inequity would have been reduced to a much lower level, or even totally camouflaged, by the struggles between the lineage and its external enemies. When danger was imminent, it is conceivable that the Hakka people had to construct their shelter in a very short time, and the shortest way to achieve their goal was to insert standardized wooden components directly into the earthen walls, leading to an evenly divided room arrangement inside the *tulou* building. Adopting this method, the room construction could be completed immediately the walls had been erected, effectively shortening the overall construction period.

1.4.2 The Resettlement in Yuantang and the Establishment of the Yongsheng-lou in the Early-Seventeenth Century

Over the following seventy-five years, the population of Qiaoxia settlement might have grown to forty to seventy people, if we assume the 0.4 percent annual population growth rate that has been suggested by Zhou (2007) as a mean rate in the areas bordering

Fig. 6 The inside of the Yongsheng-lou (with no shrine).

Fujian and Guangdong. Apart from such an estimate, according to the genealogy, the fourth-generation (that is, the second-generation in Hekeng) ancestor Liu'er moved back to Shiqiao with his wife and children. Given the fact that from the Zhengtong reign era (1436-1449), southern Fujian rural society was rapidly being reduced to chaos by the ravages of pirates and brigands, Liu'er family's reverse migration suggests that the Hekeng Zhang lineage might have intentionally controlled its population to a number that could be accommodated only in one shelter (Chaoshui-lou). However, between the 1560s and the early-seventeenth century, the population size of the Hekeng Zhang lineage grew to exceed what the Qiaoxia settlement could support. A square *tulou* as large as the Chaoshui-lou could accommodate only a very limited number of families. Within three, perhaps or even two, generations a new family would regularly split off from the old nuclear or extended family. Unquestionably, some of the lineage members would have had to move out of the Qiaoxia settlement and resettle in other localities nearby in the same river valley. It was precisely at this time that Chongzheng's family was poised to split away from the old core family in Qiaoxia. As the genealogy says, Zhang Chongde and Zhang Chongbao lived in the Chaoshui-lou with their own families, whereas their brother, Chongzheng, was forced to leave. His forced move gave rise to the resettlement in Yuantang. The concrete evidence for this resettlement is the establishment of the second square *tulou* in the Hekeng River Valley, Yongsheng-lou in Yuantang (Fig. 6).

Precisely at the time of the sixth generation of the Zhang lineage of Hekeng, Zhang Chongzheng, the grandson of Liuyi who had organized the construction of the Chaoshui-lou, directed and organized the construction of the second *tulou* building. According to the rule described by Szonyi (2002), local defense boiled down to defense of one's kin. Therefore the second shelter was probably built to protect the new settlers in Yuantang settlement, who, as a new branch (*fang*), probably shared a much closer kinship relationship and could have hived off from their Qiaoxia relatives. In this instance, the establishment of the new *tulou* building can also be taken as evidence of the emergence of a new lineage segment at a *fang* level. As the genealogy shows, from the fourth generation to the sixth generation, the rooms in the shelter had become an inheritance that could be bequeathed to the next generation. Although the *tulou* buildings on the whole must certainly have been counted as part of the collective assets of the lineage, each household of the new branch could have expected its own property inside the newly built *tulou* building.

A conservative estimate of the population size in Hekeng in the early-seventeenth century is approximately one hundred. As GIS analysis shows, the level land in Hekeng River Valley amounts to about 200 *mu*, and only part of it had actually been cultivated as agricultural land. If we take an average estimate of rice production to be 200 *jin*/*mu*/season (unhusked), we can still be fairly confident about the capacity of subsistence farming in the river valley itself to support a village of 100 people. Consequently, even relying purely on an agricultural economy, the villagers would not need to have worried too much about the decrease in the amount of arable land that would have been caused by the *tulou* construction.

At the time that the Yongsheng-lou was established, it can be postulated that a certain number of private farmhouses in the form of courtyard dwellings, cottages, thatched huts and simple structures of rammed earth still existed alongside the *tulou*. Even though people had begun to rely more on the secure environment they could find inside the *tulou*, the farmhouses might still have been important. Indeed, from time to time, they might have helped the local community to ease the severe overcrowding inside the *tulou* buildings, by providing unmarried children with the space to live apart from their married elder brothers. In short, ordinary (unfortified) farmhouses might have long been used from the inception of the village up to the recent past. Their flexible functions ranged from residences pure and simple, workshops and storehouses to courtyards for religious use.

1.4.3 The Establishment of the Shiying-tang Ancestral Temple in the Early-Seventeenth Century

As Fan (2009) and Szonyi (2002) have pointed out, from the middle Ming to the early Qing dynasty, ancestral temples on all ritual levels (clan/lineage/branch/family) began to be built throughout all the rural areas of Fujian. The establishment of the Shiying-tang Ancestral Temple (Generation Elite Temple on Nanshan)[19] in 1610 and the construction of the second *tulou* in Hekeng at roughly the same time could be clues to a heightening of an unusual tension between the lineage branches caused by the first population growth burst of the Zhang lineage in Hekeng since its initial settlement in the late-fifteenth century (Figs 7 and 8). From the late-fifteenth to the early-seventeenth century, the Zhang lineage in Hekeng was in the process of developing its first hived-off settlement in Qiaoxia. In this period, the population of the Qiaoxia settlement grew to a relatively large size. By the beginning of the seventeenth century, the *tulou* shelter even in conjunction with ordinary farmhouses could no longer house the population. Before the intra-valley resettlement to Yuantang took place, it is a reasonable assumption that the people who had lived in the settlement in Qiaoxia would already have extended their farming activities to other parts of the valley. Before the birth of the new settlement in Yuantang, all the land resources in the valley had been owned by the lineage branch in Qiaoxia. This, of course, would have encompassed the Yuantang land newly brought under cultivation by some of the families in

19. Literally, South Mountain, in fact a small hill that stretches along the southern edge of the Hekeng River Valley.

the first settlement. However, once the population movement commenced, some of the new land ownership would naturally have been transferred to the newly established Yuantang lineage branch. This would have represented a considerable loss of arable land for the Qiaoxia people. The tension would also have been deeply rooted in the fact that the Yuantang people would not only have taken away part of the lineage's land as their own farming capital, but would also have claimed their share in the right to expand their own territory throughout the whole river valley. In other words, a competitor settlement would have been established. The establishment of the Shiying-tang, the principal ancestor temple of the Hekeng people, could be a hint of the need felt to alleviate this tension between the two lineage branches.

As the genealogy says, 'It was Zhang Chongbao, Zhang Chongde and Zhang Chongzheng who built the temple on Nanshan.' Chongzheng, with his own family and probably many other families of the same descent, moved out of the first Zhang lineage settlement in Qiaoxia. Under Chongzheng's leadership, they established the second settlement in Yuantang. At this point, the three brothers represented three lineage branches of the same generation, the two in Qiaoxia and the one in Yuantang. As the key persons in the patriarchal system of the sixth generation in Hekeng, they shared the power to manage lineage affairs. It is possible to understand the establishment of the ancestral temple at this time in the much broader context of prevailing social disorder. In the early-seventeenth century, the Hekeng society – composed of two consanguine settlements – could hardly have escaped the suffering inflicted by the widespread social unrest in the southern Fujian area. Desperate times call for desperate measures. The contemporaneous general social disorder made it especially important for the two settlements to maintain an amicable relationship, although feelings between them must have been strained by the founding of the second settlement. The establishment of the Shiying-tang Ancestral Temple near Yuantang can be seen as a monument to the reunification of the two branches of the Zhang lineage in the two settlements. At this precarious moment in time, group cohesiveness needed to be strengthened by reiterating a common ancestry, paying respect to the distant male ancestors, both in temple ceremonies and on other suitable occasions such as funerals, festivals, times for religious offerings and even wedding ceremonies. Another reason the establishment of the ancestral temple at this crucial time was of great importance is that the temple itself could have served as a symbol marking the *de facto* occupation of the Hekeng River Valley by the Zhang lineage, especially given the fact that its settlements were located in the area contiguous with that of the Minnan people.

As the most important piece of monumental architecture,[20] the Shiying-tang Temple provided a public sphere in which agnates could communicate with the souls of their ancestors. In their study of lineage management in Fujian's rural areas during the Ming and Qing dynasties, Chen (2009) and Zheng (1991) state that the basic instruments through which a lineage could be managed were the ancestral temples, the genealogies and lineage-owned properties, including the lineage trust. In their very detailed research, they demonstrate how the lineage power was used to coordinate the whole settlement society on the basis of a system consisting of these three correlated instruments. Therefore, the construction of the Shiying-tang Ancestral Temple can be used as evidence to support the existence of a growing patriarchal power in Hekeng, that had just begun to direct the village affairs of the Hekeng people in the early days of the seventeenth century. The establishment of the Shiying-tang Ancestral Temple in Hekeng marked the end of the early habitation process of the Zhang lineage. Importantly, Niansanlang, the apical ancestor of the Zhang lineage in the hilly area, was buried in Hekeng and his descendents opted for Hekeng as the site at which to build their ancestral temple. These two crucial clues lead to the postulation that the temple on Nanshan actually functioned as the principal ancestral temple of the whole Zhang surname, including the Shiqiao lineage.

20. The expenditure for construction could have come from cost apportionment, whose regulation must have been understood and accepted by each member of the Zhang community.

Fig. 7 The Shiying-tang with Nanshan Hill behind.

1.4.4 The Resettlement to Xizhuba in the Late-Seventeenth Century

The two lineage heads of the ninth generation recorded in the genealogy are Zhang Shixiang and Zhang Shifa. The same generation name '*shi*' indicates that they were either siblings or cousins. They achieved prominence in the Hekeng lineage because they represented the two core families resident in Yuantang and Xizhuba, the second and third settlements of the Zhang lineage in the Hekeng River Valley, respectively.

According to the genealogical record, 'Shixiang owned rooms in the Yongsheng-lou' [in Yuantang] built by the sixth-generation ancestor. At his first appearance in the genealogy, Shifa is referred to as the founding father of the new settlement in Xizhuba: 'Shifa and his family lived in Xizhuba.' No details that describe the building arrangements in this new settlement at the time of Shifa are given. However, the genealogy goes on to say that it was the eleventh generation that built the first *tulou* in Xizhuba. On the basis of what is recorded in the *Genealogy of the Huang Lineage in Shangban*, the first two generations (Shifa and his sons) would have lived in ordinary farmhouses, courtyard complexes or even thatched huts. Although Shifa's death is not recorded, his brother (or cousin) Shixiang died in 1704, the forty-third year of the Kangxi reign of the Qing dynasty. Therefore it can plausibly be assumed that the Xizhuba settlement was established in the late-seventeenth century.

Fig. 8 The Shiying-tang in the foreground with the North Hill, where Dexin-tang was once located, in the distance.

As Zhou (2009) has pointed out, the 'tenth generation' usually marks a significant turning-point in the population growth of single-surname villages such as Hekeng. As the genealogy states, the ninth-generation ancestor Shifa, Shixiang's brother or cousin, 'moved' to Xizhuba and established the third settlement of the village there, namely: the Xizhuba settlement. This resettlement activity lends weight to the hypothesis about the size of the population growth by the tenth generation of a village. At least, it is not difficult to imagine that the first two settlements could no longer provide enough space to house more people, including Shifa and his family members. For this reason, the land in Xizhuba began to be intensively 'exploited' and cultivated in the early days of the eighteenth century. In different time periods, the intra-valley resettlements cast considerable light on the rhythm at which the whole Zhang lineage expanded in terms of population size and land resource exploitation. Between the late- fifteenth to the early-seventeenth century the population of Hekeng doubled, and it is very likely that, in the following one hundred years, the number actually tripled. In the first 240 years altogether, ten generations of Zhang clansmen had lived in the river valley; therefore, if the intergenerational age difference is taken to be around twenty years, this seems a very reasonable estimate.

On the basis of the official Ming dynasty population record of the five provinces of North China in 1393, from the twenty-sixth year of the Hongwu reign, to 1542, the twenty-first year of the Jiajing reign, Ho (1959) calculated a possible population growth

Fig. 9 Shengqing-lou.

rate of 0.34 percent. Using a similar strategy, Ge (1991) reached a rate of 0.5 percent, that he believes could be applied to the reconstruction of population processes in the period from 1600 to 1620. The average growth rate in most of pre-modern China cannot be properly estimated, simply because of the cumulative effects of high rural birth and death rates. According to the official demographics in 1981, much later than the commonly agreed upon divide between the pre-modern and modern periods set in the early 1910s, in total there were forty-six households and 116 people in Xizhuba, fifty-four households and 279 people in Yuantang, and ninety-six households and 594 people in Qiaoxia. In 1981, there were 1,084 people living in the Hekeng River Valley and this figure had increased to 1,196 in the 2005 demographic records. Examining these two thorough censuses of population in Nanjing county taken in 1981 and 2005 respectively, it is not difficult to reconstruct a possible average annual growth rate of 0.41 percent, that straddles the two estimated rates cited above. In fact, we might have many options in a wide range between 0.3 and 0.5 percent. However, a figure as low as 0.3 percent might contradict the fact that, in the very beginning, only a small number of families moved into the valley. A relatively conservative and reasonable value is 0.4 percent. When we apply this value to the calculation, we find that the population in the Hekeng River Valley might have risen to approximately 300 just prior to the 1680s. This reconstruction, although it could be criticized as representing a unilinear demographic development model, still offers the opportunity to reach a relatively correct relationship between the

Fig. 10 The *Huaiting* Ancestral Hall built inside the Shengqing-lou, in a courtyard dwelling shape.

population sizes in Hekeng at different times. Before the construction of the Shengqing-lou (Figs 9 and 10), at the time of the eleventh-generation ancestor in Xizhuba, a population size as large as 300 would have posed a real challenge to the *tulou* buildings of the whole village. At the very most, these two *tulou* buildings could have provided shelter for only around 200 to 250 people and actual permanent residence for a much smaller population. The risk is, as suggested by the figures, that some of the lineage members could not have been assigned residential spaces inside the enclosed *tulou* shelters and would therefore not have had effective protection. This inference could help us understand the basic architectural development in the river valley. At this period, farmhouses in the form of cottages, two-story earthen buildings or thatched huts might have been necessary to alleviate the shortage of residential space. The establishment of the Shengqing-lou, the first *tulou* shelter in Xizhuba during the Yongzheng reign period (1723-1735), would have effectively relieved such pressures.

1.4.5 The Establishment of the Dexin-tang Hall in Yuantang in the Early-Eighteenth Century

After Shixiang's death, the genealogy says, 'the tenth generation people began to hold offering ceremonies separately.' In 1704, nearly eighty years after the formation of the Yuantang settlement, the five brothers/cousins (Ranxiang, Renbi, Renchen, Renyin and Renwu) of the tenth generation raised funds to enable the establishment of a new ancestral hall, called the Dexin-tang or the Hall of Virtuous

Fragrance, as a place in which to hold offering ceremonies, dedicated solely to the ninth-generation ancestor, Shixiang, in recompense for his prominent role in settlement affairs and great contribution to the Yuantang settlement, as suggested by the name of the hall. This is an example of what some anthropologists call a *fensi* or *teji*, meaning a separate offering. *Fensi* can be regarded as an important indicator of social regrouping. The hall was demolished in the 1970s, but its location is still known among the local residents. Dedicated to ancestor Shixiang, the ninth-generation settlement head in Yuantang, the Dexin-tang Hall actually belongs only to the Yuantang settlement members. The separation of offering activities from those of other lineage branches in Xizhuba and Qiaoxia is based on kinship distance. In Yuantang, Ancestor Shixiang was viewed by his descendants as the most important male ancestor with a direct impact on the settlement. It is conceivable that the ancestors from the sixth to the eighth generations of Yuantang were still inscribed on the offering list of the prime ancestral temple on Nanshan. The establishment of the Dexin-tang Hall on North Hill explains why there is no ancestral shrine in the Yongsheng-lou in Yuantang. It seems feasible to assume that the people living in the Yongsheng-lou went to the Dexin-tang Hall to pay their respects to their common near ancestors. The presence of this special temple obviated the need to build an ancestral shrine inside the *tulou* building. This is also a clue that the Dexin-tang Hall was indeed built before the construction of the Yongsheng-lou, when the then-new settlers in Yuantang might still have been living in farmhouses, courtyard dwellings or other similar constructions. Clearly, the traditional non-*tulou* settlement pattern was still playing an important role in this transition period.

The establishment of the Dexin-tang Hall, devoted to the ninth generation ancestor in Yuantang by his immediate descendants of the tenth generation, marked another important event in the world of Hekeng. It reflected a desire of the Yuantang settlers to loosen the ties between the two settlements and concomitantly strengthen the internal links between the members of their own settlement. Interestingly, Yuantang only began to be inhabited by the Hekeng people in the sixth generation. As recorded in the genealogy, Zhang Chongzheng, the sixth-generation ancestor, organized the construction of the Yongsheng-lou. Nevertheless, he was not viewed by his successors in Yuantang as the founding father of the settlement and was not even accorded a place in the newly built Dexin-tang. This deliberate oversight is significant and, taken in conjunction with the overvaluation of the near ancestor, Shixiang, seems to indicate a need felt for economic independence from Qiaoxia. Nevertheless, as the high ancestor of the Yuantang settlement in the lineage pedigree, Chongzheng might still crop up in the collective memory as a person with a strong link to the Qiaoxia settlement, and therefore inappropriately a rather inconvenient link between the two settlements. All these intricate relationships led to an important decision made by the tenth-generation descendants that is summarized in the genealogy as follows: 'The [tenth-generation] five brothers jointly built the Dexin-tang Hall to conduct ceremonies dedicated to the important male patriarchs [of the Yuantang settlement] from the ninth-generation ancestor Shixiang and thereafter.'

1.4.6 The Establishment of the Shengqing-lou and the *Huaiting* Hall in the Early-Nineteenth Century

Two generations after the establishment of the Xizhuba settlement at the time of Shiyou, Zhang Shifa's grandson, the new settlers in Xizhuba built their first square *tulou* building, the Shengqing-lou inside which they constructed an ancestral hall of their own, the '*Huaiting*' (Figs 11, 12, 13, 14 and 15).[21] As its photograph illustrates, the structure and the interior arrangement of the *Huaiting* Hall is in effect analogous to the Shiying-tang Ancestral Temple and also, very probably, to the demolished Dexin-tang Hall. They both take the shape of a traditional courtyard dwellings with wooden structures that, as noted earlier, had been a popular feature in central and southern Fujian for a very long time. When it was built, the function of the *Huaiting* Hall would have been to serve as a public place in which to conduct offering ceremonies to the ancestors of the Xizhuba people, the majority of whom had lived

21. Courtyard of locust trees.

Fig. 11 The *Huaiting* Ancestral Hall, a side view.

Fig. 12 The tiled tops of the *Huaiting.*

Fig. 13 The *Huaiting* Hall viewed from outside the *tulou* gate.

Fig. 14 The 'hero' now inside the *Huaiting* Hall, Baosheng dadi, the Protector.

Fig. 15 Wooden plaque hanging on the inside gate of *Huaiting* in honor of Shengqing-lou residents, inscribed '*de shi xiang lü*', or 'village model of benevolence'.

in the Shengqing-lou. Like the Dexin-tang Hall of the Yuantang lineage branch, the *Huaiting* was also a place in which to make *fensi* offerings and belonged exclusively to the Xizhuba branch. As a newly developed lineage branch (*fang*), the core families in Xizhuba needed to legitimate their land tenure and property rights. The small wooden shrine built in the rear section of the Shengqing-lou was not sufficiently impressive to give outward expression to such an important economic requirement. Shixiang, as noted earlier, had already been accorded the most important place in the Dexin-tang Hall by his descendants in Yuantang, and this could have been a stimulus for their relatives living in Xizhuba, who, it would seem immediately felt a pressing need to build their own hall to worship the founding father of the Xizhuba settlement, Zhang Shifa, Shixiang's brother. As demonstrated earlier, the population size of Hekeng River Valley might have reached 300 in the early-eighteenth century, and the people in Xizhuba could have begun to feel the pinch of resource and cropland shortages. With land in short supply, they eventually chose to construct the courtyard-like hall inside the *tulou* building itself.

1.4.7 The Settlement Pattern in the Hekeng River Valley in the Early-Nineteenth Century

As calculated earlier, the early-eighteenth century, roughly at the time of the tenth generation of the lineage, witnessed a major population boom in the river valley. Growth in population ushered in demographic change and the new family patriarchs felt it was incumbent on themselves to conduct their own separate ancestor worship ceremonies in their newly established halls (the Dexin-tang and the *Huaiting*). *Fensi* had become established. Core families within the same settlement had begun to share more common interests and hence became more intimately and closely linked. These ties between the core families were reinforced by the *fensi* ceremonial activities. The formation of the three settlements, the sharp increase in population and the emergence of *fensi* are all indicators that a period of social reconstruction emerged in around the tenth generation of the Hekeng Zhang lineage.

The early-nineteenth century saw the formation of a Zhang lineage village consisting of three independently inhabited cores. All the three major lineage branches had already developed their own square *tulou* buildings. To assert a growing sense of independence, as well as the mother ancestral temple on Nanshan, the people living in the Yuantang and Xizhuba settlements decided to build their own ancestral halls. This tripartite settlement pattern was based primarily on the three major lineage segments (*fang*) that had gradually split away from the core families at different times since the early-seventeenth century. This evidence is backed up by the fact that the local people say that in a later period two other major lineage branches were formed but had to establish their own square *tulou* buildings inside the pre-existing settlement framework.

1.4.8 *Tulou*, the Predominant Dwelling Form

The preface provides a very brief introduction to the social background of the inception of *tulou* buildings in the southern Fujian region in the sixteenth-century. The question that has not been answered so far is why the people in the three settlements in the Hekeng River Valley eventually all moved away from an individual settlement pattern into *tulou* buildings and used the rooms allotted to them as their permanent residences. What was the driving force behind the *tulou* becoming the major dwelling form?

In the first chapter of the *Yiyan, Shengji* (The Heart Stories, Subsistence) of the *Juanshige wen jiaji* (Juanshi Hall Anthology Volume One) by the Qing Dynasty man-of-letters Hong Liangji, the author says that, 'food for one person per year is often provided by 4 *mu* of arable land; hence, around 40 *mu* of land is just enough to support an extended family of around ten people.' Following the rule proposed by Hong, it can be calculated that about 1,000 *mu* of arable land could feed a village with a population of 300 people, as Hekeng was. However, there is a rub. There is a chance that this calculation might be inappropriate when applied to the study of the agricultural land resources of southern Fujian, because the different versions of the county gazetteers report that double-crop (for some places even triple-crop) rice-farming had already begun to be practiced during the Ming dynasty at the very latest. If the weather conditions were favorable, better quality land in southern Fujian could have reached a production of 600 *jin*/*mu*/year (including the weight of the husks). Under these circumstances, 1 *mu* of arable land could feed one to two people for a single year. The only drawback to this assumption is that it is also uncertain whether the *mu* measure proposed by Hong is actually identical to the *mu* in southern Fujian, especially that in the rural areas of Nanjing county. It is certainly probable that different settlements discretely located in different river valleys might not have shared the same idea of how large a *mu* of land should be. Despite this doubt about the exact measurement of a *mu*, the *Nanjing County Gazetteer* does provide important evidence, albeit from a century later, from which to evaluate the rice-production capacity per *mu* under traditional Chinese agricultural conditions using no fertilizers and no mechanized irrigation systems. In the 1949 records, in the rural areas of Nanjing county rice production with three crops per year once reached a highest level of 605 *jin*/*mu*/year, including the rice husks. The *Gazetteer* states that changes in farming conditions, especially the use of fertilizers and irrigation machines, only began to be introduced in the 1950s. If this is so, it is plausible to suppose that the 1949, and even early 1950s, evidence is a valid tool by which to assess the yield from farming activities in pre-capital/socialist times, namely: the assumption that the annual production per *mu* in this period could have approached that of the late-Ming to the early-Qing dynasty.

This said, a *mu* yield could display a wide range of variation. A yield higher than 500 *jin*/*mu*/year is therefore only a high level value on good soil. Therefore it should be taken in conjunction with the evidence stated in the *Gazetteer* that, during the social movement called 'Land Resource Quality Improvement' in the 1950s, people discovered that there was indeed a large amount of low-quality land in the rural areas of Nanjing County. At that time, the criterion for assessing low-quality land was a yield of 300 *jin*/*mu*/year, including husks. This information helps us set the lower limit of the land average annual yield. Records (Dong, 2012) of average *mu* rice yield from the Qing dynasty Guangxi region, especially the places with fairly similar weather and agricultural conditions to Nanjing county, can also help us reconstruct the lower limit in rural Nanjing: Guilin Prefecture, 1.3 to 2.84 *dan*/*mu*; Liuzhou Prefecture, 2.39 *dan*/*mu*; Qingyuan Prefecture, 3 *dan*/*mu*; Sien Prefecture, 2.74 *dan*/*mu*; Pingle Prefecture, 2.3 *dan*/*mu*; Wuzhou Prefecture, 2.39 *dan*/*mu*; Nanning Prefecture, 1.94 *dan*/*mu*; Taiping Prefecture, 2.18 *dan*/*mu*; Yulin zhilizhou, 2.43 *dan*/*mu*; Sicheng Prefecture, 2.76 *dan*/*mu*; Zhenan Prefecture, 2.92 *dan*/*mu*. The average value of that region was approximately 2.48 *dan*/*mu*, or 297.6 *jin*/*mu* (with husks), a value nearly the same as the *mu* yield value of the low-quality land identified in Nanjing county in the 1950s. Therefore, it is very likely that the high *mu* yield played only a very minor part in the statistics, leading us to conclude that an annual yield of 300 *jin* rice (with husks) /*mu* or even less would be a reasonable average estimate.

Another fact to note in the field of agriculture is that high-yield New World crops, such as maize and sweet potatoes, only gained popularity during the Qianlong reign (1711-1799). Consequently, from the late-seventeenth century to at least the early-eighteenth century, people living in southern Fujian were still reliant on rice and low-yield vegetables.

Local residents had to balance land use among a variety of purposes: rice, vegetables, residences, temples plus anything else. It was an iron law of local farming traditions, no matter what the circumstances, level lands (*yang tian*) that are easily irrigated would have invariably been assigned to rice cultivation. An average yield even lower than 300 *jin*/*mu*, combined with a piece of arable land of less than 150 *mu*, must have presented a big challenge to the lineage heads of the Hekeng settlements who were responsible for feeding a population of approximately 300 people by the Qianlong reign period of the Qing dynasty, that is, in the early-eighteenth century. The establishment of the third settlement suggests that, by the early-eighteenth century, nearly all the level land had already been cultivated and that, until the early-eighteenth century, all three Hekeng settlements still relied heavily on subsistence rice agriculture. Unlike the population of the many settlements located in the nearby western Fujian mountain ranges, the people in the Hekeng settlements had not yet switched their economic activities to business, trade or cash crops. Hence, relying purely on the level land low-yield rice subsistence pattern, the Zhang lineage in Hekeng might have begun to suffer from food shortages as early as the late-seventeenth century.

Historians such as Xie (2007) have postulated that it might have been the increasing social chaos and wars between the Minnan Fulao people and the Hakka people from the late Ming and thereafter that gradually forced people to move into the *tulou* shelters and live there permanently. Unquestionably, in each of numerous cases (see the Appendix), the early history of Fujian earthen fortified buildings (walled villages and dwellings) does include a period from the late Ming dynasty in which people did not live permanently inside the walled enclosures. Most of the Fujian earthen 'castles' (*bao*) were still only used provisionally as shelters during times of conflict, and this could be the essential reason most of them were finally abandoned. The majority of the inner spaces of the *bao* 'castles' were arranged horizontally. Unlike these shelters, the vertically arranged inner structure of *tulou* buildings offers better opportunities for housing more people living together over a longer period. The Shengqing-lou, for example, has seventy apartments and occupies nearly 2,310 square meters, but the floor area measures 4,600 square meters. The latter is nearly twice as large as the former. If the building housed 100 people, the living space per head was 46 square meters. Were this sort of population to be housed in the usual farmhouses, it would have required at least twice the amount of level land as that occupied by the *tulou*. The construction of the *Huaiting* Hall inside the Shengqing-lou is a good example of the intention to save agricultural land. The small ancestral hall was created at some point during the late Yongzheng or early Qianlong reign. In this period, the Qing Empire was enjoying a peaceful, untroubled way of life. Raids and warfare in southern Fujian had declined dramatically since the early Kangxi reign. Therefore, in this instance, the decision to establish the hall inside the *tulou* building was not based on the need to guarantee its security; it was more realistically justified by the need to save arable land. Similarly, the true driving force that finally decided the Hekeng people to live permanently inside the *tulou* buildings might also have been the desire to save arable land. Although initially they began living in *tulou* buildings for defensive reasons, when peace came the *tulou* buildings continued to be used and the population was concentrated in them because of land shortages resulting from a sharp increase in the local population.

1.4.9 The Construction of the Square *Tulou* Chain and the Finalization of the Three-Layered Ancestral Worship System in Hekeng in the Late-Nineteenth Century

The built environment in Hekeng began to change rapidly in the early-nineteenth century. The patriarchs of the Yuantang settlement built a new *tulou* alongside the Yongsheng-lou. At this time, this is the Yongrong-lou (Figs16 and 17), or the Mansion of Eternal Honor, the second square *tulou* building in the Yuantang settlement. The construction of the Yongrong-lou in Yuantang provides a good illustration of the dilemma posed by land use in the Hekeng River Valley from the late Yongzheng to the early Qianlong reigns. In some instances, the space between the Yongrong-lou and the Yongsheng-lou measures less than 1 meter. According to the genealogical record, the tenth-generation ancestor,

Renwu, lived in the Yongsheng-lou, but his brother Renchen and most of the next-generation ancestors lived in the Yongrong-lou. Therefore, the bulk of the ownership of apartments in both *tulou* buildings was in the hands of members of the Yuantang settlement. Of the three settlements, Yuantang was the first to construct a second *tulou* building. By this time, all the level fields and gentle slopes had been nibbled away. No more land was available in the nearby river valleys. Consequently, from that period the Hekeng people had no choice but to 'double up' inside the boundaries of their own settlement. Forced by high population pressure, some of them eventually chose to emigrate new destinations, for instance, in Taiwan or Sichuan.

Rapid population growth could result in two contradictory trends: residential expansion or arable land preservation. Since the middle Qianlong reign, several strategies had been employed to cope with the tensions caused by sharp population increases. The first was to create more residential space (such as the Yongrong-lou and the later *tulou* buildings) or to save more room by taking full advantage of the space inside the *tulou* (for example, the construction of the *Huaiting* Hall inside the Shengqing-lou). The second option was to find and cultivate more arable land resources (such as land on hill slopes, commonly seen in Hakka societies scattered throughout the Jiulong River valleys). The third alternative was to emigrate to new places (for example, families from the eleventh generation began to move to Taiwan and Sichuan). The fourth course of action was to rely partially or fully on non-agricultural economic branches such as business, trade, cash crops (tea, tobacco or indigo) and paper production, all more profitable than subsistence agriculture. Finally, for those who wanted to persist in the traditional ways, the answer was to plant more high-yielding crops such as sweet potatoes and maize. Certainly, from the late Kangxi reign, the local population began to rely more heavily on these two plants.

As poor as the Hekeng people were, in the nineteenth century alone, three new square *tulou* buildings (Figs 18, 19 and 20) were erected separately in Xizhuba (the Nanxun-lou, in the 1820s to the 1850s) and Qiaoxia (the Yangzhao-lou, 1875; theYonggui-lou,

Fig. 16 The narrow alley between the Yongsheng-lou and its neighbor the Yongsheng-lou.

1876). Three *tulou* buildings in 100 years was the highest rate of building frequency in Hekeng history. As many specialists (for instance, Zhang, 1993) have pointed out, Imperial China had become a highly developed commercial society since the Wanli reign. From the early Qing dynasty, the Hakka settlements in Yongding (in the vicinity of Hekeng) were prepared to pay a large amount of money to purchase the professional services needed to construct round *tulou* buildings. The obvious conclusion has to be that construction of such huge buildings, at least at this period, was a highly professionalized job. People could afford to pay for them because the region was flourishing as the success of the tobacco trade had brought economic prosperity to the Yongding rural area. Other major sources of income included knife production and paper manufacturing. Local oral history and part of the *Gazetteer* concur that a large amount of the funding for the construction of *tulou* buildings was donated by tobacco businessmen and officials born in Yongding. Success in business and official careers had made them wealthy and some of these buildings were used as residences by big merchants, retired officials and their relatives. Taking the earthen buildings in Daxi, as an example, numerous huge buildings were constructed between the period of the Kangxi reign (1661-1722) and the Daoguang reign (1821-1851). If the calculation begins in the thirty-fourth year of the Kangxi reign era, the average frequency at which earthen forts were being built is astonishingly high, nearly one

Fig. 17 The Yongrong-lou, façade.

tulou per year. Some of them were constructed over two consecutive years. As *tulou* construction was definitely a commercial activity in Yongding, could the Hekeng people at this stage have afforded such a large outlay, given the fact that square *tulou* building would have been much cheaper than the big round mansions built in Yongding?[22] In the case of the Qiaoxia settlement, funding always seems to have been problematic, a conclusion clearly

22. There is no extant record of construction costs prior to the Republican period. The earliest extant evidence as such is dated to 1912, i.e., the first year of the Republican period. The construction of the Zhencheng-lou in Yongding cost nearly 80,000 silver *yuan*. By calculating the earth volume, we can know that the actual workload of building a square *tulou* in Hekeng was very likely only 1/8 of that of the Zhencheng-lou, perhaps even less. In other words, if the Hekeng people were to have constructed such a *tulou* building in a similar way during the Republican period, they would have to pay about 10,000 silver *yuan*. In early-20th century Shanghai, each *dan* (around 178 *jin*) of rice cost 6 silver *yuan*, i.e., 3.4 *fen/jin* rice, or 30 *jin*/silver *yuan*. With one coin, one could also buy 8 *jin* pork (12 to13 *fen/jin*). With 10,000 silver coins, one could have bought 300,000 *jin* of rice, enough to support a large village of 400 people for about 2 years. As we have discussed in previous sections, it would be impossible for a traditional Chinese village that relied heavily on rice agriculture to have paid such a large sum of money. In the traditional Chinese villages in western and southern Fujian, food shortage had always been a problem, as almost every staple and article of everyday consumption came from their own fields. In most cases, the assets of an average rural family could have been shared out in only three generations. Hence, without the introduction of new forms of economic acquisition, wealth accumulation would have always been an uphill battle for common families, and therefore for the lineage as a whole. Rice prices varied dramatically from the Ming to Qing periods. A single price fluctuated in a wide range between 1 to 4 *liang* silver/*dan* (120 *jin*). Therefore, calculations should also take inflation into account. If we take the average point to be 0.6 *liang/dan* in the Kangxi reign period and 1.5 *liang/dan* in the Qianlong reign era, then we know that it would have cost 1,500 to 3,750 *liang* silver to build a square *tulou* building.

Fig. 18 The Nanxun-lou, façade.

reflected in the much lower construction frequency there. Qiaoxia built its first *tulou* building, the Chaoshui-lou, sometime in the 1530s-1550s, and in the 300 years that followed no new *tulou* buildings were built in this settlement. This lack of building activity might indicate a wealth gap between the three settlements— or, at least, wealth accumulation in the Qiaoxia settlement might have been a more difficult undertaking than in the other two settlements. From the late-fifteenth century to the middle of the eighteenth century, the three settlements of Hekeng constructed only three *tulou* buildings, that is, one *per* 100 years. However, in the nineteenth century alone, they built three. Undoubtedly, the erection of the three *tulou* buildings cannot have been financed by their returns from the agricultural economy. From the eleventh generation, the Hekeng people began to pursue new ways of life outside of the river valley; the majority of them preferring to move to Sichuan and Taiwan. According to the incomplete statistics in the genealogy, this interregional resettlement involved nearly twenty families from the eleventh to the fourteenth generation of the Zhang lineage in Hekeng. This means that, at a conservative estimate, sixty to one hundred people would have moved out of the river valley in the course of approximately half a century. Even had there been a putative 500 people living in the village, nearly one-fifth of the population would have left by the end of the Qianlong reign. It is no coincidence that the three new buildings were all constructed by the thirteenth-to-fourteenth-generation people of the village. This fact put alongside the moving-out

Fig. 19 The Nanxun-lou, inside.

record indicates that, from the late-eighteenth to the late-nineteenth century, the population in the Hekeng River Valley had reached the upper limit that the land resources could support. This period was the second sharp population increase in Hekeng history.

Apart from the sharp increase in the population of the valley, yet another new trend emerges: the social stratification amongst the three Hekeng settlements had gradually been intensifying during this period. The construction of the two new *tulou* buildings in Qiaoxia, whose construction work was finished in 1875 and 1876 respectively, was funded by two brothers from the Yuantang settlement. It should be noted that they were not legitimate heirs of the Qiaoxia settlement, but had only recently taken up the land in Qiaoxia. Although by the late-nineteenth century, only Qiaoxia still had enough level land on which to build huge earthen buildings, the true descendants of this settlement might not have been able to provide enough funding to construct these buildings themselves. This taken in conjunction with the better economic conditions in the Yuantang settlement finally resulted in the construction of the last two square *tulou* buildings in Qiaoxia, suggests a *de facto* agreement (though not necessarily on paper) between the two settlements to redevelop what was probably the last piece of precious flat land in the Hekeng River Valley in Qiaoxia. There is no documentary evidence that a transfer of land ownership ever took place in the village, but the gap between the poor and the rich is obvious. Members of some settlement(s) could have become wealthy enough to redevelop the land of other lineage branches. How did these comparatively rich families obtain their first pot of gold?

Fig. 20 The Yangzhao-lou with lotus pond.

After the establishment of the Yangzhao-lou in 1875, the richer residents of this building constructed a completely new ancestral hall outside the *tulou* building, that is said to have been destroyed in 1975 during the Cultural Revolution. Fortunately, the hall site is still preserved and has not yet been completely built over and hence its location is unmistakable. Despite the brief lapse in time since its destruction, during the 2013 investigation no one in the village knew the name of this ancestral hall. However, all the information collected to date refers to this building as the ancestral temple dedicated solely to the near ancestors of the residents who had lived in the Yangzhao-lou since the late-nineteenth century. These data again show the close link between a *tulou* and a public ceremonial place, a socio-religious phenomenon known as *fensi*, noted earlier in this chapter. It seems highly likely that the establishment of the new *tulou* building and the ancestral hall marked the emergence of a newly established lineage segment (*fang*) in the late-nineteenth century. At this period, the Hekeng Zhang lineage as a whole would have owned: one principal ancestral temple on Nanshan (the Shiying-tang), three ancestral halls (the Dexin-tang dedicated to the Yuantang ancestors, the *Huaiting* dedicated to the Xizhuba ancestors and the unnamed one belonging to the Yangzhao-lou residents) plus a shrine in each *tulou* building, with the exception of the Yongsheng-lou. Therefore the basic settlement pattern in the Hekeng River Valley until the late-nineteenth century could be interpreted as follows: one *lou* with one shrine (*tang*), one lineage segment (*fang*) with one hall and one lineage (*zongzu*) with one temple. This is what I call a three-layered ancestral worship system (Fig. 21).

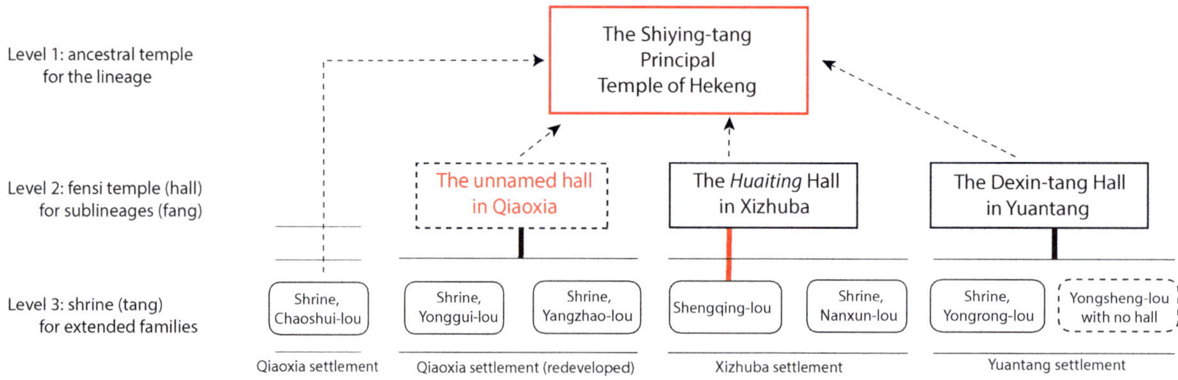

Fig. 21 Hekeng architectures for ancestral worship use.

The nineteenth century witnessed a series of rapid changes in land use, architectural development and even one redevelopment in Qiaoxia. It took nearly 400 years for the Hekeng people to construct four *tulou* buildings, yet in this century alone they built three. As noted earlier, this is an abnormally high number for an ordinary poor village relying heavily on rice agriculture. It would appear that, although housing pressure was relieved, the overall agricultural resources might have been further reduced by the appropriation of land for building. In fact, the total amount of arable land was around 5 *mu* (3333 m^2), that yielded enough to support five to ten people for one year. The proposed new land-use pattern would have provided residences for at least fifty to eighty people. Such calculations could have convinced the lineage heads that it would be worthwhile to construct new buildings. A redevelopment on this scale completely altered the housing pattern in Qiaoxia, and it eventually relocated as many as possible of the local population in the new buildings and consequently saved much land. As we have calculated in previous sections, farmhouses in non-*tulou* forms usually required more land than the *tulou* buildings. Therefore, the purpose of the construction of the two new *tulou* buildings was very likely to reduce the space required for housing use to a controllable level, namely: 5 *mu*. In every period, each settlement has had to strive with all its might to save arable land, but the population was always an incalculable factor. Nevertheless, the main solution and principal goal was to try to encourage more people to live inside the *tulou* building. In a nutshell, *tulou* construction became an effective way to save land.

However, as the brief calculation given above shows, it usually took around 2,000 *liang* of silver to build an individual *lou*, and it could have been impossible for the villagers to have been reimbursed for the outlay of such a big sum for many years to come. A wrong decision to launch a big construction project could have been disastrous for small settlements. As the case in central Fujian shows, a disastrous economic collapse of the whole settlement could follow in the decades after the establishment of the *bao* fortresses. In this case, the construction fees had been too high and the local residents had no money to pay off the debt incurred. Certainly the people would have won several *mu* of arable land and have been provided with a strong shelter in which to take refuge, but at the expense of a debt that could not be repaid with an income from a purely agricultural income. Of course, by that time the Hekeng settlements, especially the wealthy families in Yuantang, might have already relied on multiple source economy rather than on agricultural income alone.

Did any officials or retired officials from the Zhang lineage ever sponsor *tulou* construction projects in the nineteenth century? Unfortunately, the answer to this question is negative. A highly suspect but none-the-less intriguing record is given in the inscription on one of the stone pillars erected in front of the Shiying-tang Ancestral Temple, the principal temple of the whole

Fig. 22 The Shiying-tang with stone pillars and plinths.

Hekeng Zhang lineage. The inscription reads '*Daqing Xianfeng jiunian qiuyue enshou sui jinshi Zhang ... li*', meaning that the stone monument was erected in honor of a descendant of the Zhang surname who was awarded the Jinshi degree by the Great Qing Empire in the ninth year (1859) of the Xianfeng reign. The genealogy does not record in detail how his success had influenced the *tulou* construction process. However, in the late Qing empire, wealthy people could easily purchase a degree and become a '*en jinshi*' (literally, bestowed-degree holder, to differentiate them from the holders of formal degrees obtained by sitting the Imperial Examinations) from the local government (Zhen, 2005). A double-check of the official documents of that time issued by the Imperial Court in Beijing suggests that the degree-holder himself might have fabricated such a 'significant' episode in his lineage history. Even so, despite his alleged chicanery, this evidence still has its uses; it implies that by the nineteenth century some people, like that man in the Hekeng Zhang lineage, had become relatively rich, and were possessed of the ambition and the economic wherewithal to influence the settlement construction. An upward trend in the settlement economy could have led to an aspiration to expand dwellings, to build new ancestral halls and, moreover, to 'shift' from a merchant identity to an 'official' identity (Figs 22 and 23).

1.4.10 The Round *Tulou* Chain in Hekeng from the Late Qing Dynasty to the 1980s

The period from the Kangxi to the Daoguang reigns (1821-1850) can be truly said to have been a golden

Fig. 23 Stone pillar outside the Shiying-tang, erected in 1859 to commemorate a descendant's 'success' in the 'Imperial Examination' (in fact the *Jinshi* Degree was purchased from the government).

age for the round *tulou* buildings in the lower reaches of the Jiulong River. After the late Kangxi period, such buildings began to dominate the domestic architecture of the prosperous river valleys such as those of the Hongkeng and the Gaotou. As many economic historians (for instance, Jiang and Su, 2007) have pointed out, in the hilly region of southern Fujian, that straddles Longyan, Yongding, Nanjing and Pinghe counties, the thriving tobacco economy stimulated the construction of magnificent round *tulou* buildings. The round *tulou* building contests carried out among the Yongding River settlements that began in the late Kangxi reign offer proof to the assertion that these buildings could have been a newly embraced fashion advocated and followed by rich local gentlemen and retired officials. In these settlements, square *tulou* buildings, soon considered an outdated architectural style, were soon replaced by the round ones. However, the neighboring Hekeng people did not follow suit immediately.

The distance between the valleys of the Yongding River and Hekeng is only around five kilometers, but no round *tulou* buildings were ever built in Hekeng before the end of the 1940s. This does not necessarily mean its inhabitants had conservatively decided that they wanted to adhere to the square version, even though from the early eighteenth century through to the 1870s, the Hekeng people did continue to construct square *tulou* buildings, no fewer than three of them, adhering to a style had been regarded as old-fashioned by their neighbors in Yongding since the late Kangxi reign. During the social chaos that characterized the late Qing and Republican times, the whole of Nanjing county suffered large population losses in the wake of the fierce battles between forces affiliated with diverse polities. It cannot be said with any certainty which armies wreaked havoc in the Hekeng River Valley but the destruction they caused meant that, in the over seventy years from the 1870s to the beginning of the 1940s, the villagers built no *tulou* buildings at all, not even the square ones. Population loss seems to be a feasible, main reason. It was only in the late 1940 that the Hekeng people once again began to build new *tulou* buildings. Without exception, all the new buildings constructed since that time have been round *tulou*. With the encouragement of the CCP (Zheng, 2012), fresh opportunities to construct round *tulou* buildings were offered, allowing the Hekeng people to achieve a dream they had never been able to realize in the past 200 years. Since the establishment of the first round *tulou* in the late 1940s, the landscape and the built environment have both been changed dramatically. In the 1950s, the Hekeng villagers were initially divided into seven agricultural working groups. The groupings were only partially based on kinship relations. According to oral history (also see Zheng, 2012), in most parts of the village before the 1950s, only those who were close kin to one another could live together in the same square building. This time-honored pattern changed in the 1950s and people who belonged to the same working group began to be allotted living space in the same round building. What was the rationale behind the continued construction of no fewer than seven round earthen buildings? All the older villagers (over fifty years old) interviewed in 2011 and 2013 talked about the fact that, before the construction of

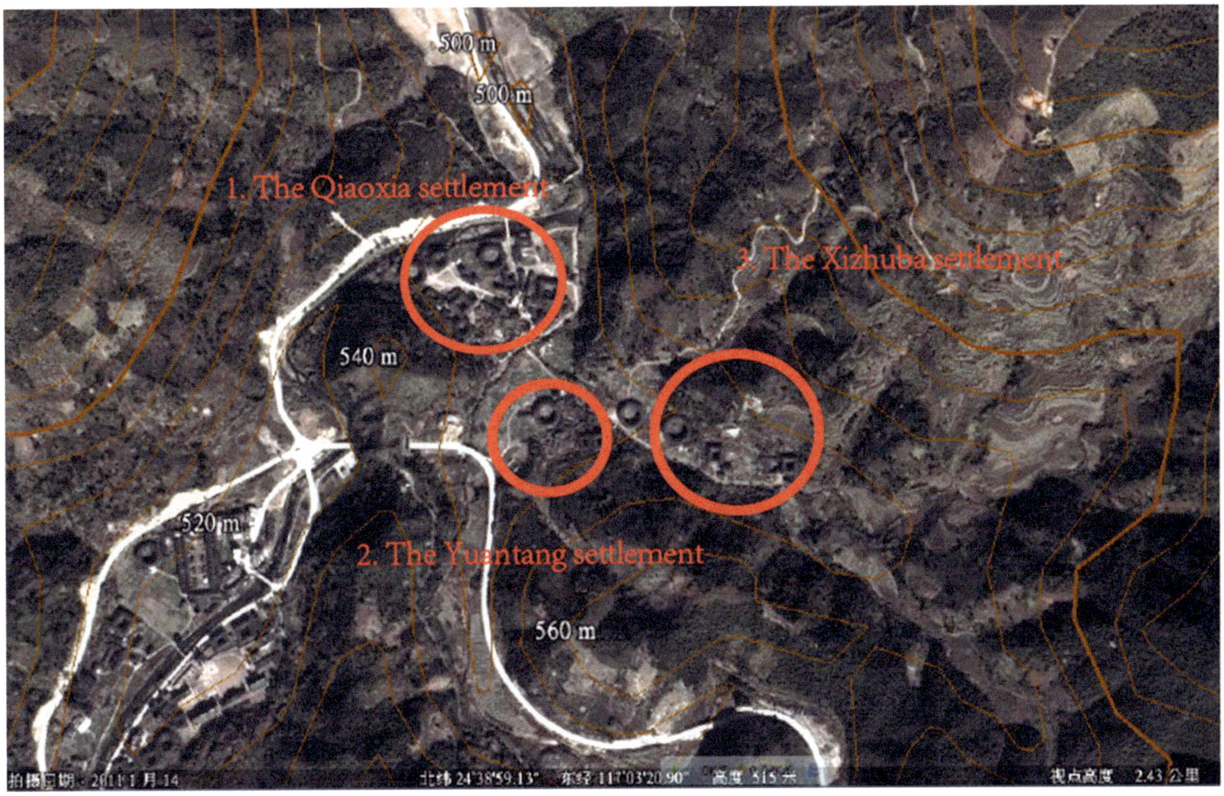

Fig. 24 The three settlements at Hekeng, Qiaoxia, Yuantang and Xizhuba.

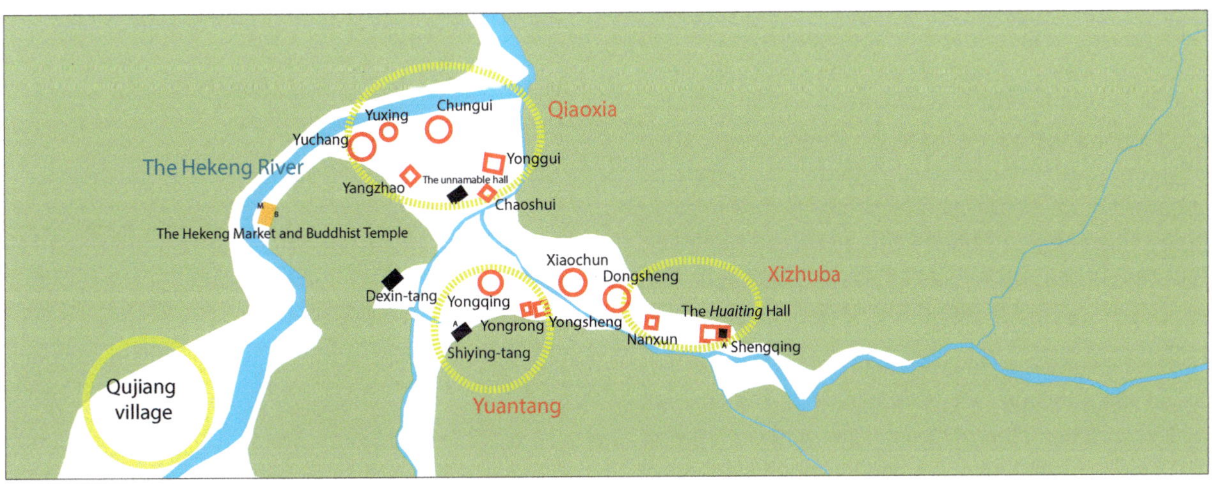

Fig. 25 The built heritage in the Hekeng River Valley.

the Chungui-lou, the third round earthen building erected between1963 and 1967, over 100 local people had been in fact piled into the Yongsheng-lou for quite some time. This information has been repeatedly confirmed by different interviewees. Their information seems to answer the question about the major reason so many round buildings had been built between the 1940s and the 1980s: the third population boom from the 1950s to the late 1970s.

What has been said above recounts the primary formation process of the Hekeng built environment (Figs 24 and 25). In this chapter, I have attempted to reconstruct the site formation process and offer a landscape biography. My main thrust has been to try to understand the relative importance of the *tulou* and other types of vernacular buildings in their historical context. It is possible that the importance of *tulou* buildings has been overstated by researchers and heritage managers. They can, of course, represent the past of the Hakka settlement history, but only part of it. Each Hakka village in this hilly area, such as Hekeng, might have had a very long pre-*tulou* history since the foundation of their first settlement, a fact that should not be forgotten. The abrupt rise in the construction of *tulou* buildings might conceivably have been a group response to the persistent tension in the region. In the following centuries, such buildings proved to be an effective method of dealing with the overgrowth of settlement population and therefore they continued to be built in each river valley. The rapid rise in the number of *tulou* buildings and the consequent homogenization of the built environment both led to the gradual elimination of non-*tulou* architectures. A thing is valued in proportion to its rarity. Therefore, architecture in non-*tulou* forms deserves more of our attention, and should be given its appropriate status not only in heritage preservation but also in representation.

In the existing site interpretations, it would be fair to say that the roles of local people in the creation of Hakka settlements have also been underestimated. As has been demonstrated in this chapter, the built environment principally reflects demographic developments in history. Changes in the built environment are usually the result of population processes, whether increases or decreases in local population size. The motivation to build can be prompted by a variety of sources. At least, what the local people invest emotionally in their public places is very different to what they invest in dwellings, including the well-known *tulou* architecture. Just as important as the *tulou* shelters, other forms of architecture in the public domain, such as temples, halls and shrines, have probably helped the local communities to coordinate social relations within the lineage. As I shall elaborate later, these buildings and structures are highly ceremonial in nature and have had rather different ways of metabolization. In short, a landscape biography, as this chapter demonstrates, can be very important to vernacular heritage management. We can only understand and evaluate the significance of each component of a built environment by seeking to pinpoint the roles it might have played in the landscape evolution process.

2. Hekeng: a Place Swamped by Regulations

In 2010, on my first visit to the Hekeng River Valley, I was told by the local residents that between 2006 to 2008 some protests had been made objecting to the World Heritage application. Interviews with the local people revealed that the main complaints had centered on three matters. The first objection was raised when, after nominating the Hekeng *tulou* buildings as World Heritage, the local government demolished some of the peasants' houses built in non-*tulou* form and failed woefully to compensate properly for the economic loss suffered by the peasants after WH status was finally achieved in 2008. The second point of friction was that, during and after the nomination process, the local residents felt that they were no longer able to live in and use the *tulou* housing facilities in the ways to which they had been accustomed. The third dissension arose from the fact that the farming and industrial activities inside the buffer zone areas are strictly controlled. As mentioned in passing in the Preface, although the private ownership of land resources is forbidden by law in China, the peasants' fundamental rights to their homesteads (*zhaijidi*) and dwellings have always been respected by Chinese law. That said, how did the conflicts between the local community and the local cultural authorities arise, and what was the real issue at stake in these controversies? This chapter seeks the answers to these questions by exploring how heritage-site planning, laws, regulations and international heritage policies have built up a discourse that has had a direct impact on the properties of the local people and their heritage counterparts.

2.1 MODIFICATIONS TO THE EXISTING BUILT ENVIRONMENT 2006 TO 2007

There is no shred of doubt that all the folk buildings in non-*tulou* forms discussed here are first and foremost an ancestral heritage. Under both the *Property Law of the PR China* (*Zhonghua Renmin Gongheguo Wuquanfa*) issued in 2007 and the *Inheritance Law of the PR China* (*Zhonghua Renmin Gongheguo Jichengfa*) issued in 1985, the owner of real estate has the right to 'bestow, to inherit, or to purchase and to sell the property he/she owns'. If this is there in black and white, why were some of these houses demolished in Hekeng village in 2006 and 2007?

As said in both the Preface and Chapter 1, vernacular buildings in non-*tulou* forms have been very actively constructed and used since the very inception of Hekeng village. The functions of these buildings are very wide ranging. Courtyard compounds were once probably the major dwelling form in the first century of Hekeng settlement history. In the following centuries, both courtyard dwellings and two-story earthen houses would have played a role in relieving recurrent housing shortages. Likewise, farmhouses in the form of either thatched or tiled huts can also have long been actively used in local farming activities, foodstuff processing, animal raising, tea processing, paper manufacturing and so forth. Historically speaking, they are also an indispensible part of household property. Furthermore, ancestral temples and halls are also constructed in the form of courtyard dwellings. All these buildings and structures are part of both the historical environment and the present settlement. They have all functioned in different ways to form the local people's cultural identity and social memories (Rowlands and Tilley, 2006). Moreover from an ethical point of view, we cannot easily dismiss or deny the cultural significance of such ordinary buildings and structures, if the local people themselves do not consider them merely functional edifices. Nonetheless, in 2006 and 2007, some of this architecture was demolished by the local cultural authorities. The rationale behind their decision was that these buildings and structures were not nominated as, and therefore not consequently acknowledged as World Heritage sites. Moreover, compared to the magnificent *tulou* houses they just faded into insignificance and were consequently overlooked.

It is certainly true that the application for WH status for the *tulou* did not include any other types of vernacular buildings and structures. Not even the ancestral temples or halls displaying typical Hakka esthetic and monumental values were registered on the World Heritage List. Obviously, although based on a series of principles approved by all States Parties, the designation of World Heritage status does indeed involve a kind of site selection process. At the heart of the matter lies the problem that, what the World Heritage Committee (WHC) can select as WH sites are only those features that have already been specifically nominated as WH candidates by the state-based cultural authorities. Unfortunately all heritage projects create conflict and destruction (Meskell, 2015). As they are technically only international policies, World Heritage regulations do not have any legal status or effect in any of the individual countries in which they might happen to be applied. To be more exact, they are not legislation in themselves. Their weakness in the implementation of heritage requirements seems to be reflected by their official denial of World Heritage status to some sites that actually violate the principles of authenticity and integrity after they have been registered. The most ironical question is: Does delisting necessarily lead to the denial of the importance of the sites in question, or do these sites need no further care? Originally on the basis of three key concepts, namely: significance, authenticity and integrity, the intention of the WHC and its major Advisory Bodies was to assist states to take a hand in the halting of intensifying physical deterioration, or at least in mitigating the repercussions on sites, particularly those caused by such social factors as urbanization and development. However, in the real world, before states submit their application to be awarded WH status, it is up to them to have read through all the relevant requirements and have transposed all these key concepts into their own heritage discourses. In a nutshell, the three key concepts have been converted into the three mandatory realms but ones that an applicant is obliged to construct itself. More precisely, to fulfill an application, local cultural authorities have to establish their position from both a regulatory and a practical perspective by inputting their own understanding of such key words as values, authenticity, integrity, buffer zone and so forth. To achieve the basic requirements of the WHC in their own minds, applicants might feel it necessary to make some modifications to the landscape with reference to their own scenario that, in their perception, closely adheres to the WHC stipulations. Under these circumstances, the key concepts advocated by the WHC are gradually metamorphosed into the cultural constructs of the applicants. Usually, what the WHC and its Advisory Bodies (represented by commissioned experts) might know about a proposed WH site commences only at the time the application is submitted, not before. The unfortunate upshot is that the WHC might be presented with no more than an outcome that panders to its taste. This begs the question: What might have happened before the application submission?

In the Hekeng case, any 'modifications' were certainly not made haphazardly. Rather, all the 'edits' made on the flatland within the Hekeng River Valley followed a series of principles founded on historical events, opinions about heritage, Chinese laws of inheritance and diverse regulations, commonplace knowledge about *wenwu* (literally cultural materials), especially vernacular houses, a balance of costs and benefits and, most importantly, the local government's own understanding of the key WHC concepts. When push comes to shove, the local cultural authorities can have created their own theory to support their heritage modifications, especially the demolition of some of the peasants' non-*tulou* houses. The best way to explain this theory is in examining the terms of several key concepts usually appearing in pairs.

2.1.1 Traditional *versus* Modern

From the late Qing dynasty right through the early Republican period, a large number of overseas descendants of the Hakka communities returned to their own or their ancestors' birthplaces in the areas adjacent to Shuyang township, for example, to the Zhuta (now Qujiang) settlements to the south of the Hekeng River Valley. These rich merchants funded the construction of a large proportion of the local infrastructure, contributing to the building of an assortment of schools, bridges, roads, temples, *tulou* buildings and markets. The most representative of their contributions is the market in Qujiang (Fig. 26). Compared to the economic prosperity of the Qujiang settlements, particularly the new buildings and facilities with Western architectural features, in that period Hekeng was still rather 'backward', as all it had to offer was several old-fashioned square *tulou* buildings. Unlike what has been written into the American *National Historic Preservation Act* in 1966 (Duerken, 1983; King, 2004), no particular date is stated in the *Chinese Cultural Heritage Law* (1982) as clear starting point for designating cultural heritage (*wenwu*) in China. The truth is that, in practice, materials dating from later than the early Qing dynasty are usually underrated, even overlooked. In typological terms, from the Ming to Qing periods *guanshi jianzhu*, or official buildings, usually attract more attention in conservation disciplines than do vernacular buildings (*minju jianzhu*) in the rural areas. This preferential system inevitably leads to a weakness in the study of traditional Chinese folk buildings and structures. To date, no manuals or guidebooks for the significance assessment, designation process or conservation principles of rural folk buildings have ever been formally published by the Chinese cultural authorities on the national level. Crucially, no criterion has ever been established solely to make a differentiation between the traditional and the modern. Therefore, in the world of rural vernacular architecture, the boundary between the traditional and modern still remains very blurred.

Fig. 26 Qujiang market, built in the Republican period.

According to the inventory in the *Zhongguo Wenwu Dituji* (An Atlas of the Chinese Cultural Heritage) (Zhongguo Guojia Wenwuju, 2007), the practical major lower time-limit for making a cultural resource designation is conventionally set at the Republican period, although new sites and buildings from the PRC age might be occasionally added to the inventory as a 'red memory', if and when appropriate. In the Hekeng River Valley, only a very few structures dating from the Republican period still exist. In fact, the lower time limit of traditional times in Hekeng is quite vague, simply because all the seven huge, magnificent round *tulou* buildings date from the post-1940s (Chapter 1), clearly a very recent date. The latest one was constructed in the 1980s, and nearly all the extant *tulou* buildings are still inhabited by the lineage community that built them. It is very important to be aware of all this information in order to be able to understand why some of the non-*tulou* houses in Hekeng have been demolished. In theory, the Hekeng site planners might have nurtured hopes that such an edifice in itself might incorporate a number of Hakka history elements, nevertheless they have chosen to select huge *tulou* buildings as the sole representations of the Hakka past. In their efforts to create a place imbued with valued Hakka cultural traditions (Graburn, 2016), the site managers decided to erase the atypical architectural elements displaying fewer historical attributes. Their choice leads to a strong suspicion that the *tulou* buildings have been designated representative of traditional times, whereas the non-*tulou* buildings are lumped together as representative of the modern times; and this is of course historically incorrect.

The traditional *versus* modern divide is also viewed as equal to the proportion between old and new materials, and as the opposition between the old-fashioned and new-fashioned in terms of architectural styles. For all these reasons, non-*tulou* buildings and structures have been accorded a much lower level of significance by local site managers and planners. Old building materials, in the eyes of the local site managers, are primarily earth, wood, bamboo and metal, particularly iron. The Shiying-tang Ancestral Temple of the Hekeng lineage is now nearly a complete reconstruction. As described previously, the architecture, although in the style of a traditional courtyard dwelling, has already been transformed into a new building, part-brick, part-cement. Therefore, in the strict sense of physical composition, it cannot be described as 'traditional'. This is the main reason the principal ancestral temple has not been registered on the cultural resource list and was not stressed in the cultural heritage discourse. In short, the temple is not so 'traditional' that the experts could give it any statement of significance from a CRM standpoint, despite the fact that for centuries it has served as the major place for making sacrifices to the ancestors of the Zhang lineage and its construction commenced in the early-seventeenth century and therefore has a much longer history than over 70 percent of the traditional buildings and structures in the Hekeng River Valley.

With *tulou* buildings as their major target of preservation and without any direct source of reference for dating criteria for the ordinary folk dwellings in the existing heritage legislation, it was up to the local heritage managers to judge the importance of the non-*tulou* buildings and structures themselves. In all fairness, in most cases they also relied on local cultural resource experts. In the Chinese cultural resource management system, it is usually the cultural authorities on the county (the lowest) level who set the designation process of a place or a building complex in motion. According to some of the local cultural resource managers with whom I talked when investigating cultural resources in Qionglai in Sichuan province in 2009, the cultural authorities on the county level have usually had to work out whether they have the economic capacity to preserve a designated heritage and still balance their budgets. This consideration overrides all other factors. Although the *Zhongguo Guojia Wenwuju* or the State Administration for Cultural Heritage (SACH) is supposed to play the leading role in looking after all kinds of cultural heritage throughout the country, it should be underlined that the SACH does not exercise any executive power over the cultural authorities on the county level, simply because it is the local county government (*xian zhengfu*), not the SACH, who pays the office expenses of the local cultural authorities (*difang wenwu bumen*). Similar situations to that in Qionglai also frequently arise in Fujian rural areas. If local government finances tend to be running low, in most cases, it might not be worth adding a new county-level site or building to the existing local cultural resource map at the price of costing for the expense of employing more caretakers. For all these reasons, the county cultural authorities might actually go as far as deliberately concealing some of the sites or buildings that do require good care and consequently such sites and buildings never appear in the preservation list of the SACH. Therefore, in most Chinese counties it is a county's financial state that finally decides in what proportion of the old buildings can be registered and therefore preserved. The long and short of it is that the local cultural resource managers play a key role in deciding what to preserve for the country. The fate of Chinese vernacular buildings in rural areas especially is in their hands. It can be disastrous for a vernacular building of high historical value, if it is 'omitted' from the list of the local cultural resource managers. Generally speaking, although frequently running short of money, the local county cultural resource managers are in effect the most powerful decision makers in shaping the final list of endangered folk buildings. Their financial resources, their taste in particular dates and forms (as demonstrated in the traditional *versus* modern dichotomy discussed above), could both exert a direct impact on outcome of the heritage preservation. Unfortunately, since the 1990s by and large in the *tulou* settlements, all the attention of the local Hakka cultural resource managers was directed toward the huge earthen 'castles', when they began a campaign in the name of Hakka *tulou* architecture in order to attract more tourists. From a theoretical perspective, with the exception of a very small number of ancestral hall buildings, the local CR managers had also already overlooked the non-*tulou* buildings when designating the endangered cultural resources. Paradoxically, ancestral halls and temples are not as important in the cultural resource world as they might be in the everyday life of the ordinary people; indeed they are, as viewed by many local cultural resource managers, not cultural heritage at all.

Experts in China usually tend to think more about the technical aspects of heritage; and such elements as memories, emotions and the identity of people that are anchored in certain places are rarely taken into account when establishing the criteria for making a heritage designation. Therefore, a house as such might be preserved for its rarity, architectural achievement, esthetic and scientific value, but almost invariably not for its importance in local people's memories.

2.1.2 Non-Heritage *versus* Heritage Site Planning

After having achieved the legal status of an ancestral heritage, the common farmhouses in the Hekeng River Valley still had to face the hurdle of heritage site planning (*yichan baohu guihua*). The SACH usually requires that the architectures or sites enlisted under national-level protection should be provided with a concrete *baohu guihua*. This *baohu guihua* has two major goals. The first target is to identify the significance of the built environment, whether the place in question is an archaeological site, a village, a town, a building complex or a landscape and, on this basis, decide what, for which reasons and how to preserve the physical parts that have proven to be important. The second objective is to set rules by which to begin a new relationship between the 'place' preserved and the people settling in or around it. In China, a *zongti baohu guihua*, or principal heritage planning, designates a legal status, denoting that once the major plan for site preservation has been established, the land-use in and around the site area should scrupulously adhere to the methods that have been prescribed in that plan, and therefore any violation of the plan is deemed a violation of the law (National Congress, 2007). Sometimes, colleagues in this discipline even use the term '*guihua fa*' (literally planning law) directly when referring to the *zongti baohu guihua*.

In practice, when setting the rules, planners are more concerned about the future (use) of the heritage (indeed the land), the first goal, rather than the new relationship, namely, the second goal. In most cases, local governments usually want to transform the existing land-use patterns in the site area once and for all into theme park or ethnic culture village (*minzu wenhua cunluo*). This trend has been widely observed in Chinese *guihua* practice since the late 1990s. The truth of the matter can often be that, even long before the heritage evaluation work took place, the final goal of creating a theme park or a culture village had already preoccupied the minds of the planners. Once it has become 'a law of the Medes and Persians', it is usually the case that anything deviating from that preoccupation is deemed an obstacle. The upshot if existing land-use patterns such as farmland, industrial land, vernacular buildings, or even the local people in many cases, can be seen as obstacles, the planning, when it takes place, usually involves intensive removals of the elements of the existing built environment in the name of clearing away the 'irrelevant'. Typical examples in China include the National Daming Palace Archaeological Site Park[23] (Guo, 2011), the

23. The clearance of population from archaeological sites can result in complicated and radical social changes. The National Daming Palace Archaeological Site Park on the northern outskirts of Xi'an is one instructive example. The site is located to the north of Xi'an railway station. It dates from the Tang dynasty and is regarded by the majority of archaeologists and historians as the most important Imperial Court palace complex during the Tang dynasty. From the beginning of the 20th century, for a long time the site area was occupied by refugees from Henan province. Located outside the urban center, it became home to large numbers of immigrants from outside the Guanzhong river corridor. In 2009, the population inside the site area had reached over 100,000. (Zhou, 2009) In the process of urbanization, some external companies had long nurtured hopes of redeveloping the area around this important archaeological site. What worried these these developers most was the low price that the future 'rural' apartments might fetch. This consideration aside, they also hesitated at the price they would have had to pay for protecting the Daming palace site and the compensation due to the local people, who were supposed to be moved off the site and redevelopment areas. The only solution was to raise the price of the apartments. At this point, the transposition of the archaeological site to a park seemed to be the best excuse for raising the price. Their reasoning was clear: A good park is equivalent to providing a better environment for the future residents living in the new neighborhoods. A good environment has to be paid for. The advantage of this is: If the houses can be sold at a much higher rate, all the costs of the site transformation could be easily repaid by only part of the profits. With mutual benefit uppermost in their minds, the developers decided to support the site park project first. In the following years, the funding for the development project gradually ran out, posing the managers of the archaeological park a big financial challenge. They had to find new financial sources for maintaining the park facilities. The establishment of the National Daming Palace Archaeologi-

Anyang Yinxu National Archaeological Park (Wang, 2013) and the burial garden of the Qinshihuang Mausoleum (Institute of Archaeology CASS and Architecture School of Tsinghua University, 2013). In Japan, the equivalent would be the Yoshinogari Site Park (Wang, 2010). Admittedly all these are extreme cases. The themes of such newly invented cultural spaces are in fact the remains of ancient built environments and are deemed irrelevant to modern, contemporary local society. Similarly, in the Hekeng case, as discussed above, non-*tulou* buildings are usually labeled 'modern' and consequently deemed irrelevant to the architectural theme whose aim is to represent the 'imagined' past of a Hakka village in South China. Naturally this is a wrong perception, as discussed in Chapter 1 and earlier in this chapter. In the case of these heritage sites, the unwanted parts of the land features are often totally removed. The most challenging questions is: Is it really impossible to have the recent past involved in the future of the landscape? Is the representation of the past really incompatible with other land-use patterns? As the Daming case shows, a site park can prove to be a big economic burden even for a metropolitan city like Xi'an. Therefore to 'museumize'[24] (Kolb, 2007) a place completely by ruling out other possible land-uses is sometimes a very risky venture. In the matter of the loss of farmhouses, especially the diverse structures housing industrial facilities, the overriding factor is that, compared to the once-and-for-all transformation leading to a theme park or a fully museumized atmosphere like Hekeng village after 2008, the economic advantages of which are not always rose-colored, the retention of some of the pre-existing land-uses does at the very least maintain multiple sources of income for the local residents.

In 2006 and 2007 the demolition of some two-story earthen houses, courtyard dwellings and tea workshops was complicated by the delay in compensation that resulted in some local residents protesting against the local cultural authorities. Under the general practice of heritage site planning in China, house demolition is also one of the basic strategies resorted to to improve the environmental quality (*huanjing zhengzhi* or *huanjing zhili*) for future touristic use. Important places like sites, towns, villages or even whole landscapes are more often than not very densely inhabited and used. According to the 2012 statistics in the Ford-funded cultural heritage project (also, Zhang *et al.*, 2008), nearly half of the most important Chinese heritage is located in rural areas, and in urban situations, even the traditional *guanshi jianzhu* in the capital can have been transformed into an overcrowded area (*dazayuan*). The degradation of the site environment as a result of population influxes and subsequent disorderly habitations is the fundamental reason dwellings and facilities of later dates usually have to be demolished in site plans. In the Hekeng case, the houses in non-*tulou* forms are usually viewed as new constructions, as mentioned in Chapter1, although the buildings of these sorts might have housed many of the lineage people who could not find enough room to accommodate themselves inside the *tulou* buildings. Apart from that, the local residents in Hekeng also built some 'modern'-style brick houses that were all deemed insignificant in comparison to the magnificent mansions representing the themes of the Hakka past. Both Yan (2014) and Ye (2006) have discussed similar events in great detail in their works on the southern Fujian region.

The most controversial issue is the demolition of the two-story earthen houses, that traditionally supplement the *tulou* dwellings. As briefly mentioned above, each of the three settlements in the Hekeng River Valley had its early core dwellings, including both major *tulou* buildings and supplementary residences in diverse forms, one of which is called a '*yizixing lou*' or one-wing earthen building by the local people. They are usually two-story structures. In Tianluokeng, people also refer to such buildings '*zhugan cuo*', or bamboo post houses (Xiamen University, 2009). These buildings are actually stylized versions of *tulou* buildings. They are composed of a thick but truncated wall into which wooden beams and posts can be inserted to support

cal Site Park has been a milestone in Chinese heritage management history. All the stakeholders in the heritage-making process had used the cultural resource in some way but, when the urbanization process had been finished, no one wanted to pay for the future of the park. The sustainability of the site park therefore presented a big problem.

24. As McCannell (1989) says, 'The separation of non-modern culture traits from their original contexts and their distribution as modern playthings.'

Fig. 27 The Yangzhao-lou with a supplementary simplified-version earthen building.

the joists for the floor boards (Fig. 27). Various such small buildings of this sort are attached to a major *tulou* building. Other two-story structures can also stand as separate dwellings. Unlike the completely earthen *tulou* architecture, they are much easier to construct and could have helped alleviate the periodically crowded living conditions. In the past, these buildings might have been fairly numerous in the Hekeng River Valley. When asked how important such buildings are, Zhang Mintai, one of my informants, replied by asking a question,' Do you know any village with just one big *lou* yet no small *lou*?' His answer, again, affirmed the importance of these smaller *cuo* structures in local people's mind, and highlights the wrong choice made by the local site managers when they decided to remove some of these buildings between 2006 and 2007.

For a long time, Chinese heritage settlements have been managed in a particular way. For a goodly number of years, the State Administration of Cultural Heritage has required that every settlement that has been registered on the National Cultural Heritage List be cared for and protected by the county government of the heritage place. The responsibility for finding accredited academic institutions or companies to undertake the conservation, management and representation plans usually devolves on the county government (*Regulations on the Preservation of the Famous Cities, Townships and Settlements*, issued by the State Council in collaboration with the Ministry of Housing and Urban-rural Development Department of China, 2008). In practice, planners are often required to do their work on the basis of the heritage values assigned by the local cultural resource managers or experts in relevant research areas. Socioeconomic considerations are usually overridden by such plans. When it's all said and done, it is usually not what the local communities perceive as important that leads to a policy decision but the experts' point of view. This leads to two results: (1) the local people's demand for socioeconomic development is underestimated and hence underrepresented in the planning process; (2) heritage planning is usually divorced from the socioeconomic planning made separately by urban design institutions.

2.1.3 Buffer Zone *versus* Core Zone

Buffer zones, though not 'mandatory' as the *Convention* states, have become extremely popular in Chinese heritage protection and management practices. In Chinese, they are known as the *jianzhu kongzhi didai*, or 'construction control areas'.

Mürner (2009) has pointed out that buffer zones 'are not formal (mandatory) components of World Heritage sites', and the protective agenda involved should be considered on a case by case basis. In the *World Heritage Convention*[25] and *Operational Guidelines for the Implementation of the World Heritage Convention* (the 2014 edition), a buffer zone is described as an area surrounding the nominated property, and therefore offering an 'added layer of protection'. Buffer zones, first used in the area of natural heritage, are intrinsically a tool for separating the significant protected area from 'incompatible human use' (ICCROM position paper, 2009). In a cultural heritage area, it is also frequently applied to differentiate compatible from incompatible land-uses to protect a target site. In practice, when creating the buffer zone, site planners usually take the following points into account: view horizons (Mürner, 2009), immediate settings, building heights, massing, location of public open spaces, safety and sanitary issues. All these aspects are established and taken into consideration with only the interests of the protected properties in mind. As a separating instrument, the prime purpose of a buffer zone is to mitigate or even totally eliminate the negative impacts emanating from a human society. Consequently, the local populaceand its use of the land can be largely deterred from taking any action. Consequently, the buffer zone of a cultural heritage area might have acquired the essential attributes of its predecessors and counterparts in the natural heritage area in that it, to a large extent, is put in place to discourage any actions by the surrounding society that is viewed as the major source of negative impacts, and hence antithetical to the preservation activities. In these discourses, a natural-social divide is replaced by a cultural-social divide. However, the WHC believes that a buffer zone should usually be neutral and, theoretically, even an unnecessary buffer zone should not threaten the properties in the 'core zone'.

When evaluating situations in which a buffer zone is not necessary, the ICCROM has proposed the following likelihoods: '(a) the drawing of the World Heritage site boundaries amply enough to ensure protection of the OUV within the site itself; (b) the physical geography of a site (either mountainous or flat) which would render a buffer zone meaningless; (c) the OUV of a site which is located underground, inside, or in some other way not subject to the types of threats that a buffer zone is meant to protect against; (d) an instance where the setting of the site has already radically changed and for which a buffer zone would no longer be useful.' One important situation, in relation to the physical geography point made in (b), has been excluded from the discussion: What happens if it is impossible to differentiate a so-called 'core zone' from the whole inhabitation area?

In the Hekeng case, the site planners took the 'buffer zone' matter very seriously for fear of any trouble arising in the evaluation and decision-making processes (ICCROM position paper, 2009), given

25. 'Many World Heritage properties face problems that directly or indirectly derive from the situation of their buffer zone. New constructions within a buffer zone may have an impact on the World Heritage property and could threaten its Outstanding Universal Value; a different legal status of a buffer zone could also impact the conservation, the protection or management plan of a site.' *World Heritage Convention* 'A buffer zone is intended to avert the effect of negative environmental or human influences, whether or not it embodies great natural or cultural value itself. The importance and function of a buffer zone and the necessary protective measures derived thereof is a relatively new concept in conservation science and can differ greatly for each site.' International Expert meeting on World Heritage and buffer zones (Retrieved 10:03 AM 11/24/2010. 'Background and contents').

the fact that a buffer zone is not mandatory for registration on the WHL. In creating a buffer zone, the site planners chose to follow the view-horizon approach, that has been used for a long time to determine the boundaries of the buffer zone areas of cultural corridors/routes, for example, the Rhaetian Railway (Mürner, 2009). By linking the apexes of the foothills surrounding the village, the planners' first step was to form a contour line; subsequently the area between the edge of the central flatland and the contour line constituted the buffer zone. What did this buffer zone mean in the Hekeng River Valley? To follow the very definition of the term scrupulously, a buffer zone should separate the core zone from the rest of the outer environment/atmosphere in order to reduce undisclosed threats. This gives rise to the next question: Is it possible to make such a difference between a 'core zone' and the 'outer' atmosphere in the Hekeng village context? Unfortunately, the answer is negative. As discussed in Chapter 1, the thirteen nominated *tulou* buildings in the three inhabited cores are all dispersed along the Hekeng River Valley, taking up nearly 30 percent of the total flatland area, leaving the remainder of the arable fields situated only at sporadic intervals among the earthen structures. The dispersion of the *tulou* buildings leaves no room between the residential area and the hillsides, making it impossible for the planners to differentiate any 'core zone' within the densely inhabited flatland area. Faced with the dilemma of fulfilling their task as they interpreted it successfully, the site planners finally chose to transform the hillside area into the buffer zone. Beyond this area also lie other hillsides on which farming and rural industrial work such as tea processing are usually carried out or that are just still just a wilderness with no inhabitation at all. In fact, no appreciable negative impacts could be identified, and so the proposed buffer zone was totally devoid of any reason and hence invalidated. Moreover, in Chapter 1 I have noted that all the flatland inside the river valley has long been densely populated, and the terraced fields and slopes in the foothills, that were finally designated the buffer zone area, are the sites of the major local subsistence and rural industries pursued since the very beginning of the settlement history, and hence an absolutely essential element in the local people's living heritage. Consequently, what has been totally ignored is that these fields are actually crammed with cultural significance and should on no account be directly transposed into a (meaningless) buffer zone.

Obviously, zoning was devised to separate historical space to comply with the needs of protection, tourism, scenic preservation and so forth. As noted earlier, the buffer zone is regarded by many as a solution to the negative impact of human activities but in fact, as also said above, historically the local people have always had their own ways of zoning a landscape. Dwellings, cemeteries, rice-paddies, ancestral temples and mountain slopes are usually intersected by waterways, channels or small paths. The settlement pattern is therefore a specific reflection of the Hakka people's innate knowledge of how to manage their land, and hence a living heritage of local people. The conflicts between the local residents and local cultural authorities all had their roots in the dramatic change in land zoning that was introduced in 2006 and 2007.

2.2 HEKENG TULOU BUILDINGS AS ARCHITECTURAL EXHIBITS

The dispersion of the nominated *tulou* 'properties' resulted in a decision to designate the whole flatland area the 'core zone', in which, according to strict regulations on authenticity and the local site manager's specific tastes in dates and forms mentioned previously, no 'eyesore' buildings could any longer be allowed to be 'a blot on the landscape'. However, this is not the only consequence of such zoning activities. Its effects range from such obvious examples as the physical removal of the 'irrelevant' to a prohibition on stalls (Xiamen University, 2009) and tea-processing facilities in the designated area. This creates the problem that the making of heritage can directly affect the pre-existing built environment in many ways in both the preparation and the post-registration stages. From the perspective of site planning, a new relationship between the inhabitants and their own place is gradually generated in the process that has been set in motion. Although they might be guaranteed the legal ownership and usufruct of their own properties, people's private feelings about life in the newly created set-up might be quite different. Unquestionably, the World Heritage title attracts more tourists to their place but this means that, to some extent at least, their settlements have been transformed into a sort of public space.

The public use of the local built environment as heritage can have two outcomes. One is that the built environment is eventually reduced to a living museum,[26] displacing the local inhabitants into other outer areas (Shepherd and Yu, 2013).[27] The Daming site park is a prime example of this. People have good reason to doubt that these situations are confined only to the creation of archaeological parks. Indubitably, we were also able to identify a local government tendency to try to displace local people from the 'core zone' in the creation of 'culture villages' in some Fujian WH *tulou* sites. During my 2010 investigation, a letter from the ICOMOS addressed to the Nanjing *Tulou* Management Committee was discovered. In this letter, the examiners commissioned by ICOMOS expressed their concern about displacing local people from their own villages. ICOMOS suggested that the local county government should be very careful about making this decision (several inquiries by the ICOMOS in 2008, date unclear, information collected from the Archives of Nanjing County Government in July, 2011):

> *We understand a decision has been made by county governments to move some of the tulou population in some of the nominated areas from within the core and buffer zones to reserved land beyond the buffer zone in order to relax population pressure within the nominated area and meet the requirements of the visiting public. However, at the same time, at some nominated properties, there appears to be a problem with depopulation and the need to find new and viable uses for vacated units. ICOMOS would welcome further clarification on these two issues. It would be helpful if more information could be provided on the reasons for moving people out of the core and buffer zones and on the overall policy for sustaining the buildings as living units rather than museums.*

The second outcome is that, although the local people are still permitted to live in their original places, they are obliged to adjust their previous uses of house and land so as not to violate the newly issued site plans, laws, regulations and government policies. They are able to 'negotiate' with the government through dialogue, resistance, conflict or other possible means, and a compromise can eventually be achieved. Unlike the situation in what are called 'living museums' in which nearly every possible impact from the local society, as the local cultural authorities perceive these, is completely controlled, the local residents who still live in *tulou* houses are viewed dismissively by the local cultural authorities as the major source of negative impacts. It is ironic that the negative impacts are thought to have originated primarily from the inside, even though the defining buffer zone is an external imposition. To protect the *tulou* properties on the flatland inside the core zone properly, the cultural authorities of the Nanjing county government have built up a regulatory system consisting of a heterogeneous mixture of national heritage laws, county-level regulations and transactional policies. In many *tulou* villages, including Hekeng, the many direct impacts on the local communities from the local regulatory system are clearly visible.

Since the late 1980s, a resurgence in traditional culture began in China (Oxfeld, 2010). This newly awakened enthusiasm led to heritage display being treated as field of government and social regulation (Oakes, 2012). Following the registration of the Kaiping Diaolou and the South China Karst Landscapes on the WHL in 2007, a passion for World Heritage nomination (*shenyi re*) gradually gathered pace throughout the country. In many places, the acceptance of World Heritage applications has even been considered one of the local officials' major

26. A similar concern addressed by some delegates at the Davos Conference in 2009 was about the possible effects resulting from the establishment of buffer zone in some cases. Turner (2009) states that this can be delineated as follows: 'The division between core and buffer zone further isolates and differentiates the HUL from the remaining urban context as it accentuates the differences between historic urban fabrics from other fabrics perceived as insignificant from the heritage point of view often resulting in polarization of 'living museum' or tourism theme parks.'

27. As Shepherd and Yu (2013) have pointed out, 'this global model, which is supposed to strengthen cultural diversity, may paradoxically have the opposite effect, transforming world heritage sites into remarkably similar spatial zones while displacing local residents in the name of preservation.'

political achievements (Hou, L., *et al.*, 2009). In order to win the coveted WH designation, government officials began to pay serious attention to the regulations and key concepts of the WHC. There is a widely known old saying in the Chinese architectural conservation discipline: 'Try to conserve ancient architecture by following the way that it was constructed, and try to prolong the lifespan of what is being conserved by curing the diseases here and there.'[28] This idea, I would argue, is to a large extent applicable to the conservation of the Chinese *guanshi jianzhu*, that is, the Imperial and official buildings or large temple structures built by scrupulously following a very detailed blueprint (*yangshi* in royal cases). For obvious reasons, these buildings have had a very strong symbolic meaning and most of them have been preserved and transformed into open spaces since the early Republican period in the 1920s (Wang, 2003). In legal terms, they are the property of the Chinese people. The spatial transformation has made them into exhibits that represent the Chinese past. Their new role as examples of the nation's pride emerged much earlier than their role as World Heritage sites. To preserve the typically symbolic traits, attention has always been paid to the conservation of the layout, form, structure, arrangement, configuration, color, design, façade and other similar attributes. To be more exact, I see no appreciable differences between the Chinese *guanshi jianzhu* conservation strategies and the World Heritage conservation requirements, with particular reference to the 1994 Nara Conference[29] on the contextualization of the authenticity of Japanese wooden architectures. In other words, their status as national symbol means that it is much easier for the restoration of *guanshi jianzhu* to follow the principles set out for conserving the 'monuments' advocated by the international cultural heritage regimes. In fact, their resplendent title of 'national pride' has reduced their role purely to the reception of visitors. Although the difference in the conceptualization of authenticity between different cultural areas was revealed during the 1994 Nara Conference, the *guanshi jianzhu* in China and their counterparts in Japan have rather similar public uses to those in European approaches to architectural monuments. Obviously, official buildings are no longer commissioned to house people and, in particular, their original purpose was eclipsed a very long time ago. The spontaneous metabolization (see Preface) carried out by the residents/users has been terminated. Eventually the sites have been transformed into a kind of architectural exhibit. The exception that proves the rule is Buddhist temples, that have been used for centuries as religious symbols. This is especially true of architectural elements with ritual significance, such as the Mountain Gate, the Buddhist Halls, in some cases, the Drum Tower and the Bell Tower. As has been mentioned earlier in passing, the authenticity of a ceremonial place requires first and foremost that all its ritual significance should be preserved fully intact so that it can fulfill its functions. Consequently, cultural traits represented by what Rapoport called 'cues' are the foremost goals when a conservation is undertaken. The result is that Chinese official buildings, as exemplified by the Forbidden City, plus huge temples of various kinds, are in themselves carriers of cultural traits and hence are basically architectural specimens.

At this point, I see no difference between a Chinese or Japanese architectural specimen and a monument in Europe, but I do see a big gap between a carefully conserved architectural exhibit and a vernacular building in the foothills of South China, whether or

28. Translated by following the interpretation of Li Xiaojie, Director of the SACH, 2012 to 2015. http://culture.people.com.cn/n/2014/0224/c87423-24447158.html

29. The *Nara Document on Authenticity* is the first significant international document acknowledging the cultural diversity and heritage diversity in different social contexts. The contribution of this document lies in that it begins to recognize the complexity of heritage authenticity and the fact that a purely European viewpoint of what authenticity is is not enough to provide a rationale for non-European heritage management in the world, especially East Asia. For people living in less modernized areas, life cannot be arbitrarily simplified into a dichotomy of the present and the past. These people have their own attitudes about what conservation is about. Roughly their concept of conservation can be reduced to building maintenance. The idea of making anything a collectable museum object does come from a European antiquarian tradition, that can be traced back to the late Middle Ages. This type of thinking tends to blur the boundary between 'their' past and the world's past. Moreover, as analyzed previously, it usually transforms the objects into a heritage category by deliberately creating a boundary between the past and the present, or at least a set of phenomenological criteria for making such a differentiation.

not a *tulou* building. A fudged boundary between the two categories can lead not only to incorrect conservation strategies but also to disputes about the use of vernacular buildings. Unlike the interior of an ordinary folk building, the adaptability to modern use of such monuments is not mandatory.

It stands to reason that the foremost legislation under discussion in the field of *wenwu baohu* (heritage conservation) is the *Chinese Cultural Heritage Law* (*Zhonghua Renmin Gongheguo Wenwu Baohufa*), that is, the cultural heritage laws passed in 1982. Another two related laws are the *Inheritance Law of the P.R. China* (*Zhonghua Renmin Gongheguo Jicheng fa*) issued in 1985 and the *Property Law of the P.R. China* (*Zhonghua Renmin Gongheguo Wuquan fa*) issued in 2007. However, under the terms of the *Chinese Cultural Heritage Law*, once 'unmovable property' such as buildings and structures is designated the cultural property of a county, province, or is said to be of national significance or even registered on the World Heritage List, it falls under the strict control of the government. On paper, according to the *Regulations on the Preservation of the Cities, Townships and Settlements of Great Historical and Cultural Significances* (*Lishi Mingcheng Mingzhen Mingcun Baohu Tiaoli*, issued by the State Council in collaboration with the Ministry of Housing and Urban-rural Development Department of China in 2008, any modifications in structure, arrangement or façade of highly significant personal real-estate (*xianji*, *shengji*, *guojiaji* and World Heritage sites) should be 'approved' by the local government authorities on or above the county level. In practice, as far as we know, most of these modifications are prohibited by the cultural resource department of the local government, because the worry exclusively occupying the officials' minds is the potential loss of any heritage traits in the wake of building renovation activities. These rules apply to not only *guanshi jianzhu*, but also to most of the highly significant vernacular buildings on different levels in Chinese rural areas, especially those inscribed on the National Registration of Cultural Heritage (*Quanguo Zhongdian Wenwu Baohu Danwei Minglu*)[30] and the WHL. In places like Hekeng village, strict restrictions on *tulou* building renovation was already in force in 2006. Spontaneous renovation activities inside the buildings are strictly prohibited if they might lead to possible changes to the approved cultural attributes representing the Outstanding Universal Values. To make it a better place in which to receive tourists, the feeding of animals, acknowledged as part of traditional subsistence agriculture, was also banned inside the *tulou* building. If the truth be told, its World Heritage site status has turned the Hekeng River Valley into a museum-like environment for the display of Hakka *tulou* architecture, not of ordinary villages. Hence, the *tulou* buildings are also in part cultural exhibits. Caught between the devil and the deep blue sea, they are faced with the requirements of two major sources. On the one hand, the *tulou* buildings are required to be conserved following very strict Chinese traditional conservation principles, '*xiu jiu ru jiu*', by the local cultural authorities so that they meet the basic requirements of the WHC. Any demand to improve the housing conditions by changing the structure itself or wooden sections is therefore unacceptable to the local government. On the other hand, as ordinary houses, the *tulou* buildings are also often required to be used adaptively by the local residents. In fact, we have already discovered these sorts of spontaneous adaptations in other non-WH villages, for instance, Taxia and Shiqiao. In local people's opinion, the primary purpose of maintenance is to improve the housing conditions. In fact, the Hakka people, like any other cultural group in rural China, have long regarded habitation as the most essential way of maintaining houses, but this is just their own conservation philosophy.

For centuries, Taxia village served as a transfer stop on the crossroads between the hill settlements and the Nanjing county seat. As a hub of local trade, it has a long commercial tradition. Its commercial importance means that the culture of Taxia communities is very different from the cultures in other river valleys. The Taxia people have a reputation for being good at business. Compared with other settlements in Nanou, Hekeng and Shiqiao, Taxia is home to a large number of small retail shops built along the major watercourse in the center of the valley. Apart from this, since their renovation, some of the *tulou* buildings facing the river have now been adapted and are even used as bars and restaurants.

30. http://www.sach.gov.cn/col/col1644/index.html.

Fig. 28 The Banyue-lou in Taxia village.

This change in use has involved not only an external renovation, it has also entailed the alteration of some inner structures, particularly the addition of toilets in the corners of the wings. The narrow space between these *tulou* buildings and the river has now been paved with asphalt, making it impossible for any new pipes to be laid. Furthermore, no drain outlets, essential to the adaptive use of *tulou* buildings, are to be detected in the area of the rivers banks. This indicates that the local people have probably installed sealed septic tanks under the squatting pans and flush tanks inside the toilets. If this supposition is correct, this will surely have changed the floor structure at the corners but these alterations will not have upset the stability of the whole building. Similar adaptations can also be observed in some locally well-known *tulou* buildings, such as the Banyue (Crescent) (Fig. 28). This round example of *tulou* architecture was so seriously damaged by fire that half of the wooden framework has had to be demolished, and the extant half looks like a crescent. Some of the rooms on the second floor of this building have been adaptively used as hotel rooms. Usually, if one room is used as a living room, its neighbor has been adapted for use as a water closet. They have also installed squatting pans inside. The room in the same position on the first floor is also used as water closet allowing the drainage system to be designed, installed and managed vertically. The hotel managers have changed all the floor boards inside the living rooms and the water closets on the second and third floors. This has greatly improved the internal housing conditions (Figs 29 and 30). Some rooms are even equipped with air-conditioning. During the 2013 investigation, Taxia emerged as one of the earliest villages to have embarked on an adaptive use of the *tulou* buildings, not to mention that of many other vernacular architectures.

Spontaneous renovation activities make up the most essential part of the metabolic process of vernacular buildings in Fujian and, in what has happened in Taxia, we came across some key changes to the earlier renovation methods. By and large, in the past the local residents never used varnishes when constructing or repairing the houses, but such new coating materials have now been commonly used on the wooden floor boards. Air conditioning is also widely installed in the rooms in these adapted *tulou* rooms. Toilet facilities and showers are all new additions to the original domestic amenities. Walls have to be strengthened so that new devices can be hung. Damp courses have to be built for the water closet, on ceilings, and on walls and floors, and this inevitably introduces new materials such as plastic. In any old building, the rooms on the top floors all share the same roof and therefore do not have separate ceilings of their own. In the newly adapted buildings, ceilings have to be added to each new hotel room, and this innovation can lead to big changes in the superstructure of the original buildings. In living-rooms, wooden panels have been attached to the original rammed-earthen walls, and sometimes, electric wires have to be buried inside the small troughs on the earthen walls behind these panels. In comparison to this rather drastic adaptive use of old buildings in both Shiqiao and Taxia, the renovations to the buildings in Hekeng and Nanou are more conservative. In Hekeng, 'WH principles' have undoubtedly prevailed in local managers' minds and these have inhibited any adaptive use. In Nanou, economic depression has been the main force preventing the local communities from undertaking any radical alterations. At this point it is important to pause to and recall that the changes that have modernized buildings and structures in the *tulou* settlements have been part and parcel of these structures since the dawn of the twenty-first century. Although they do not seriously influence the WH-registered architecture or those building on the Chinese National Cultural Heritage List, new materials and new ways of adaptation have challenged the more static views of 'authenticity' held by the local cultural authorities.

In countries such as Britain (Ross, 1996; Wang, 2003), if the owner of a heritage attraction architecture can preserve and keep the façade as it was, that person might be granted permission to adapt the interior of that building in some approved ways, but is always subject to the restrictions imposed by the status of the listed building. However, to date no such a regulation setting out 'to what extent a renovation/ an adaptation of an old building with high heritage values is acceptable as appropriate' has been introduced in China. The 'façade' authenticity principle is certainly a practical measure by which to assess changes, but any alterations to *tulou* architecture only occur inside. In many non-WH *tulou* villages, such as Taxia, the local residents can modify their properties just as they wish, without having to make a preliminary assessment of the load-bearing capacity of wooden structures. This indicates that new adaptive uses of old buildings might be confronted with two major problems. The first is a possible violation of the authenticity principle; the second the risks the new materials and structural modifications might pose. Adaptive use as hotel rooms involves the installation of ceramic sanitary devices such as water basins, squatting pans, toilet seats and seepage floor pavements. There is a good chance that the ensuing weight could overload the posts, floor boards and joists. For safety reasons, the local residents have to substitute completely new modern materials for the posts and joists. If they want to preserve the original interior appearance, no bricks can be used for this purpose. These stipulations will eventually lead to the use of such new materials as lightweight steel. As we are aware, posts also bear the upper load exerted by such structural elements as rafters, roof beams and tiles. Substitutions for such wooden supports can cast the stability of the whole architecture to the winds. This is a speaking example of the low adaptability threshold of the old structures to modern use. In fact, this concern has already been formally, though briefly stated, in relation to the sustainable use of the *tulou* houses, in the same letter from the ICOMOS addressed to the Nanjing *Tulou* Management Committee:

If the tulou *are to continue to be lived in as workable houses, there is clearly a need to upgrade them to provide modern services for the residents. How to achieve this transformation without impacting the authenticity of the buildings needs guidance and advice. We understand currently there is no overall guidance for residents on how this type of work should be carried out. ICOMOS would welcome further information on how advice of this sort might be put in place so that the buildings might be upgraded in the most sympathetic way possible. Similarly, it would be helpful to know if such guidance might also be considered for public facilities in order that visitor laboratories, for instance, might be constructed and sited in the least distractive and most sympathetic way...*

This letter makes it palpably clear that the ICOMOS does not encourage local authorities to impose a rigid conservation approach in preserving authenticity. Unfortunately, for all the above reasons, it is impossible to preserve every cultural attribute that has played a part in the WH registration while satisfying basic demands to improve internal housing conditions. The goals of WH conservation and the needs of the local people are at complete odds with one another; they might not even be compatible. Unquestionably, the cultural/touristic resource designated by the cultural authorities in the case of the *tulou* is legally the property of the local communities. The *Property Law* and the *Inheritance Law* protect a person's basic rights to inherit, preserve and transfer his/her own real-estate ownership and also the right to do make modifications to the property he/she owns to satisfy his/her basic housing needs in rural social contexts. In the matter of the basic rights to use personal property in accordance with needs and wishes, the regulations in the cultural heritage laws obviously collide with the what has been promulgated in the *Property Law* and the *Inheritance Law*, both regarded by many as the most fundamental laws of China.

2.3 THE CREATION OF THE HEKENG TULOU HERITAGE: A REGULATED PLACE

The creation of a World Heritage site involved the establishment of professional or management bodies, the passing of laws and the formulation of regulations and policies, many dynamic changes in socio-cultural rights plus profit-sharing agreements. This is especially pertinent when we consider how the insiders' assets are being used by outsiders as tourist attractions, or simply as architectural specimens preserved purely in the public interest. More often than not, spatial transformation in itself is rather passive from the local perspective. To maintain the *tulou* WH sites, the local cultural authorities have been forced to establish certain social mechanisms in the form of a series of official documents in order to proceed with the heritage-making process during and after the WHL registration succeeded in 2008. These stipulate the prerequisites for transforming a village into a regulated place.

In response to the requirements of the *Operational Guidelines* (108 and 117), a government-based organization, the *Nanjing* Tulou *Guanli Weiyuanhui* or the Nanjing Committee for *Tulou* Buildings Management, was formally established in 2011. According to the stipulations set out in the *Notice of the Decision to Establish the Nanjing Committee for Tulou Buildings Management 2007*, the organization was to take the responsibility for making social and economic plans for the protected areas, for protecting, exploiting and managing the cultural, touristic and natural resources, putting WHC requirements, rules and regulations in law into practice, managing the routine work on the agrarian property as well as in construction, forestry, environmental, real-estate and cultural heritage. Regulations governing the WH *tulou* sites protection were issued by the People's Government of Fujian Province. In fact, even before the WH registration succeeded in 2008, *Regulations on Fujian* Tulou *Buildings Protection* had already been issued in 2006 in preparation for the WHL application in 2007. In 2008, the Fujian Government finally established *Regulations for the Protection of the* Tulou *Buildings Registered on the World Heritage List*. Important information relevant to the present discussion can be paraphrased and summarized as follows:

2.3.1 Conservation and Maintenance Responsibilities

The listed *tulou* buildings should be cared for and protected in a way that adheres closely in both its strategic and practical aspects to the conservation

Fig. 29 Renovation inside a *tulou* room in Taxia village.

Fig. 30 Renovation inside a *tulou* room in Taxia village.

requirements advocated by the World Heritage Committee in its approval documents issued in 2007; special emphasis is placed on the stipulation that any proposed management plans should be made and implemented by implementing an explicit bipartite conservation zoning methods, namely: core zones and buffer zones. The delineation of the latter is conventionally set out along the view horizons of the nearest mountains in the vicinity of the property. It should be the responsibility of the municipal and provincial governments to supervise and oversee the management of the WH sites. The governments/committees of the counties, townships and villages in which the World Heritage buildings are located should be responsible for the preservation and protection of the buildings. Administrative villages (*xingzheng cun*) and hamlets (*ziran cun*) are entitled to establish their own protection units to undertake the duty of the day-to-day care and routine inspections. However, the physical conservation and restoration should be funded directly by the central government and undertaken by qualified institutions under the supervision of the central government. The day-to-day care and maintenance should be the responsibility of the owners or the actual users of the *tulou* apartments. (In the *Meeting Notes of the 23rd Conference of the Standing Committee, Fujian People's Congress, May 2011.*)

2.3.2 Funding, Ticket Income and Reimbursement

One of the responsibilities of each county government is to raise funds for the protection and management of World Heritage buildings. This is easier said than done as this huge task has overburdened local officials who are obliged to maintain all forty-six registered buildings simultaneously. This problem is not insuperable. Drawing on the experience of World Heritage management work in China and abroad, the obvious conclusion is that it would be advantageous if the conservation and management work could be reimbursed by making over a proportion of the ticket income. A fixed proportion of the ticket income could be used to compensate the owners of the apartments in World Heritage *tulou* buildings. To satisfy sightseeing stipulations, the forests in the nearest mountains should be purchased by the government and gradually made a part of the themed landscape. Multiple funding sources, such as the central government, the non-government organizations, as well as international or any appropriate funding agencies, should be encouraged. (In the *Meeting Notes of the 23rd Conference of the Standing Committee, Fujian People's Congress, May 2011.*)

2.3.3 Business

Commodification is a relevant and inevitable challenge with which any managers and planners are constantly confronted and are forced to consider thoroughly. Effective control of such spontaneous activities tend to focus mainly on the limitation to the adaptive use of the listed buildings. Under no circumstances should any of the World Heritage buildings be allowed to be transformed into any type of hotel, shop, restaurant, workshop or other facility for the purpose of making a profit. The theme of residential dwellings should not be altered or shifted to any other use. Commercial activities should be cleared away from the core zones. A fee should be charged for making videos for commercial use. The World Heritage *tulou* building residents' commercial activities should be planned appropriately and managed so that none of the authenticity principles is infringed. (In the *Meeting Notes of the 23rd Conference of the Standing Committee, Fujian People's Congress, May 2011.*)

2.3.4 Land-Use

Land and other natural resources within both the core and buffer zones cannot be occupied by anyone for any purpose other than what is allowed by the WH guidelines and it should be kept intact as required in the basic stipulations in the *Operational Guidelines*. Quarries, sandpits, burials and trash pits are all prohibited in the core and buffer zones. Combustible and explosive substances are also forbidden within these areas. New tourist attractions (artificial landscapes) should be allowed to be created in the open areas. (In the *Meeting Notes of the 23rd Conference of the Standing Committee, Fujian People's Congress, May 2011.*)

2.3.5 Facilities

County governments are expected to take responsibility for establishing museums, galleries or information centers to house and exhibit the intangible heritage that cannot be conveniently exhibited *in situ*. (In the *Meeting Notes of the 23rd Conference of the Standing Committee, Fujian People's Congress, May 2011.*)

2.3.6 Economic Benefits

If any profits are made from the local people's properties on the *World Heritage List*, the relevant owners of *tulou* apartments should be kept completely informed about the total sum of the annual tourist income the tourism exploiters have earned. (In the *Meeting Notes of the 23rd Conference of the Standing Committee, Fujian People's Congress, May 2011.*)

2.3.7 Penal Clause

(a) No one, including the local residents, without a permit issued by the Urban-Rural Development (*Chengxiang jianshe bu*) of the People's Republic of China, is allowed to construct any buildings or structures inside the core and buffer zones in which the World Heritage *tulou* buildings are located. (b) Anyone without proper qualifications issued by the State Administration of Cultural Heritage is not allowed to undertake any conservation, restoration or reconstruction work. (In the *Meeting Notes of the 23rd Conference of the Standing Committee, Fujian People's Congress, May 2011.*)

How did the local site managers implement all these regulations and to what extent has the Nanjing County government fulfilled its roles in shaping the newly regulated places, for example, Hekeng village? What challenges did the local government and local people have to face? Thinking about this, it is worth our while to go through some possible impacts each of the abovementioned regulations could have on both the cultural resource authorities and the local communities.

2.3.8 Theming a Regulated Place

Heritage theming is an inevitable aspect of the shaping of a regulated place, because the theme mirrors how the site managers evaluate and interpret the site, and indeed what they want to present to the visitors. The present assumption seems to be that only theming can make future touristic use possible. As discussed previously, to preserve the authenticity of the most representative buildings within the village, the local government has deliberately sanitized some of the contemporary buildings and structures. In step with the current conservation strategies popular in Fujian, local site managers and planners believe that the past cannot coexist with the present — and the theme required by the UNESCO is certainly a representation of the past, not the present. After 'modifying' the landscape, the river valley has been restored to its 'pre-modern look'; in fact a complete fantasy. When 'theming' the place, local site managers chose to preserve the authenticity of the architecture, not that of the landscape or the living heritage. As has been elaborated in Chapter 1, site interpretation of a built environment is still generally very problematic in Fujian. Without a thorough multidisciplinary study on the WH sites, the local site managers might have to rule the significance of local people and their living heritage out of the themes of heritage representation. Even in the WH application materials, the interpretation of *tulou* sites remained focused on the explanation of the *tulou* architecture itself (Fujian *Tulou* Compilation Group, 2009). In essence, misunderstanding of the authenticity concept and the lack of an appropriate interpretive framework eventually both result in a *de facto* scenic spot selection. The past is not represented by what the local Hakka people actually believe to be their past, but by all the old buildings authenticated by experts. All those disparaged as irrelevant have been hidden. The above regulations established by the local government set out the rules for a representation of the past. As noted earlier, in the course of 'theming as narrowing' (Kolb, 2008), the regulations narrows Hekeng's past to the display of only the thirteen *tulou* buildings, but the place to be exhibited is in fact the whole village landscape. It is very clear that the past of the local people has been interpreted controversially and simplistically. In addition, as the *Shuyang Township Government Announcement about the Control of Land use and Building Forms* (2011) regulated, since 2011 the built environment in each river valley settlement of Shuyang township has been placed under the strict control of the government: 'No one is allowed to build new architectures or change the forms of the buildings and structures without the permission of the government.' Consequently, a village like Hekeng has been transformed into a regulated place in which to display architectural exhibits, or a living museum, not a place in which the local people can live in harmony with their past.

Does all this make the assumption that the theming of the Hakka heritage was successful? In 2013 I briefly interviewed various tourists to the Hekeng River Valley, all of them first-time visitors. The purpose of these interviews was to test the performance of the heritage representation and interpretation on the site to see if the ongoing Hakka heritage-making process might help tourists to learn more about the heritage and the people behind it. The questions asked included: How many settlements are there in this river valley? Where do the Hakka people live now? Where did they come from? Who first created the *tulou* buildings and did you hear anything about it when you visited the village? What do you think are the differences between your life and their life here? Do you know of any other types of Hakka architecture besides the *tulou* buildings? What do you think are the basic characteristics of Hakka culture?

These are difficult questions. None of the interviewees could answer them satisfactorily. Obviously, if there were no professional interpretation, the visitors would not even know what they were looking at, simply because these community-related inquiries had never even been recognized by the site managers and planners as the fundamental questions that the proposed themes should try to answer. WHL does provide an opportunity to spread the fame of the registered cultural heritage and therefore improve the condition of these heritage sites, financially and technologically. However, WHL registration and regular reviews by the World Heritage Committee do not necessarily guarantee a sound interpretation. In essence, they can only provide a list of values and periodically review whether or not such values still exist after the listing of the heritage has been successfully completed; they are responsible only for the registered parts.

2.3.9 Budget for Sustaining a Regulated Place

Dramatic changes in land-use usually involve huge costs. As discussed previously, the management of such heritage sites as the Hekeng *tulou* village did follow a rigid conservation approach characterized by excessively strict restrictions on tourist hygiene. McCannell (1989) describes such as a museumization process as indeed a 'separation of non-modern culture traits from their original contexts and their distribution as modern playthings'. Because the local cultural authorities transformed the *tulou* into building specimens, the spontaneous metabolic process has been lowered to its minimum level. As in many other heritage places, to conserve a huge earthen *tulou* 'castle' in its entirety can cost a very large sum. In China, it is usually the SACH that provides the funding for undertaking the site planning and making the site management plans. Conventionally, the local governments on the municipality or county levels can apply for such funds. They can use these to hire experienced specialists or organizations with expertise in cultural resource management to make management and conservation plans. Site conservation costs are also covered by the SACH. However, the SACH is not supposed to have the responsibility to provide further support for the practical construction of the heritage attractions in the forms of heritage parks, ethnic culture tourism villages or historical streets. Generally speaking, maintenance fees and expenditure on tourist facilities should be paid for by the local government from its annual income. These costs can amount to a large sum of money. Again, taking the Daming Site Park as an example, its chief designer, Zhou Bing, has calculated (2009) that the construction of the National Daming Palace Site Park cost nearly 2.8 billion *yuan* and it requires annual maintenance costs amounting to about 0.2 billion. This has placed a big burden on the Xi'an government, whose annual financial income is around 12.5 billion (Zhou, 2009). In a nutshell, it gave birth to a child who does not seem as easy to bring up as it had expected. This financial burden is especially pressing in counties as small as Nanjing. What would be a realistic price if the country wants to conserve a *tulou* building fully by scrupulously following the most rigorous conservation methods? If the Chinese cultural resource management authorities decide to conserve/repair an unoccupied wooden building fully, they could be faced with a bill much higher than just the daily maintenance costs. Using China fir tree wood, the conservation of an ordinary courtyard dwelling measuring between 200 and 300 square meters could cost on average100,000 to 200,000 *yuan* RMB.[31] For single *tulou* buildings, the conservation budgets announced by the Fujian Local Cultural Resource Management Authority are often very large: In 2002 the SACH spent 2 million *yuan* RMB in conserving the rammed-earthen walls, the inside wooden parts (posts, beams, rafters and staircases), plus the stone and wood carvings and the wall paintings of the Eryi-lou (Chen and Chen, 2002).[32] In 2002 the Hua'an County government spent 3 million *yuan* RMB on improving the immediate environs of the Dadi *tulou* clusters (Chen and Chen, 2002).[33] In 2011 the Yongding County government drew up a budget of over 5 million *yuan* RMB for conserving the twenty-three enlisted *tulou* buildings over the following five years.[34] In 2013 the Yongding County government budgeted 16 million *yuan* RMB to conserve the Wuyuan-lou in the course of the next two years.[35]

As Meng (2013) has pointed out, the bulk of the funds for conserving *tulou* buildings come primarily from two sources. The major part of the funding comes from the financial budget of the Chinese central government. Usually, it is the SACH on behalf of the central government that allocates the funds to the counties in which the heritage sites that qualify to be looked after are located. Nonetheless, it is also quite clearly regulated[36] that the local governments have to find funds to make up for the shortfalls themselves. This can be an uphill battle as they know from bitter experience that these shortfalls can turn out to be a sizeable sum. It is no easy matter for the county government to find the money for conservation costs

31. A personal communication from the CRM researcher of Fujian Provincial Institute of Archaeology Zhang Jinde.
32. Chen and Chen, *The People's Daily*, April 16, 2002.
33. *Ibid.*
34. *Information on Fujian Investment*, January 17, 2011.
35. *China News*, September 24, 2013.
36. *Regulations on the protection of the well-known towns and villages*, issued by the State Council, 2008.

Table 1. The demographics of Hekeng residents living in *tulou* buildings, 2011.

Building	*household*	*permanent*	*male*	*female*	*age over 60*	*age above 50*	*age under 16*	*rooms*
Chaoshui-lou	7	16	8	8	12	3	2	60
Yongsheng-lou	0	0	0	0	0	0	0	120
Shengqing-lou	6	10	6	4	5	1	4	78
Yongrong-lou	2	2	2	0	0	0	0	54
Nanxun-lou	2	3	2	1	1	0	2	63
Yangzhao-lou	7	16	8	8	5	2	3	96
Yonggui-lou	8	25	12	13	9	2	8	78
Yuchang-lou	11	26	13	13	4	7	5	108
Dongsheng-lou	9	19	9	10	4	8	3	66
Chungui-lou	11	16	16	14	8	7	10	96
Chunxiao-lou	15	17	17	18	14	4	17	96
Yongqing-lou	11	19	19	12	6	7	18	96
Yuxing-lou	7	11	11	8	7	4	8	60

at such a high rate. 'Money is always a big problem in doing conservation in these *tulou* settlements', Meng said. Current management plans, even if desirable, will not be economically sustainable. As an indispensible source of conservation funds, the local county governments are often forced into a very embarrassing position. The more heritage attractions that are designated, the more economically overburdened they feel. As some of the architectural conservators say, in some settlements of extremely high cultural value, only one-third of the vernacular buildings have been designated heritage buildings of county-level significance by the local government. Many cultural resource authorities on the county level throughout China withhold information about local cultural resources to varying degrees when they are compiling cultural resource inventories. This is not a bolt from the blue; the sustainability of conservation has always been a problem.

2.3.10 Maintenance Responsibility

Each year, every resident living inside the *tulou* buildings in Hekeng is awarded19 *yuan* RMB for room maintenance. For example, there are only nineteen people still living inside the Yuxing-lou; therefore, the total expenditures spent on the building maintenance of that *tulou* building is only 361 *yuan* RMB per year. Not to put too fine a point on it, by paying each person who still lives in it 19 *yuan*, the local cultural resource, on behalf of the county government, have in fact completely shifted the responsibility of day-to-day maintenance of the *tulou* buildings on to the local communities. The assumptions they use to support this shift in responsibility include: (1) As a resident who lives in the building, a person enjoys the ownership of the rooms he/she possesses. Therefore, (2) he/she has the requirement, indeed the duty to keep his/her own property in good condition. (3) If a person accepts the 19 *yuan* reward from the government, this is tantamount to him/her agreeing to repair their *tulou* apartment under the stipulations of the *World Heritage Convention* and the *Operational Guidelines*. (4) The person who accepts the money also tacitly has the duty to look after his/her own property, keeping it as 'traditional' as the cultural resource managers require. In fact, 19 *yuan* is a ridiculous sum to undertake any repair work. Nevertheless, with the lure of 19 *yuan*, the local government has successfully attracted many *tulou*-keepers. In a nutshell, by paying only a small amount of money, the local government has successfully involved itself in the housing property management in the Hakka people's daily life.

As Table 1 shows, there is always only a very small population still living in the *tulou* rooms. Only those living in the apartments are eligible to receive the 19 *yuan* and to assume responsibility for maintenance as the managers direct, but the majority of the present owners, who live elsewhere most of the time, neither receive anything nor do they have any responsibility. Nineteen *yuan* means nothing to these residents; yet it does indicate a sort of right that the local government could claim or even use as a basis to intervene directly in the daily management of the Hakka heritage. Ever since the 1990s, the Hekeng economy has been on the wane. The loss of its young labor force means that not only are there high vacancy rates in the *tulou* apartments and consequently poor conditions for preservation, but also the land resources have been badly neglected. Moreover, the shift in the labor force demographic has eventually resulted in the collapse of the agricultural economy in such rural settlements as those in the Hekeng River Valley. While it is certainly true that the changes in the agricultural landscapes must have emerged long before the decline in the local economy, before the 1990s no one could have imagined the collapse of the rice- cultivation system. Interviews with the Hekeng people suggest that nearly all the younger generation have chosen to work in Zhangzhou and Xiamen. The rice cultivation has been totally abandoned since the early twenty-first century. Agriculture no longer brings the local people large profits; working in urban centers, young peasants can earn more. The elderly and children usually do very little in the fields; their major income comes from the earnings of the 'peasant workers' (migrant workers) outside the valleys. The result is serious; urban centers have become the predominant source of income. Although not highly profitable and not particularly reliable, the new economy has still been strong enough to make the local people decide to quit working in the fields. Some old people might still grow tea on terraced fields, but tea is subject to large fluctuations in the market. Slowly but surely, Hekeng village has shed its agricultural image. The old have depend heavily on their children working outside the hilly region. Like many rural places elsewhere in China, Hekeng is now a village relying heavily on 'money transfers'. Although the residents cannot use the 19 *yuan* RMB to repair their roofs properly, they can still fall back on their children's bank transfers to fulfill such tasks. Presenting these data, I would argue the repair jobs are funded *de facto* by the young peasant workers.

In fact, the use of cultural resources as site parks, museums or museumized places usually involves the exploitation of rural cultural resources by urban centers. In the case of Hekeng, although almost every travel agency prefers to choose this village as a heritage attraction to lure the tourists, no one wants to reimburse the settlement for the exploitation of its heritage. Likewise, the county government is also set on making good use of 'its' heritage, and the way that it achieves this goal is to set strict limits to human activities inside the *tulou* settlements. It believes that the World Heritage status can conjure up development opportunities. Therefore, it is very important to keep this title by doing as UNESCO requires. As analyzed above, the local government usually follows the 'keep it as it was' principle. Human activities are strictly limited to ensure that the basic security and authenticity requirements are met. By the consistent implementation of its own regulations, it has successfully museumized the *tulou* buildings. The buffer zone requirement has meant that the Hekeng people are losing even more chances to process tea in the buffer zone areas. In the Hekeng people's own words, they are not allowed to do what they did in the past; 'they are not kept as they were'. The Hekeng people have lost not only their traditional way of life but their chance indeed their good right to develop their own society. In legal terms, they are the inalienable owners of the *tulou* rooms, but their rights to use the spaces fully as they would wish are limited not by law but by local regulations. In this case, we can see how the principles are being juggled by the local authorities to achieve their own goals. By paying the 19 *yuan* RMB, the local government successfully involves itself in the preservation and protection of the *tulou* buildings, and it has given itself the right to a say in the management of 'its' property. When it's all said and done, the property of the Hekeng people is heavily exploited by outsiders. Museumization as a World Heritage attraction is not necessarily a pleasant fate.

2.3.11 Redevelopment[37] and Authenticity

The local people's desire to redevelop their village area is another practical problem that the local government has to face from time to time. Their property is now no longer regarded as innately or self-evidently important as it was in the past. Compared with modern frame-type architecture, the quality and durability of earthen buildings is fairly poor. The enclosing outer walls usually measure about 2 meters in thickness (Dai, 2012) and therefore a solid foundation is an absolute must. The sheer thickness makes it impossible to reserve enough space underneath to install huge pipes; the upshot is that the sewage system is fairly restricted. Looked at from every angle, the adaptability of the *tulou* to modern use is rather limited. Unable to put in sewerage pipes the local residents have to build toilets outside the *tulou* buildings and their waste water has to flow into the open ditches first before it

37. *The Appleton Charter for the Protection and Enhancement of the Built Environment* defines redevelopment as 'insertion of contemporary structures or additions sympathetic to the setting'. For vernacular settlements in Fujian, as in most of the rural settlements elsewhere in China, rural redevelopment has always been carried out in a fairly decentralized way. Redevelopment of its very nature is the main social mechanism that leads to new land-use patterns. As it is extremely 'deconstructive', redevelopment is usually viewed by many as one of the major threats to heritage preservation, even when it is carried out by the local communities themselves. As analyzed in this part of the discussion, redevelopment is in effect a quite spontaneous construction activity of local residents in response to the changing demands of life. This sort of redevelopment has happened all the time throughout settlement history. Spatial compensation should also be considered as the outlet of new housing demands. For many reasons, spatial compensation is usually the weakest part of heritage site planning. Without any guidance about the locus in which redevelopment is allowed to happen, local residents can improve their use of even a densely inhabited part of a settlement. This is not a result of the failure of heritage conservation practice, but of the incompetence of site planning and the low adaptability to new uses in an old rural built environment.

runs into the pipes or gutters under the gateway and is finally discharged outside the building. Many local residents have to use the night-stools. Most such facilities are placed along the floor corridors in the daytime. Another sanitary hazard is that chickens, ducks and big domestic animals such as cattle and pigs are usually raised inside the buildings, so when it is all said and done, the inside of a *tulou* building is terribly overcrowded and insanitary. The younger generation of Hekeng people have spent almost their entire childhood with their parents in urban areas and cannot stand these unhygienic conditions. They simply cannot accept such a basic humble flat as their home. Their dilemma begs a very challenging question: Who will want to live here in the future? The second-generation peasant workers aged from 20 to 30-plus are more open-minded than their parents, the first-generation peasant-workers. When interviewed, young and middle-aged people both talked about their own futures. Having been long alienated from the farming society, they have lost basic agrarian skills and would no longer be able to make a living from agriculture and are totally unfamiliar with the rural environment. Even though they are still registered as permanent rural residents in official demographic documents, the majority have made a decision to settle down in the urban areas in which they work. Consequently, although stability of ownership is assured, it does not necessarily guarantee the permanent residential use that would gladden the heart of the ICOMOS. In fact, if the WHL had not intervened, local residents might have redeveloped the whole river valley by building brick or timber-frame-type residences.

Right now, the local people are trapped in a dilemma. They do not want to live in old buildings, but they are not allowed to build modern residences inside the settlement area (core zone). As far as the local residents are concerned, the WH nomination came at an inopportune moment when a radical change in the traditional built environment was poised to happen in the Hekeng River Valley. The urge for 'authenticity' is largely to blame for thwarting the redevelopment of the local Hakka society. In such international documents as the *Aoi An Protocols for Best Conservation Practice in Asia* (2009), and also in ICOMOS suggestions, local residents are frequently encouraged to live at home, in the old houses. Although this has not been set out in black and white in these documents, the essential purpose of such encouragement is that people keep using the buildings, constant habitation being a condition particularly important to the maintenance of wooden-earthen type architectures. However, apparently completely absorbed with preserving the past, these principles have never made any mention of methods that might improve the internal living conditions in the old houses.

As mentioned above, one of the major duties of the local government is to preserve cultural heritage. The primary legal doctrines on which it relies to do this are the articles in the *Chinese Cultural Heritage Law* pure and simple. The snag is that the law fails to offer any clear-cut suggestions about to what extent a building or structure of cultural significance can be modified, in the event that redevelopment is not allowed as it would interfere with the cultural significance of the built environment. Apart from this oversight, no regulations in the form of operational guidelines or any equivalent have ever been worked out. Therefore, when talking about cultural heritage protection, officials usually take an 'intact' attitude toward those houses and *tulou* buildings that have been designated culturally significant on different levels. Pragmatically, it goes without saying that people might need to change the inner structure in order to improve the internal living conditions. Such an operation might involve changing the floor boards, plastering the surfaces of the earthen walls inside the rooms and installing new bathroom facilities such as toilet seats, that would be a totally new innovation. Unfortunately, no basic laws address a problem like is the installing a toilet seat in a World Heritage site building 'legal'. Up the creek without a paddle, on behalf of the government the heritage site managers have to fall back on a plethora of regulations to make their judgments. I would argue that the feasibility of the regulations in the *Chinese Cultural Heritage Law* that cover the preservation of real estate is quite limited, and that the regulations themselves have not been compiled rigorously. The ambiguity lies in the fact that, on the one hand, houses are symbols of the cultural heritage of the country, but on the other hand they still serve the residential needs of the local people. Caught in this dilemma, officials who are responsible for the preservation and protection of cultural resource therefore hesitate to take any decision. Nowhere do the fundamental laws (for example, land management laws, property laws) state concisely and to the point that a property of cultural significance should be used in strict accordance with the 'intact' principles advocated in such professional laws as the *Cultural Heritage Law*. In other words, a person's basic rights should encompass the right 'to modify personal property as he/she wishes, provided that he/she has the ownership of it'. No one knows what should be done to transpose a historical space into a modern residential area without violating the heritage requirements. The embarrassment of such officials is that: In their duties as public cultural resource managers, they have no room to manoeuver and have no choice but to apply the 'intact' rules. Despite the fact that the fundamental laws surely have a much higher status than the bylaws, they say nothing about the legitimacy of spatial transformation. Although it has less legal force, the cultural heritage law does say something about this transformation, but this is both vague and negative. By keeping to the latter, at least, the government authorities lower the risk of being blamed for misconduct. In practice, without appropriate guidance to the making trade-offs between preserving authenticity and improving the adaptability of the *tulou* to modern use, the local cultural resource managers find themselves having to defend the baseline of authenticity principles very strictly. Everyone knows that adaptive use is not completely prohibited, but no one knows to what extent he/she can undertake any moderations. A local conservation specialist criticized as follows:

> '*... We need not only the regulations and laws. They are, of course, important, but you know, the* Chinese Cultural Heritage Law *was first issued in 1982. Therefore, it may be outdated. When it first came out, vernacular buildings were even not regarded as places of cultural heritage significances, so nothing about such buildings has ever been clearly written into the conservation regulations of that law. We cannot find even a single word about what are wrong doings in the conservation of vernacular buildings in that law. This has brought us troubles in management work. For instance, can it be a violation of any regulations if a peasant would like to change the structure of his/her own property for accommodating other uses, or they simply hope to change the wideness of a window or other features of their own property? We've got no answers. According to our basic knowledge about cultural heritage authenticity, such activities are surely not encouraged, but you know, these essential requirements on authenticity are foreign rules, international principles. They are not clearly written in any Chinese laws. They are not illegal. They just make changes on their own houses. We cannot stop them doing such things. We protect, we conserve, and we persuade, only following our basic sense about authenticity principles advocated by foreign NGOs, not any Chinese law articles in written forms.*'[38]

During the 2013 investigation in the Hekeng River Valley, I was informed that the local county government had just launched a new project, that was called *'Fu Mei Xiangcun'* (Wealthy and Beautiful Countryside). The core of the project is the construction of some basic infrastructures for the villages; however, the rules were adamant: Hekeng was not allowed to pave the roads in the valley. Again, the reasoning behind this prohibition is that new materials could interfere with the authenticity of the traditional settlements and negatively affect the OUV on whose basis the buildings were registered on the WHL. WHL is, as many, especially the local government officials, have perceived, provides the basis for a better tourism economy. What the Hekeng people have been complaining about for a long time is that the local government, in conjunction with external travel agencies, have made use of their property but at the price of sacrificing the future of Hekeng village.

Among all the *tulou* villages scattered throughout Fujian, Hekeng is very special. It is the only one in which all the *tulou* buildings have been nominated for and registered on the World Heritage List. This is the most important difference between this small river valley village and other Hakka and Minnan villages.

---

38. Meng, Z., 'The Fujian *Tulou* Buildings Trapped in the Post-inscription Dilemma, the More Well-known, the More Difficult to Protect?', *Xinhua News*, September 24, 2013.

Some the villages have only one *tulou* building registered on the WHL. Usually, the buffer zone in these villages is quite limited in area. In the ICOMOS letter cited previously, the commissioned experts have even stipulated that the local cultural authorities enlarge the buffer zone of such villages.[39] Obviously, development pressures in these villages are much less than those in the Hekeng River Valley, in which the built environment has been transformed into a representation of the past or into functional zones serving the same purpose. Hekeng could be said to be a fully regulated place. The people there have long been walking the tight-rope between the property law and the heritage law and that between their desire to modernize their settlements and the requirements of the local cultural authorities. The chief embarrassment of the Hekeng people is that, although they have done everything the cultural heritage principles require of them, they are unable to squeeze any acceptable compensation from the county administrators for the resultant inconvenience and economic backwardness, largely derived from the need to keep the tourist resource 'intact'. By contrast, Shiqiao, where the Zhang surname established their first settlement, is also very famous for its *tulou* buildings. Registered on the National Famous Village List, it has been less impacted by heritage regulations than Hekeng, that really is a fully regulated place. The investigation in 2013 discovered that more new, modern buildings had already been built in the peripheral areas of Shiqiao village. Most of them have been constructed using bricks and cement. As the local people said, the local cultural resource managers have permitted them to build these small buildings that are in the style of either courtyards or small two-storied bungalows. Some have been built in the buffer zone and are located quite near the old *tulou* houses. In recent years, some outsiders have also paid rent for using the land of the local peasants, and some of the small bungalows are theirs. As it is not a World Heritage attraction, land-use at Shiqiao village is much more flexible.

39. 'It was the opinion of the ICOMOS Mission experts that it would be beneficial to extend the buffer zone for Zhenfu-lou further down the valley. ICOMOS would welcome a response to whether consideration has been given a slightly larger buffer zone for this complex or if one could be considered.' (Several inquiries by the ICOMOS in 2008, date unclear, information collected from the archives of Nanjing County government in July, 2011).

2.3.12 Profit-sharing and Compensation

At the time of the investigations, nothing to do with the profit-sharing issues had been regulated.[40] Hekeng, like most of the *tulou* settlements in Fujian, has been a major tourist destination since the 1990s. Many believe that the local people, especially the owners of the *tulou* apartments, could be reimbursed from the tourist-generated income; however, this is still a pipe dream. Tianluokeng and Yunshuiyao are the best examples of the tourist economy in the hilly region. Their success, I would argue, derives from the local people's participation in cultural resource management. Unlike these two places, in most other settlements, including Hekeng, Nanou, Taxia and Shiqiao, visitors are free to enter any buildings, and no one is going to be charged. In these places, the *tulou* buildings are still sites of daily use and residence; they have not yet been developed as tourist attractions. In 2007, 420,000 tourists came to visit the hilly region. In 2009, this had risen substantially to 518,000 people. In 2010, the settlements in Yongding had to handle a tourist 'invasion' of around 710,000. It is estimated by the local government that Yongding county alone generated a total tourist income of 0.3 billion *yuan* RMB in 2007.[41] This figure is only a rough estimate. In 2011, Tianluokeng settlement for the first time in its post-developed (tourism) era, even welcomed a migrant-workers' backflow from the urban centers. The wanderers returned home to help their families manage their businesses. The local residents and tourists immediately began to complain about a deterioration in the environment. Stalls are scattered throughout the buffer zone, that is extremely crowded, dirty and disorderly. This 'return to base' is evidence that tourism had already generated copious economic benefits and had therefore become the

40. Profit-sharing can always be a problem. Ye (2006) has recorded the income-sharing at Eryi-lou heritage site, also a WH site in southern Fujian. According to Ye, an ordinary visitor who wanted to visit Eryi-lou and the small museum housed in another *tulou* building might be charged 30 *yuan* RMB. At that time, the local government alleged that the ticket income was used for the maintenance of the buildings and employing caretakers. In short, none of the income was allotted to the *tulou* residents as compensation.

41. The Chinese Tourism Planning Academy. 2008. *Yongding Tulou Settlement Tourism Design*. Unpublished.

major income source of the local people in Shangban. No one knows how many people will come to Hekeng each year, but surely 'there will be a great many', as some of the residents said. It seems that Hekeng has been a tourist 'hot spot' for quite a long time. The disappointing news is, in the settlements in Hekeng and Nanou, people cannot expect more from tourism; they are only stations on the way to somewhere else. In the 2011 investigation, I began to sense a tension between the local residents and the outsiders. Some of the local people even refused to allow the tourists to go inside the *tulou* buildings. At the time of the investigation, the Hekeng people were all talking about their wish to develop settlement tourism. As noted earlier, the local government was encouraging people to live inside their real estate. On the one hand, only residents would have the right and feel the necessity to repair their dwelling and thereby preserve the buildings. On the other hand, this might certainly reinforce the impression that the village is still densely occupied and actively used (which it is obviously not, owing to younger generation's exodus), one salient condition for attracting more tourists. The sad truth is that almost every tourist line passes the '*tulou* village in Hekeng', the well-known World Heritage site, by. Before reaching their final destination, perhaps Yunshuiyao, perhaps Shangban, visitors are able to get their first glimpse of the magnificent buildings of the Hakka people in the Hekeng settlements from their bus without paying a penny. Indeed, although a WH site, tourism development in Hekeng lags far behind that in many other places nearby. Between 2006 and 2012, the Hekeng River Valley became a tourist destination generating no ticket income. According to communications with some of my informants, it is possible that some of the local residents in these two site villages, namely: Shangban and Yunshuiyao, are 'government cadres' and were adept at making good use of these 'advantages' to initiate the tourism development process there very early. This is a very feasible reflection of the uneven distribution of political influence and the advantageous position of rural cadres in the use of local heritage resources. In reality, a WH title might not necessarily lead to an advantageous position in regional tourism competitions.

Compared to Shangban and Yunshuiyao, whose tourism economy is run basically by the local people themselves, the local residents in Nanou, Shiqiao and Hekeng rarely have the chance to participate in any form of tourism development. In 2011, in an interview, the staff member of a travel agency in Taxia said that the local people were never invited to play any part in tourism management. Theoretically, tourism would seem to be one of their best options. However, as mentioned earlier, the taxes from tourism companies only find their way into government coffers: they are not the gateway to a better quality of life for the *tulou* residents in Hekeng. The companies share the tourist income with only the local government. As noted earlier, a fairly paltry 19 *yuan* RMB is given to each Hekeng resident as recompense. Only when the residents began to realize what role they had been allotted to play did they begin to voice their complaints about the museumization process and the tourism development in which they are pawns.

In many instances in China, compensation for heritage preservation is usually closely linked to the relocation of the local people. The relocated local communities are entitled to compensation for the loss of their property as well as subsidies for both relocation and interim housing. A good example of this process is the Fangyan cultural heritage site in Zhejiang province. Zhao (2013) claims that a total number of 3,500 people were moved out of the site area. Some of the local people were able to obtain additional compensation for the decorative components of their houses. Some of them received 'one-time' compensation for having had to close a business. The local government even issued *Detailed Guidelines for Demolition, Compensation and Settlement Plan for the Central Scenic Area of Fangyan*. The Fangyan case sets a good example for other local governments in the compensation of local people for the economic loss incurred during the creation of national heritage. In a situation radically different to the Fangyan case, the Hekeng people have suffered two kinds of losses. The most appreciable one is the loss of their real-estate, including the two-story earthen houses and tea processing places. The compensation for these losses was actually underlined in the Fangyan compensation plan cited above. However significant this material loss is, there is also another important loss that should be paid more attention, but this has been overlooked in the details of that plan, namely: the complete or partial loss of the local people's right to inhabit or use their own properties conveniently and in the way in which they were intended to be used. As most people were not satisfied with the two relocation places proposed by the local township government, the plans for relocation in the Hekeng River Valley did not go ahead. To add insult to injury, as their properties were treated as a national treasure, they were not eligible for damages. That said, as discussed previously, the Hekeng people's right to use their built environment has already been seriously eroded. Therefore, the compensation for this invisible loss should take the form of renting.

2.4 THE LEGITIMACY OF 'OVERREGULATED PLACES' IN THE CHINESE LAND RESOURCE MANAGEMENT FRAMEWORK: A BROADER VIEW

As Silverman and Blumenfield (2013) have observed, since 2000 on many formal occasions Chinese officials have begun to lay a growing emphasis on the importance of cultural heritage resources, domestic tourism and economic development as a whole. They have often raised the question:' How should the contradictions of simultaneously destroying and protecting heritage be understood?' If they go back to the drawing-board, they might well discover that such contradictions can be the direct result of the contested zoning activities in land resource management.

The term 'regulated place' refers to those Chinese cultural places registered on the international, national, provincial and county cultural heritage lists, that are subject to being influenced to various degrees by certain laws and regulations pertaining to land-use. The Chinese cultural heritage is 'administered' in a hierarchical top-down system. On the one hand, the Chinese heritage management system, like that of any other countries, is used to place all the cultural resources on a ladder ascending from the sites of least significance to those of overriding importance. Although this might seem all clear and above board, 'cultural significance' does not necessarily make sense in the overall Chinese land resource management system. At least five Chinese ministries can have a direct impact on the preservation of Chinese cultural resources. The most significant is, of course, the Chinese Ministry of Culture (*Zhongguo Guojia Wenhuabu*) with which the SACH is affiliated, whose role is to guard the cultural resources of the country. Second in descending order of importance is the Ministry of Land and Resources of the PRC (*Zhongguo Guotu Ziyuanbu*), or the MLR. This government department was established to manage all Chinese land resources (*tudi ziyuan*), most pertinently such natural resources such coal-mines, forests, other natural reserves and so forth. The third one in the pecking order is the National Committee for Development and Reforms (*Guojia Fazhan yu Gaige Weiyuanhui*), or the NCDR, whose major role is to make plans for urban and rural development. It is followed in influence by the fourth one, the Ministry of Housing and Urban-Rural Development of the PRC (*Zhonghua Renmin Gongheguo Zhufang ji Chengxiang Jianshebu*), or the MHUD, that is responsible for overseeing and managing Chinese infrastructure, real estate and public facilities in urban and rural areas. Finally the Ministry of Agriculture, that has complete charge of Chinese agriculture and rural development is also entitled to have its say as well.

In view of the inconsistency and inconvenience that inevitably result from these cross-managing practices, since 2007, the National Committee for Development and Reforms has embarked on a new program: 'One Map for the Whole Country' (*Quanguo Yizhang Tu*) whose purpose is to draw all the urban and rural land resources into one geographical mapping system. It states unequivocally that there is absolutely no doubt that cultural heritage is one of the primary land resources, and on this ground, in seeking its support they proposed various notions to the SACH. However, for reasons unknown the then incumbent director of the SACH was not prepared to lend a willing ear to whatever it had to say.[42] Abashed by the director's refusal, the officials of the NCDR turned directly to the local governments

42. Personal communication from Prof. Wang Xuerong in 2014.

for their help. Finally, in 2014 the NCDR put forward its periodic plan in the form of a series of zoning plans, entitled *Quanguo ji Gediqu Zhuti Gongnengqu Guihua* or the *Primary Plans for National and Provincial Function Zoning*. As the primary strategy for guiding Chinese development in both urban and rural areas, the plan re-divided the total land area of China into four principal categories, namely: redevelopment areas (*youhua kaifaqu*), development areas (*zhongdian kaifaqu*), limited development areas (*xianzhi kaifaqu*) and cultural and natural reserves (*jinzhi kaifaqu*). As the officials of the NCDR might have initially assumed, cultural resources such as archaeological sites, official buildings in historical urban areas and vernacular buildings in rural areas should have been incorporated into the reserves category. Under the plans published in 2014, their goal was only partially achieved. Without the help of the SACH, the NCDR could have only included the WH sites and natural heritage parks in the reserves, and this limitation would have entailed an oversight of nearly all other important cultural heritage sites. Obviously, the existing Chinese CR management hierarchy cannot match the new land resource management orientations. Its impotence can only expose the cultural sites and buildings to a greater threat from urban and rural development and redevelopment, especially those sites located in or around the areas belonging to the first two newly developed land resource categories. As I mentioned previously, in urban and rural planning in China zoning activities play an enforcing role in legislation. When this affects Chinese cultural heritage preservation and protection, it is highly likely that a vernacular building site, such as the Hekeng *tulou* heritage, could be subject to the regulations and laws from at least seven sources: (1) the NCDR function zone regulations that do recognize the *World Heritage Conventions* and follow the authenticity and buffer zone principles of the *Operational Guidelines*; (2) the *Regulations on the Preservation of the Cities, Townships and Settlements of Great Historical and Cultural Significances* (*Lishi Mingcheng Mingzhen Mingcun Baohu Tiaoli*) issued by the State Council in collaboration with the MHUD; (3) the *Chinese Cultural Heritage Law* (*Zhonghua Renmin Gongheguo Wenwu Baohufa*) issued by the State Council in collaboration with the SACH; (4) local government regulations, decisions, policies in relation to cultural heritage protection, such as the ones cited in this chapter; (5) *Land Resources Management Law of the PRC* (*Zhonghua Renmin Gongheguo Tudi Guanlifa*) issued by the State Council in collaboration with the MLR; (6) the *Chinese Property Law* (*Zhonghua Renmin Gongheguo Wuquanfa*) issued by the National People's Congress; and (7) the *Chinese Inheritance Law* (*Zhonghua Renmin Gongheguo Jichengfa*) also issued by the National People's Congress. Excessively burdened with rules and regulations, Hekeng has had to wrestle with many serious restrictions on land and house use, ensuing economic hardship, unpromising compensation for the transference of right of usufruct and a nugatory tourism income.

Hekeng was once a small but densely inhabited lineage village located along a brook in southern Fujian region, particularly well known for its high density of *tulou* houses. From 2006 to 2012, using the rules and regulations laid down in WH policies, regulations and concepts as an excuse, the local county government, in collaboration with site planners invited from other parts of China, transformed the village into a 'museum' in which the *tulou* architectural specimens are the principal exhibit. During this spatial transformation, even though the local residents were still living there, the built environment began to change dramatically. Essentially, a new function, that of serving visitors, was imposed upon the inhabited area. To create a heritage theme that would attract more tourists, the local site managers accorded representation of the past the most prominent status among the many other *tulou* uses. Not to put too fine a point on it, between 2006 and 2012, Hekeng was swamped in regulations.

3. Hekeng: a Place of 'Placelessness'

This chapter focuses on the representation of the past in the Hekeng River Valley. As the most important international cultural heritage organization, the WHC, tries to help each State Party preserve the outstanding cultural attributes embodied in the heritage sites on which that particular state places a high value. As the leading CRM organization globally, it has sought out the way to construct a universal value methodology that, as it has long put into practice, can apply to the World Heritage site selection in each State Party. For a long time, the WHC and its Advisory Bodies have endeavored to preserve all the essential characteristics of the physical part of heritage in each registered place; features that are apparently meaningful to the local people and might therefore represent their past. Unfortunately, for many reasons, attaining this goal is not as easy as might have been expected. Deviations from these expectations seem to be inevitable. One factor of overriding importance is that the built environment changes constantly throughout any settlement history. Many socio-cultural mechanisms can give rise to the spontaneous metabolization of the heritage, and inexorably also to the loss of the physical fabric and the memories attached to it. Theming would seem to be the answer but, as demonstrated to some extent at least in Chapter 2, when creating a heritage place, in many ways theming can also adversely result in the greater loss of not just the material fabric but also of the social memories bound up in it. Moreover, in recent times social changes such as depopulation[43] and relocation have also often incurred the disuse, abandonment and demolition of the traditional built environment. What is put on the final stage in a WH representation is nothing but the outcome of these social processes. This realization prompts the next questions: To what extent does the representation of a place achieved by the application of the WH methods relate to the past in the minds of the local people, if they are the group best qualified to judge the value of their properties? If the local people have their own ways of commemorating the past, what is the best way for WH creation to accommodate these traditions? What are the major changes in the identity of the place and identity of the local people in a heritage-making process?

43. After the mid-1980s, large numbers of rural Chinese moved to the urban areas to find jobs. This trend has continued for almost over 25 years. In contrast to other places in China, the western and southern rural areas of Fujian have had a long reputation for high population mobility in historical times in response to their inhabitants' quest for scarce resources.

3.1 THE LOCAL PEOPLE'S PLACE AND THE REPRESENTED PLACE

Tuan (1977) argues that most definitions of place are quite arbitrary. In the context of the present discussion, as Tuan writes, places are locations in which people have long memories, 'reaching back beyond the indelible impressions of their own individual childhoods to the common lores of bygone generations'. He also points out that the smallest size space that can be thought of as a place by geographers is a settlement. Inevitably as night follows day, a place is destined to be intertwined with time (Lowenthal, 1966) and people. The former statement covers the dynamic spatial changes throughout the whole history of the place, whereas the latter is mainly concerned with the individuals and communities who open up a space and build up experiences there. In the phenomenology of place (Relph, 1976), human spatial experience is stated to be an important factor in a place. Relph's conception of a place is that it has the power to order and focus people's intentions, actions, experiences, and perhaps emotions as well. As David Seamon and Jacob Sowers (2008) argue, Relph's ideas of place and identity of place are quite useful and can be thought of as the first step leading toward a thorough understanding of a real place. In his work, Relph proposed three components of place identity: (a) the physical setting of a place; (b) its activities, situations and events; and (c) the individual and group meanings created through people's experiences and intentions in relation to that place. In fact, these three key components correspond respectively to space, time and people, that are all closely related, in Relph's terms, to the restoration or creation of a place. What matters to the present discussion is Relph's concern about the loss of the 'insideness' of a place, or what he called 'the feeling of placelessness', that are the outcome of 'the casual eradication of distinctive places and the making of standardized landscapes that results from an insensitivity to the significance of place'. Essentially, Relph ascribes placelessness to an 'uncritical acceptance of mass values'. Echoing Relph's inspiring theory, I would like to probe the process of the dissolution of Hekeng, once just a very small riverside settlement. In this process, a new place has replaced an old one; heritage creation, allied with many other socioeconomic factors, has turned placeness into placelessness, and imbued the local people with a sense of 'outsideness'.

Insideness is grounded in the use of the buildings, structures and the whole settlement landscape, all of which can be conceived of as the physical setting of the settlement place. This use was made up of the daily activities, situations and events that happened in or around the settlement landscape from historical times to the contemporary past. In the long process of lineage life, the use of land helped the local people form a relatively steady and stable relationship with their built and natural environments. In the eyes of any lineage member, the house he inhabited, the land he cultivated, the hall or temple in which he attended lineage ceremonies, the paths leading to other settlements and markets near or far constituted his life setting and helped in the construction of his own insideness, self-identity, and sentimental/attitudinal attachment (Tuan, 1977) to the place in which he lived out his lifespan. The use of the built and natural environments also provided chance and fixed occasions on which interactions between lineage members took place. It is no exaggeration to claim that the use of buildings and structures linked the local residents and their environments. The other side of the coin is that changes in the manner of inhabitation, farming processes, offering ceremonies, place attachments and land-use patterns can also initiate a series of changes in the built and natural environments and in this process the place in which one was born can become quite unfamiliar and no longer as meaningful as it was in the past. Undoubtedly, an innovative intention to use the environment in one way or another is usually the very first step leading towards changes in a place, and in turn these can influence the local people personally. When a settlement such as Hekeng is used as a heritage place, it is particularly important to differentiate these land-use intentions, understand the stakeholders[44] and be absolutely clear about the impacts that changes in land-use orientations might introduce in both a historical and a present perspective. Basically, we can classify these intentions into three groups, namely: those of the historical insiders (to metabolize); those of the present insiders (to develop or redevelop); and those of the outsiders (to museumize). These outsiders can be either local government authorities or international cultural heritage organizations.

Before I proceed with the assessment of land-use intentions, I would like to draw a basic demarcation along the border between the local people's place and the represented place from a spatial perspective. In 2008, altogether forty-six *tulou* houses scattered throughout ten settlements in the south Fujian region were eventually registered on the World Heritage List. For unknown reasons, the heritage was not nominated as traditional settlement sites or cultural landscapes, but in the form of single *tulou* architectures or building clusters. The reasons I find it important to stress this negative comment are as follows: First and foremost, the nomination was in itself a violation of the authenticity and integrity principles of the WHC and, secondly, the nomination has generated an apparently new, spatial realm in terms of 'building clusters' arbitrarily coined by heritage management professionals that is obvious neither to people from outside nor, more importantly,

44. Stakeholders are those social groups that get themselves deeply involved in the use of cultural resources. As a matter of course, they have different views about how the past should be used. By introducing different land-uses, they can impose significant impacts on the built environment and consequently the daily life of the local people. Those stakeholders who might get involved in the land-use issues in Hakka heritage sites are both insiders and outsiders. The majority of the former are the Hakka communities; the latter are primarily government authorities, cultural resource managers, site planners, conservators, tourists and cultural resource developers.

to the local residents themselves. The crux of the matter is that it artificially divorces some of the buildings from their original settlement and their social context. The upshot is two parallel spatial scales are emerging on the same heritage stage. The first of these is the real place that a local resident recognizes by recourse to his or her own place experiences built up since childhood and from the collective memories of the past of the lineage settlement. The other is an artificial spatial concept composed of the property and the buffer zone surrounding it. The former is a 'place' recognized by humanistic geographers, whereas the latter is really nothing more than a representational zone having no spatial overlap with the local communities and no reference to the historical/existing settlement pattern, as demonstrated in Chapter 2. Finally, the space in *tulou* settlements such as Hekeng is dragged into an arbitrary differentiation between the past and the present, as mentioned in Chapter 2, forming contradictions between a local people's place and a represented place. If these assertions are accepted, to what extent should we recognize what we see today in these highly-modified places as the representation of a real past, both temporally and spatially?

There are at least three points omitted from the authenticity list of the Hekeng historical representation, or have otherwise only been noted ambiguously in the site interpretation. The most conspicuous is the omission of some non-*tulou* buildings and structures. This oversight has already incurred a spatial incompleteness of historical preservation and representation. I have already discussed this point in Chapter 1. Agnew (1993) has pointed out that a place can be constituted by all kinds of buildings and structures in an area, and these buildings and structures form 'nodes', at and around which the sense of a place can be generated and structured. This point is very important as it underlines that all the relevant buildings and structures that helped shape the insideness of a settlement member should be included in the representation of the place, because all these 'nodes' built up the authenticity and integrity of that place. The second oversight is the time. How can time be represented? Granted this is a very difficult task. We are very aware that in many heritage places, representation is flattened. Apart from the time order in which the architecture was built, as suggested in Chapter 1, both the metabolization of the built environment and the former appearance of the buildings themselves can be used as evidence of time. The sticking-point is that historical metabolization is not directly visible but it has already been intertwined with the feelings about the place felt by the local people. Any traces of previous physical changes have already disappeared in the metabolic processes. In Hekeng, for instance, the metabolization is about all the evolution process of the whole settlement landscape in which changes in building forms and structures must have played a significant role. Some basic episodes of these changes have already been unequivocally identified in Chapter 1. The historical use of and changes in the built environment make up the basic timeline along which the whole landscape developed into its last organic shape in the late 1980s. The third point omitted, and indeed the most important one, is the sense of the place. Lineage members who possess this insideness are indisputably an indispensible part of the historical environment. They have acquired some of the feelings about their place from their parents and other older relatives. They are also able to sense a long history when they participate in ceremonies in temples or pay their respects at graves. Such emotions, feelings and attachments are difficult for outsiders to perceive. Local residents are intrinsically part of their place. Unlike the actual physical settings of a place, a sense of a place cannot and need not be represented directly. Although it is recessive, *insideness* is a useful measure for testing whether a local resident still retains the feeling that the place is his place, and hence also a useful measure for testing the authenticity of a place.

3.2 SPATIAL METABOLIZATION AND THE CREATION OF INSIDENESS OVER TIME

How people have used and modified their built and natural environments lies at the core of any local history. As has been touched on in Chapter 1, it is a series of social processes in which the local population has waxed and waned, the arable land curtailed in area, in which settlement expansions and relocations have occurred from time to time and spontaneous environmental metabolization has continued in many guises, running the gamut from building establishment, renovation, use and disuse to demolition, all processes which have happened in response to the population increases and decreases. The changes in the built environment usually echoed either the perpetual or instant needs of local communities in the past. New buildings replaced old ones, leading to a new look for the whole place. Besides, if they were to survive in such river valleys with the very sparse agricultural resources at their disposal, the local residents needed to prolong the lifespan of their buildings and structures and maintain the important physical attributes and cultural 'cues' in them, long justified as in some way useful, by making renovations and doing repair work from time to time. These sorts of undertakings also unavoidably led to the physical metabolization of the built environment, affecting different types of buildings, carried out on different architectural scales and at different rates. This metabolization was more than just the local way of life, it was the force that generated the basic mechanisms which had allowed the buildings and structures to continue to exist through time. The traditional ways of maintaining the built environment expressed in terms of building skills, materials, attitudes, emotions, procedures and so on are also part and parcel of heritage authenticity. These capabilities and intentions of the local people are intrinsic evidence of time. They are very important in that they might not only be able to be used to justify the validity of historical alterations in built environments but in that they also underline the reasonableness of the changes made by the local people to their properties in the early modern times, indeed even today. Changes constitute the time dimension of authenticity. The preliminary investigations in 2011 and 2013 revealed a traditional Hakka settlement landscape (as a place) in the Nanjing rural area usually consisted of seven parts: temples and halls, residences, cemeteries, agricultural fields, workshops and animal husbandry facilities and communal structures. A knowledge of how local people interacted with their built environment and how this environment changed would considerably enrich our understanding of the representation of the settlement place in Hekeng. Through their interactions with their environments, local people created a micro-society in which the sense of *insideness* was grounded in the lineage glories kept very much alive in the ancestor worship culture, people's emotional attachment[45] to the place and the spatial and temporal geography constituted by the intergenerational gaps (expressed in building dates, burial dates, generation names), monumental buildings and structures and the experience of land-use learned since their youth. All these elements were the building blocks of a local person's identity, bonding it with the whole built environment. At this point it would be useful to present some cases demonstrating the real relationships between the local people and their settlement place under traditional conditions.

3.2.1 Temples, Halls, Shrines and Lineage Ceremonies

As noted earlier in Chapter 1, temples and halls in the southern Fujian area are all in courtyard form and are the most durable part of the settlements. The majority of the extant temples and halls were first built in the late Ming and the early Qing dynasty. The Hakka people had many uses for these structures but, as said, there is usually only one principal ancestral temple (*zongci*) for the whole lineage. In the Hekeng Zhang lineage village, each strong sub-lineage (*fang*) also had its own ancestral hall (*zhici*) to commemorate its own common near ancestors (*fensi*). An ancestral shrine (*tang*) is a public space located inside a *tulou* building, built in the rear portion of the first floor. The sort of shrine inside a *tulou* building is actually a transformation of the shrine (*tang*) in a typical courtyard dwelling (*heyuan*). By and large, the structure of a courtyard residence is characterized by a central shrine (*tang*) with two or more houses in its wings (*heng*). In former times, every resident inside the same *tulou* had equal access to this small place in which they could get together to make daily offerings to their common ancestors (or deities in later times) and discuss the affairs of the households. Therefore,

45. Like 'collective memory' defined by Connerton (1989), lineage attachment is also a way of interpreting a settlement's own past and includes all the activities that 'go into making a version of the past resonate with group members'. In Chinese vernacular cases, ancestral temples, genealogies and the lineage properties are the major means (Chen, 2011) that shape a common sense of belonging. Temples are primarily monuments that, according to Rowlands and Tilley (2006), make the people believe in the permanence of identity.

viewed as a whole, the complete Hakka ancestral worship system of the Hekeng Zhang lineage would have consisted of three levels from bottom to top: ancestral shrine (joint families), ancestral halls (sub-lineages) and principal temple (lineage). Their presence underlines the great importance of the Hekeng settlements. To a very large extent, the extant temples (that is, the principal temple Shiying-tang and the *fensi* temple the *Huaiting* Hall and another two that have been completely devastated) as well as the shrine structure inside each *tulou* building (except the Yongsheng-lou) represent the whole spectrum of the ancestral worship architecture of the Hekeng Zhang lineage. In traditional times, the shrines inside the *tulou* buildings were also the places in which wedding ceremonies were conducted and this tradition has continued to the present day.

Ancestral temples, especially the principal ones, were used in many different ways. They could serve as a place for conducting the major offering ceremonies of the lineage (*hezu gongji*), holding meeting, and the invocation of spirits in funerary rituals. As the major temple of the whole Zhang lineage, in the past the Shiying-tang provided opportunities to strengthen the cohesiveness of the lineage members from time to time. For instance, the *hezu gongji* observance still takes place every year. The *toujia* or the family that takes the lead is often determined by drawing lots. That year it is the principal family responsible for raising funds and organizing offering rituals in the principal ancestral temple. The time for observing the *hezu gongji* offering varies from lineage to lineage, but is usually held in winter. The series of ancestral offering ceremonies and the later harvest celebrations are called the *zuo dafu* or the grand ceremonies asking for the blessing of the gods by the local people. In Hekeng, every winter, the Protector or *Baosheng dadi* (whose statue is now enshrined inside the *Huaiting* Hall) is invited to meet the Common Lord or *Minzhu gongwang* in the shrine at the entrance to the village. This encounter is the fundamental part of the *zuo dafu* activities. Apart from its religious use, the principal temple was also used as a place in which to exhibit the history and glories of the Zhang lineage.[46] The lineage erected numerous stone pillars (*shi qigan*) around the small square in front of the temple. Each and every stone pillar is a memorial that celebrates an individual's success in the Imperial exams, business or other great achievements. Therefore every one represents a kind of monument that commemorates the honor and glory of the Zhang surname as a whole. All in all, it was a place in which the Zhang lineage members created both a religious atmosphere in which they immersed themselves emotionally and a place in which they announced their existence to the outside world.

The *Huaiting*, built inside the Shengqing-lou and used in conjunction with the shrine at the rear of the building, is the sole representation of a *fensi* temple in Hekeng, and therefore of particular cultural significance. Although it now serves as a place for making offerings to *Baosheng dadi,* in the past this small hall inside the Shengqing-lou was used as a place for making offerings to the common ancestors of the Xizhuba settlement residents. In the late Qing dynasty, the role of the Xizhuba settlement people was to tend to the needs of the travelers on the nearby mountain path, providing them with drinking water and chairs on which they could rest. This small path traverses the Hekeng River Valley, linking Yongding to Meilin and Chuanchang. The late Qing local government was generous in its praise of the contribution of the Xizhuba residents and in 1832 (the *guiwei* year of the Jiaqing reign era) awarded

46. Ancestral temples are places created to strengthen lineage identity by means of all kinds of ceremonies at particular points of the lunar calendar year. A past recurs periodically when settlement residents gather together to remember the benevolence of the ancestors. Consequently, the repetition of the same descent identity is the primary form of collective memory construction. Genealogies, even though the early days of the lineages might be misrepresented, embellished or even distorted, are the primary written source of their own histories. Intangible features play a key role in the creation and continuation of the lineage identities. This is the reason that the desire to make the ancestors feel proud of their offspring by renovating temple architecture is always accorded paramount significance. This has always been a higher priority than any considerations of architectural authenticity. The sacred places provided an appropriate atmosphere (in fact, the setting) in which ancestors could be respected and honored, but they also serve the living psychologically. Improving the quality of serving the ancestors could make the lineage members who participate in the ceremonies feel better in themselves.

them a wooden plaque bearing the inscription '*de shi xiang lü*', or model of village benevolence. Ever since it has hung on the inner gate of the *Huaiting* Hall to honor the Xizhuba descendants in perpetuity. This information is important to understanding the use of the *Huaiting* in the late-nineteenth and early-twentieth century. Like the stone pillars erected in front of the Shiying-tang, the plaque bearing praise from the Qing government can be hung only in an ancestral hall, in which it bears eternal evidence of the glories of that lineage segment.[47]

Shrines (*tang*) are quite common structures inside *tulou* buildings. Playing a similar role to that of a principal temple and branch hall, this public space usually serves as a place in which worship the ancestral tablets, hold weddings and sometimes meetings of the extended families in the *tulou* buildings.[48] Functionally, though smaller in size and simpler in style compared to the temples, these public spaces might represent the oldest building tradition (*tang-heng shi jianzhu*) of the Hakka people in southern Fujian. The Hakka people deliberately took great care to preserve this semi-open structure in the middle rear portion inside their *tulou* shelters, in the same fashion as their forebears had once built the central *tang* structure in their courtyard dwellings.

Unlike the robustly constructed *tulou* buildings, temples, halls, shrines and other facilities with similar functions can be the most variable part of a settlement in terms of metabolization in East Asia, particularly China, Japan and perhaps Korea. What we have discovered seems to bear out the idea that the ancestral temples in southern Fujian could be 'improved' (repaired/restored/reconstructed) every fifty to one hundred years or so. The Shiying-tang Ancestral Temple of Hekeng village, for example, was first established in 1610, the thirty-eighth year of the Wanli reign, and in the following centuries it was 'improved' in 1732 (the tenth year of the Yongzheng reign), 1776 (the forty-first year of the Qianlong reign), 1823 (the third year of the Daoguang reign) and 1928 (the seventeenth year of the Republic of China) respectively. The frequency is nearly once per century. In the past, there could have been diverse changes in the use and maintenance of the Shiying-tang, which could have encompassed not just repairs but also reconstruction, expansion and so forth. As I explained in Chapter 1, the extant Shiying-tang is a grayish brick building in the form of a courtyard-dwelling. This is substantial evidence for arguing that ancestral temples could have been changing all the time, and therefore are the most unstable part of a settlement. However, this might be running before we can walk. In the present study of Hakka villages, we also need to consider the whole scenario of the evolutional built environment, especially the radical changes in the residential section that have taken place since the mid-sixteenth century, namely: the major transformation from an ordinary Chinese courtyard dwelling settlement into a *tulou* settlement. It is important to emphasize that ancestral temples are possibly the only extant architectural type that reflects the long pre-*tulou* history (roughly from the late-fourteenth century to the early-sixteenth century) of the local Hakka people in southern Fujian's hilly regions. Bearing in mind the revolutionary change in residential building form that took occurred between the middle Ming dynasty and the early Qing period, it is crucial to note that, when the Xizhuba people built the *Huaiting* Hall inside the Shengqing-lou, they still chose to construct it in full courtyard form. There can be no doubt whatsoever that the local residents rigorously followed the pre-existing *tang-heng* building styles when they were constructing the most important symbol of ancestral worship of the settlement. Therefore, it can be said with certainty that although they have been extensively repaired or even reconstructed periodically, ancestral temples and halls have preserved metabolically the most stable

47. This is a piece of hard evidence supporting the hypothesis that the tang in each *tulou* building should be the place for making offerings to the ancestors of the *tulou* residents, rather than a deity-offering place as Zheng first proposed in 2012. Indeed, the ceremony Zheng witnessed has only gained popularity in more recent times. On the evidence of the 2011 field investigation, it can be said with certainty that the metamorphosis of the ancestral shrine into a Protector shrine occurred only very late, in the early twentieth century in fact. As a *fensi* temple, the *Huaiting* shares many architectural traits with the principal temple. The other two *fensi* temples, the Dexin-tang and its unnamed counterpart in Qiaoxia, were completely demolished in the mid-1970s during the Cultural Revolution.

48. Interviews with local residents Zhang Enhan and Zhang Mintai in 2011.

form of traditional Hakka architecture. Therefore we can categorize these buildings as very stable. Having said this, in order that the temple be a place worth of representing the lineage honor and accommodating the souls of ancestors, renewals of adornment, improved internal conditions and more spacious central yards have perhaps been the foremost wishes of each lineage head. On behalf of the whole lineage, the head of the Zhang lineage in Hekeng, accepted donations from rich relatives to maintain and renovate.[49] Furthermore, the yields of the *gongtian* and the *jitian* (two major kinds of lineage trust) were also set aside to be sold to support the repair work. In fact, there was a series of social activities bound up with the management and renovation of the ancestral temples. Therefore, in their original form, temple renovations cannot be reduced to purely physical phenomenon; they must also have involved a significant number of community members. Today, the expenses incurred in making renovations still come mainly from donations. The latest renovation was carried out in the late 1990s. As the local residents were quick to point out, the 1990s renovation was virtually a complete reconstruction.[50] Compared to ordinary houses, the metabolic changes in the temples were inspired more by social and ceremonial considerations. Such modifications were undertaken not only when the compounds were damaged but also at particular points in time at which people felt it appropriate to strengthen the unity of the whole lineage or at the very least the bonds between several major families. Enhan says that since the 2000s, the temple, hall and shrines in the Hekeng River Valley have been rarely used. The local people tend to think of these places only when they need to organize wedding ceremonies and *zuo dafu* rituals.

3.2.2 *Tulou* Houses, Lineage Identity and Inheritance

Strictly speaking, in the present Hekeng village, the residential parts inside the *tulou* buildings are confined to the upper-story rooms supported by wooden posts and floor-boards/joists. Taking a four-story square *tulou* building as an example, the sections on the first floor are used as livestock stables, kitchens and sometimes bathrooms. Toilets have not been installed inside the *tulou* buildings and are usually located behind them. The rooms on the second floor are used as storehouses and barns. Only the rooms on the third and fourth floors are used for residential apartments. It is the custom of the old people to place their coffins in the corners of the corridors on the fourth floor. It is a folk belief that having your coffin ready while you are still alive will make you live much longer. The shrine on the first floor, in conjunction with the central open area, constitutes the public space of a *tulou* house. Wells are also customarily dug in this open area. A similar residential pattern is also observable in round *tulou* buildings. As noted earlier, windows are constructed only on the third and fourth floors. In the eyes of the local communities, residences also help to create a person's own lineage identity.

49. Renovation: Refurbishing and/or adding to the appearance of an original building or elements of a building in an attempt to 'renew' its appearance in keeping with contemporary tastes and perceptions of conservation. *(Aoi An Protocols: for Best Conservation Practice in Asia)*

50. Architecture in traditional Fujian settlements evolved at different rates. Religious buildings might seem to have been more stable in their morphology than common dwellings, but the wooden parts of this architecture also evolved. In fact, the '*xiu*' activities (see later) undertaken on religious buildings might have been even more radical and intensive. The *Nara Document on Authenticity* deconstructs the existing heritage conservation approach and proposes appropriate ways of assessing the authenticity of the building heritage in the East Asian context. As the Document comments, authenticity is by no means a static conservation criterion; information sources, knowledge background and cultural diversity should therefore be given a more important status in evaluation work. Basically, what the local people at heritage sites believe is authentic should also be taken into account, and the authenticity criteria should therefore be localized. Some members of the Japanese delegation to the 1994 ICOMOS conference in Nara explained that the Shinto building they wanted to nominate as a World Heritage site has been reconstructed regularly since antiquity. They have long rebuilt temples keeping to the original plan, design and strict requirements for the fabric and building techniques. Their contribution to World Heritage conservation methodologies could be rephrased as: Being faithful to the original architectural design plus the materials and techniques should be viewed as a basic component of authenticity criteria. However, as demonstrated in this section, the later repair work in most Chinese temples might not have scrupulously followed the original designs. Some of the reconstructions have even turned the original plans upside-down. In most vernacular architecture, change is inevitable. I would say that physical metabolism is the intrinsic nature of Chinese vernacular buildings.

The close link between people and their *tulou* building is especially reflected in the ways that local people make introductions to their fellows, 'who lived in which *lou*' and 'such and such a *lou*'s person'. These linguistic materials also reveal that the local people's personal identity has been largely intertwined with the 'identity' of the *tulou* houses. The combination of a person's name with a specific *tulou* building can even be an indication that the person being introduced was indeed born in that building. The link is quite clear and is very much in evidence when they introduce themselves to outsiders. It is not simply a building belonging to the Hakka people as a whole (collective identity); it really did belong to someone who has and had lived inside it during his/her lifespan from birth to death. They are not abstract architectural representations or specimens; they lived together with the specified descendants of the Zhang lineage. Conventionally, within the lineage village, a *lou*'s name and its position in the establishing sequence can be a direct signification of the introduced person's position in the generational hierarchy. Therefore, the personal identity expressed by involving a *lou*'s identity can even be a reflection of the interpersonal relationships between different lineage members of the same or different generations. The dispersal of the thirteen *tulou* houses along the Hekeng River Valley also represents the major time period in which the local people interacted with their immediate surroundings and went about constructing *tulou* houses.

A typical characteristic of Fujian rural society is a clear divide between the collective (lineage or lineage segments) and the private domains in settlement wealth. The inheritance of communal lineage property and the privately owned *tulou* rooms both constituted an important route by which the Hakka people's materialized past could be passed on to later generations. The collective domain usually encompassed the religious amenities, lineage trust (*zutian*) and such other public facilities as bridges, irrigation channels, roads and rivers. Usually, it was the lineage heads who bore responsibility for caring for the legacies of the whole settlement on behalf of the lineage members. They were required by settlement convention to organize the construction and maintenance of the lineage facilities, control the use of the lineage trust, expand lineage wealth by reclaiming land whose owners have either died or are heirless and raise funds for the compilation of the lineage pedigrees. These key persons were basically those who managed, or perhaps manipulated, the past of the settlement by maintaining the lineage's communal legacies and presiding over the ceremonies. At the same time, the collective memory of these settlements was fundamentally structured by the compilation of lineage genealogies and was represented by all the structures and buildings in the collective domain known as the bestowal of the ancestors. A lineage agnate could obtain a position in the collective memory simply by adding his name to the lineage genealogy. This sort of recognition could also heighten his sense of responsibility about caring for collectively owned wealth. All these intimate community ties culminate in the question: How could the Hakka people 'materialize' a past through their own *tulou* apartments and fields? The answer is quite simple. They kept a past by transferring the room ownership from generation to generation. As said in the last chapter, when speaking of the residential dwellings and farmlands, they usually use the terms '*zuwu*' and '*zuchan*'. The former indicates the houses transmitted down from the forebears, whereas the latter means the paddies bestowed by the ancestors. In a nutshell, the right to inherit things from the past legitimizes the basic right of a person to hold the means of subsistence in the present. Although it is conceivable that dwellings could have been used as a physical symbol for memorializing elderly people who had passed away a long time ago, it can be said with certainty that they are not 'monumental' in nature.

3.2.3 Constructing and Maintaining Buildings for the Descendants

In the 2013 investigation in some of the central Fujian settlements, the investigators discovered that all the occupied houses are actually being changed all the time. Some of the buildings had been renovated or even reconstructed as early as the late Qing dynasty or the early Republican period, precisely on the sites on which earlier building frameworks had been erected. In some inscriptions on the wooden plaques, the geomancers used '*xiu*' or '*chong xiu*' to denote the basic ways in which the local residents interacted with their buildings and structures.[51] Although the buildings on which these observations were based were not *tulou* houses, this information is very important for understanding the essential attitude a common Fujian rural resident might nurture towards vernacular buildings and structures, hence, relevant to the present discussion in general. *'Xiu'* usually translates as 'repair' or 'restore', a maintenance job on a limited scale, an undertaking quite frequently seen on traditional Chinese dwellings. However, in many other contexts, the word can also mean 'establish' or 'construct', for instance, as observed in the inscriptions introduced in central Fujian. These wooden plaques inscribed with the word *'xiu'* were indeed made to memorialize the establishment of the dwellings, hence they are themselves monuments. *'Chong xiu'*, literally translated as 'repair again' or 'construct again', might refer to the indifferent condition of the architectures. In the case of some, *'chong xiu'* indicates that the buildings had been repaired or renovated on a large scale. In the case of others, it could suggest that the buildings had been totally reconstructed. In the latter instance, the earlier section of the original buildings could have been completely devastated or in a state of total collapse. I would argue that this is a very precise description of most of the vernacular buildings. *'Xiu'* and *'chong xiu'*, with five meanings in all (construct, repair, restore, reconstruct and enlarge/expand) encompass the core metabolic processes of most Chinese vernacular buildings. Essentially, the purpose of such activities has been to repair or rebuild an architecture, and consequently to restore it to an appropriately functional state.[52] Historically, the upshot of residential repairs in diverse forms has meant that the buildings and structures are the product of a physical metabolization. On consideration, structure, layout, inner wooden

51. Five of these building biographies were found in the 2013 investigation in the central Fujian area. Building biography inscription A.: [the first line] The diviner, Zheng Daosheng, is invited to hold and perform the ceremony. The residence is built (*xiu*) in a roughly *geng-jia* direction [on compass], three points [degrees on compass] passing the '*you*' mark... [the second line] Time: the Great Qing dynasty, the twenty-first year of the Jiaqing reign era [official time, AD 1817]; a *bingzi* year, a *xinchou* month and the eleventh day (*shuoyue wuri*), a *jiashen* day, a *yichou* time, a gentleman of the Zhangs commenced building a magnificent residence...[auspicious verses] best wishes for children and good fortune for the family...[the third year] signed by the Heavenly Generalissimo [*taishang dutian tongling zongguan zongbing dayuanshuai*], the house is named 'Longwen-tang' [Longwen Hall], desiring a place of vitality and outstanding achievements of the family descendants... (The *Longwen-tang Wooden Plaque Inscription* from Dongren village). Building biography inscription B.: [the first line] Time: the Great Qing dynasty, the thirty-fifth year of the Kangxi reign [official time, AD 1696], a *bingzi* year, in the eleventh month, on the eighth day, wushi [11 a.m. to 1 p.m.], an auspicious time to construct (*xiu*) the residence; [the second line] approved by Commissioner of Hell, the Demon-Queller, Earthly Generalissimo Yin. (The *Lian'an-tang Wooden Plaque Inscription* from Zaoxing village). Building biography inscription C.: [the first line] The diviner, Zheng Xuanzong, is invited to hold and perform the ceremony. The residence has been rebuilt (*xiu*) in a roughly *shen-yin* direction [on compass] ... renamed *Shengwu-tang*. [the second line] Time: the Great Qing dynasty, the twenty-sixth year of the Guangxu reign [official time, AD 1900]; a *gengzi* year, a *wuzi* month and the fourth day (*renshen ri*), a *xinchou* time, the wooden ridge-pole is to be installed. A gentleman of the Zhengs is inaugurating the restoration of a magnificent house...[auspicious verses] best wishes for a good place in which to live, the continuation of the family line and promising prospects for each generation... desiring a place of vitality and outstanding achievements for the family descendants... (The *Shengwu-tang Wooden Plaque Inscription* from Dongren village.) Building biography inscription D.: [the first line] The diviner, Zheng Xuan..., is invited to hold and perform the ceremony. This ancestral hall is being built (*xiu*) in a *geng-jia* direction, and named *Youqi-tang*. [the second line] The fifth year of Republican China [1916], a *bingchen* year, *dingyou* month, the fourth day, *xinsi shi* [9:30 a.m.], the wooden ridge-pole is to be installed. The gentleman of the Zhangs builds this ancestral hall... [auspicious verses] best wishes for a good place in which to live, the continuation of the family line and promising prospects for each generation... desiring a place of vitality and outstanding achievements of the family descendants... (The *Youqi-tang Wooden Plaque Inscription* from Dongren village.) Building biography inscription E.: [the first line] The diviner, Zheng Xuanchang, is invited to hold and perform the ceremony. The house is being built (*xiu*) in a roughly *kun*-[?] direction... [the second line] Time: the Great Qing dynasty, the eighteenth year of the Guangxu reign [official time, AD 1892]; a *renchen* year, a wushen month (indeed the eighteenth day of the seventh month), a *guichou* day, a *guichou* time... a good time for the ridge-pole to be installed. A gentleman of the Zhangs is inaugurating the restoration of his ancestral hall...[auspicious verses] best wishes for offspring and good fortune for the family...[the third year] signed by the Heavenly Generalissimo [*taishang dutian tongling zongguan zongbing dayuanshuai*], desiring a place of vitality and outstanding achievements for the family descendants... (An ancestral hall wooden plaque inscription from Dongren village.)

52. This said, it should be noted that the term 'restore' in this sort of context does not necessarily refer to being faithful to the original design.

Fig. 31 The Longwentang Wooden Plaque Inscription, dating the courtyard building to Jiaqing 21.

Fig. 32 Hall section, the Lian'antang, Zaoxing village.

framework design and room arrangement are very probably the backbones later buildings have acquired intact from their predecessors, whereas fabrics, tiles, adornments and single wooden parts are unstable elements, liable to replacement. Reconstruction and restoration are two very drastic types of interventions, therefore running repair work is the most frequently seen treatment of dwellings. Nobody would deny that constant maintenance can prolong the lifespan of buildings but the unstable elements of buildings are also highly sensitive indicators, easily influenced by esthetic affectations as well as such cultural and natural factors as rain, insects and fluctuations in levels of humidity. Therefore, these latter, including tiles, window frames, wooden carvings, mats and so forth, have to be periodically substituted in response to the immediate preferences and needs of the residents. This provides a feasible explanation of the mismatches we frequently find between the founding dates given by the building biographies and their architectural styles, reflected in the physical details. Changes in residential buildings are in essence a process of physical evolution. The buildings are 'alive' (living organisms), unless physical metabolization is terminated. Therefore, it is of paramount importance to remember that the builders of Chinese vernacular architecture made no differentiation in their minds between 'authentic' and 'inauthentic'. A statement that is equally applicable to today's rural builders.

This discussion prompts us to ask: What about the metabolization of *tulou* structures? In other words, how did the local people interact with such huge earthen buildings in the past? As are the courtyard dwellings, *tulou* architectures are also composed of earthen and wooden parts. The substitution rates of the rooftops (for example, tiles and rafters) are therefore similar to those of the ordinary houses mentioned earlier in this chapter. 'They replace the tiles here and there and repair the wooden parts occasionally', some local experts commented. However, in one respect they are most assuredly different from the ordinary courtyard dwellings: When established, any major interventions in the major wooden frameworks of *tulou* buildings are usually discouraged and people are usually reluctant to suggest that any massive repair work be undertaken. If the posts and beams have to be substituted for unavoidable reasons, the repair rate of the internal wooden structure might consequently increase sharply in the following decades. 'Therefore, they prefer to patch up here

Fig. 33 A *tulou* ruin in Shiqiao village.

and there rather than completely reframe the whole building... Also for that matter, more frequently, if they find huge cracks in the walls or irreversible problems with the wooden structure that is beyond patching up, and if they could afford to do so, they would prefer to rebuild the buildings somewhere else...', local conservators said.[53] Many of these abandoned *tulou* ruins lie scattered around such settlements as Shiqiao and Nanou (Fig. 33). Given this situation, the metabolic changes in the *tulou* buildings are therefore mainly represented by rooftop renovations, the substitution of decayed wooden parts (mostly boards and planks) *in situ*, and, in extreme cases, building relocations. Structural reframing is rarely resorted to by the local *tulou* residents if the building is still in use as a dwelling. These ideas diverge from those that underpin modern conservation treatment.

What might be the sentiment of a builder when he was constructing, maintaining or reconstructing his own houses or apartments? In what ways might he have related such a new or reconstructed house to his family? The building biographies newly discovered in central Fujian might provide some answers (see Note 9). First and foremost, he probably hoped that the site of the construction or reconstruction would be auspicious and hence offer his family enough protection. The second idea uppermost in his mind

53. Personal communication from Zhang Jinde in 2013.

Fig. 34 A *fengzixing mu* at Nanou.

might have been that that house would bring his offspring good fortune and guarantee the fertility and continuity of his family. His third hope was probably that all his best wishes and the construction or reconstruction activities would be legitimized by the gods and spirits. Therefore, each time a local peasant constructed or reconstructed a house or an ancestral hall, he might have linked himself, his family, the construction site, the house to the local supernatural powers, forming or reiterating the hope of an auspicious future for the homestead. Although the situation described here is that of the courtyard dwellings, it is feasible to assume that the *tulou* builders would have entertained much the same feelings and ideas.

3.2.4 Grave Monuments Used in Conjunction with Buildings

Two types of burials are popular in the southern Fujian region. One is the *fengzixing mu*, or stone-plate-sealed burials (Fig. 34). These burial chambers are usually dug perpendicularly into the hillsides. The first action of the local people might sometimes have been to dig a burial pit; afterward they would insert the coffins into holes dug into the pit wall. The opening to such a compartment would finally be sealed with a semi-circular stone plate carrying a relief epitaph carved in its center. The rest of the ground space could be set aside as a small area in which to make offerings to the occupant of the tomb. Besides these compartmental graves, there are also numerous small earthen pit burials with no burial furniture. The locations of cemeteries have usually been selected by geomancers. Three locations have been preferred by the local people, as observed in Hekeng, Nanou, Taxia and Shiqiao. A small number of tombs are located in the rice-paddies; they are all *fengzixing mu*. Some have been carved out of the hillsides. Most of these burials are also *fengzixing mu* and are not necessarily located within the valley. They can sometimes even be found on hillsides outside the valley or very close to the entrance to the river valley. Ordinary or even poor families usually choose to bury their members next to their terraced fields. These graves are often the second type mentioned above – small burials with single burial pits and no epitaphs. The differentiation in land-use pattern explicitly reflects the social stratification among the households of a settlement. In terms of *fengshui*, the appropriate burial loci of the forebears could ensure protection and benefits for their descendants (*li hou*). Ostensibly, this is the reason these tombs were frequently in the flat fields but still very close to the *tulou* buildings; that is, near the residences of their descendants. Interestingly, instead of referring to *fengshui*, villagers give a very different reason some people are buried in the paddies instead of on the slopes or other places, for instance, invariably selected by geomancers: They are undoubtedly the 'grave monuments' of the families with dignity.[54] This begs the question: What is the relationship of the local rich people with these monuments? Again, Hekeng village provides important evidence. Each year the Hekeng lineage conducts a *xindingji* or the neonates ceremony. Newborn baby boys delivered in the same lunar calendar year are brought by their parents to such burial sites to pay routine respect to a certain renowned ancestor, sometimes a female such as the principal wife of Ancestor Shiliang (*Shiliang Gong*). Unlike those buried on the hills, those buried in the paddies near the residents, along with the ancestral halls and temples, embody part of the symbolism of ancestor worship. The Hekeng people knew they could meet their ancestors inside the residences (shrines), in the paddies and in the temples. Residence, cemetery and temple could also be used as one whole. As the elderly people[55] in Hekeng recalled, in their childhood, when someone in the village passed away, his/her relatives first took the coffin out of the corner of the upper floor of the *tulou* building; then, in the first night after his/her death, they placed the deceased in the coffin. A total of eight men carried the coffin to the burial place that had been determined in advance by a local diviner. There, the people gathered to conduct the whole burial ceremony. Throughout the ceremony, an oil lamp was kept alight in the darkness. After all the stipulated procedures had been observed, people had to take that oil lamp back to the ancestral temple. It was the local people's belief that they should not let the lamp go out on the way back because it symbolized the soul of the deceased. The mourners should do all in their power to keep it alight and by so doing conduct the soul of the deceased back to the principal temple in which those of his/her ancestors had long resided. Later, on certain days, relatives would be summoned to gather in the ancestral temple where they would recall the virtuous deeds of the dead and placate his/her soul. Had the dead been very kindly to his/her fellow villagers when alive, the numbers attending this 'requiem' ritual would swell as more people would want to pay their respects. Residence, cemetery and temple all figure at specific points on the same funeral chain.

3.2.5 The Obvious Time System on Memorials Leading to Insideness

When examining the time phrases used by the local people in epitaphs, genealogies and on stone monuments (for example, the stone pillars/steles) and in their everyday spoken language, we immediately discover that formerly the local Hakka residents actually had two temporal frameworks: political time and lineage time. The principal words and phrases denoting political time included '*Da Qing*' (the Great Qing) or *Zhonghua Minguo* (Republican China). The other is the lineage time, indicating intergenerational relations. Each individual could find his or her position along the generational timeline running from the very beginning of the Zhang lineage, when the first generation ancestor had just arrived in this hilly area. In genealogies, particularly, events, interpersonal relations and settlement affairs were frequently recorded and 'measured' with reference to the generation sequence, not natural time, not even political time. Such time traditions actually continued into the first decade of twenty-first century, when interpersonal relations were still partially reflected in the language used in the pedigrees, family trees, settlement committee posters and temple prayers, for

54. Interviews with Zhang Enhan in 2011.
55. Interviews with Zhang Enhan in 2013.

instance, 'the twentieth generation descendant',[56] 'the ninth generation ancestor' and so forth. These time phrases recurred in nearly all the small places inside the settlement, highlighting lineage continuity and the cohesiveness of kinship relations. Time phrases inscribed on monuments, reiterating a person's own position in the lineage history, could evoke a sense of belonging to the place in which he/she grew up.

3.2.6 Agricultural Fields, Workshops, Traffic Systems, Markets and Regional Identity

Chapter 1 touched briefly on the division of the land into agricultural field systems: level fields for rice cultivation, terraced fields for rice cultivation and fields on hillsides for high-yield vegetable cultivation. As just said, fields could also be used as sites for burials. When the traditional rural conditions still prevailed, open fields in the Nanjing rural area presented a diversity of farming activities and a variety of produce, including rice crops, tobacco crops, bananas and vegetables cultivated on the level fields along the major watercourses, sweet potatoes, maize crops and tea on the terraced fields along the slopes of mounds, and bamboo and China fir tree forests in the hills. These patterns of cultivation and seasonal species adjustment in the rhythm with the changes of micro-geomorphology represented the pre-modern (traditional) ways of Hakka land-use, and these very flexible indeed.[57] Workshops usually took the form of thatched or tiled huts and slightly larger cottages. Their locations tended to differ with the functions of the architecture. For instance, tea-processing huts were usually located near the terraced tea fields on the hillsides, whereas the paper-manufacturing workshops were frequently located on the banks of brooks, streams or man-made water channels. Tobacco-processing workshops were built near major residences, as observed in the settlements in Yongding. Husbandry facilities include pigsties, cattle byres, chicken and duck coops and so forth. As observed in the *tulou* buildings in Shiqiao, the bulk of the husbandry facilities were located on the first floor directly inside the *tulou* buildings. As they were regarded as important family part of property, the animals usually lived together with the owners. Workshop buildings and facilities were usually located near watercourses or on mountain slopes, and they were often 'coarsely fabricated'. By and large, their structures and immediate surroundings were arranged to suit the production process, be that drying and processing tea leaves, depositing paper pulp and curing tobacco leaves. Generally speaking the metabolic rate of change of these buildings was

56. The local people use two different words to denote 'generation': '*shi*' for the dead and '*dai*' for the living.

57. According to the Qianlong period *Nanjing Gazetteer*, from the late Ming to the middle Qing period in the rural areas of Nanjing County the major agricultural produce and cash crops included: Japonica rice: crops planted in mountain ranges could bear a crop only once a season. Sticky rice: crops are divided into four primary sub-types; one is called *chigushu* and is used for making rice wine. Wheat: usually of low quality here in Southern Fujian, and should not be viewed as a staple food. Legumes: types include black beans, white peas, soybeans, red beans, hyacinth beans, broad beans and so forth. Broom-corn millets: some could be used for making wines. Foxtail millets: low yield. Sesame plants: two types, black and white, good oil-manufacturing plants. Vegetables: leaf mustards, *huangmao*, celeries, Chinese kale, rapes, water spinach, spinages (old word from spinaches), *Bata vulgaris L. var.cicla L*, romaine lettuces, crown daisy chrysanthemums, edible amaranths, turnips, radishes, carrots, *Pteridium aquilinum* (*Linn.*) *Kuhn var. latiusculum* (*Desv.*) *Undenw. ex Heller*, *Osmunda Japonica*, egg-plants, bamboo shoots, cattails, gingers, onions, garlic, leeks, parsleys, sweet potatoes, white (wax) gourds, watermelons, pumpkins, *tugua*, taros. Fruits: Litchi, longan, oranges, shaddocks, persimmons, bananas, pears, peaches, olives, sugar-cane, peanuts. Herbs: Chinese yams, Chinese wolfberries, wormwoods, mints, motherwort, *Fructus rosae laevigatae*, *Semen plantaginis*, *Pinellia ternata*, *Herba lycopi*. Woods: cypress, camphor, willows, banyans, mulberries, fir trees, birch-leaf pears. Bamboos: diverse types of bamboos: *changzhi*, *ma*, *maoer*, *lü*, *renmian*, *chi*, *han*, *Guanyin*, *fengwei*. Livestock: cattle, sheep, pigs, ducks, chickens, geese. Sugar: red and white. Tobacco: officially introduced into China from Japan (*dongyang*) in the late Wanli reign of the Ming dynasty, also known as *xiangsicao*, or lovesickness herbs. Indigos: two types, known as *dajing* and *xiaojing*. Blue dyestuff. Safflower: red dyestuff. Gardenias: yellow-reddish dyestuff. *Dioscorea matsudae Hayata*: black dyestuff. Vegetable oils: coleseed oil, camellia oil, peanut oil. Alumilite: dyestuff in stone shape. Palm fibers: used for making twisted cords and ropes. Charcoals: no details. Hessians: usually good for making cloth. Crystals: rarely seen, fewer details. Cotton cloths (*jibei bu*): very rare, but a specialty plant of Guangdong. *Ko*-hemp cloths(from *kudzu* vine]: more commonly seen than cotton cloths. Ramie cloths: commonly seen. Banana-leaf cloths: no more details. *Jialuo bu*: cloths made from cotton and silk fibers. Bee honeys: no more details. Bee waxes: no more details. Porcelains: Shancheng town [next to the county seat] is well known for porcelain production. Mats: Maping township is famous for mat manufacture. Ceramic tea-water boiler: Maping is also the most important place of ceramic boiler production.

relatively low but as a part of the local industrial heritage, they were always very susceptible to changes in modes of production. As briefly noted above, from the early Qing dynasty, the settlements in the rural areas of Yongding county had enjoyed a reputation throughout the country for tobacco plantations and processing. However, during the early Republican period, when Japanese cigarettes were introduced, most of the tobacco-processing workshops seemed to be on the wane, and were subsequently torn down in the following decades. The huts used for paper-production scattered throughout the Nanjing hills were likewise finally dismantled in the late 1960s because of the advent of new types of paper that could be sold at a much lower price as its production had been mechanized. Local markets usually had a very fixed in location and scale, but by their very nature were rather easily influenced by fluctuations in the local economy. The closure of the Hekeng market was largely attributable to the rise of the nearby Qujiang market in the early Republican period. The latter market owed its existence to rich businessmen living abroad who made large donations to support the commercial activities of their relatives in Qujiang. By their very nature, workshops and markets were variable and unfixed elements in a local economy. Sometimes they even appeared ephemeral; but sometimes they could also be very stable structures and facilities. Susceptible to the rise and fall of the local economy, especially the economic mainstays, and the uncertainty of supply-and-demand relationships in both the short and long term, more frequently than not the existence of these buildings and facilities was extremely unstable. Unlike the gradual changes in residential and religious architecture, they usually shared a polarized metabolic rate.Nowadays,the thriving local markets[58] in such places as Hekeng,[59] Qujiang and Taxia are all dilapidated or have even disappeared. Taken as a whole, the agricultural fields, workshops, traffic systems[60] and markets provided the local people with an economic mechanism whose tentacles penetrated the boundary of each settlement place, each river

58. Important local markets in the hilly area included the following (Xiamen University, 2009): Luxi, Pinghe (on the border between Nanjing and Pinghe); Trade items: rice, vegetables, livestock, salt, bamboo good. Possible foundation date: Qing dynasty. Opening days: the fourth and ninety days in every ten day of a lunar calendar month. Travel time there and back: one to two days. Shancheng, Nanjing: Trade items: bamboo paper, bamboo and wood goods, salt, fish and other sea products. Possible founding date: Ming dynasty. Opening date: the second and seventh days in every ten days of a lunar calendar month. Travel time there and back: four to five days. Transfer towns: Chuanchang. Shuyang, Nanjing: Trade items: bamboo paper, rice, China fir-wood. Possible founding date: Ming or early Qing dynasty. Opening days: the third and eighth days in every ten days of a lunar calendar month. Travel time there and back: within one day. Dabu, Guangdong: Trade items: bamboo paper, salt, fish and other sea products. Possible founding date: Ming dynasty. Opening days: unknown. Travel time there and back: four to five days. Transfer towns: Xiayang. Banliao, Shangban, Shuyang: Trade items: rice, salt, meat, sugarcane, cloth and textiles, piglets, fish and other sea products. Possible founding date: Qing dynasty. Opening days: the second and seventh days in every ten days of a lunar calendar month. Travel time there and back: within one day. Gaotou, Yongding: Trade items: rice, salt, cloth and textiles. Possible founding date: Qing dynasty. Opening days: the third and eighth days in every ten days of a lunar calendar month. Travel time there and back: within one day. Hukeng, Yongding: Trade items: sugar, clothes. Possible founding date: Qing dynasty. Opening days: the fourth and sixth days in every ten days of a lunar calendar month. Travel time there and back: within one day. Qujiang, Nanjing: Trade items: rice, paper, livestock. Possible founding date: Qing dynasty or Republican period. Opening days: the fourth and ninth days in every ten days of a lunar calendar month. Travel time there and back: within one day. Changjiao, Nanjing: Trade items: rice, paper, bamboo. Possible founding date: Qing dynasty. Opening days: the fifth and tenth days in every ten days of a lunar calendar month. Travel time there and back: within one day.

59. During the Republican period, Hekeng established a small flea market near the Hekeng River, located at a crossroads where the mountain paths to Meilin, Yongding and Shiqiao met. As the villager Zhang Mintai recalled, a small Buddhist temple was once built near the market but was devastated in the mid-20th century. To help the traders, the Hekeng people built two stone bridges over the river running around the flea market and temple.

60. Public structures and facilities include primarily bridges, roads and river traffic lines. The metabolic rates at which they developed are quite different. As interregional traffic resources, roads and rivers are usually fixed. Taking the extant rivers and mountain paths linking the settlements in the rural areas of Nanjing, Pinghe, Longyan and Yongding, for instance, the use of most of them could be traced back to the founding era of these settlements, that is, the early to late Ming dynasty. By contrast, such small structures as wooden pavilion-bridges, stone bridges and ordinary wooden bridges might have been changed only irregularly in response to damage resulting from storms, fires and river floods. Compared to other facilities, such structures as bridges could be more fragile and therefore repaired, restored or even reconstructed more frequently. Therefore, we rarely find bridge structures preserved in the completely 'original' way.

valley and each lineage. As the major sources of the livelihood of the local people, these small places formed a large yet loose network linking each small river valley settlement to the whole hilly area and the townships as well. Undoubtedly, all these buildings, structures and small localities had made their contribution to the coalescence of regional recognition between different lineage settlements. However, the interpretation of all these interrelated elements constitutes the weakest point in the present representation of the Hakka heritage, leading to an unjustified impression that all the settlements were isolated units standing alone and independently of each other.

3.3 BUILT ENVIRONMENT METABOLISM AND THE LOSS OF INSIDENESS

What has been said above constitutes a very brief reconstruction of the Hakka traditional land-use pattern. As was to be expected, the local people had built up their lineage identity and place-attachment by actively interacting with the local environment. Nevertheless, this is not to say that land-use pattern might not have changed over time. As I have explained in the landscape biography section in Chapter 1, driving forces for change could have been exerted by either sharp population growth or changes in the economy, or sometimes both. What the heritage managers regard as the destruction of cultural heritage pure and simple can be justified by the local Hakka residents as quite reasonable changes in earthen architecture and the advantageous adjustment of land-use patterns to improve their daily lives. This has been referred to as 'landscape metabolism' in the previous chapters. Metabolic activities can include those leading to changes in form, location, the structure and arrangement of the built environment, sometimes even the landform, as people responded to the immediate or long-term needs of the traditional lifestyle. It is not unusual for radical changes in the built environment to usher in a sense of outsideness (Relph, 1976) and be a prelude to the eclipse of community life (Stein, 1960). These truly dramatic changes cut the existing bond between a resident and the original place with which he or she had been familiar with since they were very young. Changes in lifestyle can give rise to emotional maladjustment. Sometimes, local people deliberately reserved some basic architectural elements in their newly fashioned house in order to counteract this feeling of sentimental loss. In the 2013 investigation, for example, we came across a very interesting phenomenon: in some settlements in central Fujian, the local residents were constructing new two-story houses using totally new materials such as bricks, ceramic mosaics, cement, glass and so forth. Nevertheless, they deliberately 'replicated' the *tang* (shrine) structure in their new homes (Fig.35). As we have already noted, the *tang* structure is the most representative ceremonial component in vernacular architecture throughout the central and southern Fujian. Interestingly, these local residents have even hung horizontal inscribed plaques above the doorframes on which the names of the buildings are inscribed. Without exception, they are called 'such and such *tang*'. They are named in exactly the same way as their predecessors were, for instance, the *Longwen-tang*.[61] That said, we cannot ascribe all this loss to the metabolization of built environment. Sometimes, it is the outcome of radical changes in social practices and customs, funerals, burial, marriage, depopulation and heritage-making for instance. All these radical social changes can lead to immediate abandonment of some land-use patterns, and hence place-detachment.

3.3.1 Separation of the Dead and the Living

Radical change in the treatment of dead bodies in the southern Fujian region is a good example of the rise in the separation of the living and dead. New funeral regulations[62] advocated by the local government

61. The local residents actually emulated the essential structure in their old houses (*zuwu*), in which they or their ancestors had lived for a very long time. This is very reminiscent of the *tang* structure in the *tulou* buildings in the southern Fujian hilly region. During their transformation from ordinary to *tulou* settlements, the Hakka builders also copied, and thereby preserved, the *tang* section inside the *tulou* shelters. Using old structures innovatively has been a very widespread practice since the middle Ming dynasty. Therefore, without outside intervention, the local residents might still have changed the architectural styles keep old (traditional) elements in the newly established buildings and structures.

62. The *2001-2005 Plan for Funeral and Internment Reform of Fujian Province*, issued in January 2001 by the Government of

have already affected rural burial activities and cut the links between different parts of the built environment. In 2003, the local governments in the hilly region of the three counties in southern Fujian began to enforce cremation. When talking about this 'big issue', the elderly people in Hekeng looked worried. In their recent experience, no bereaved family has ever brought the ashes of the deceased back to Hekeng because the crematoria near the urban center provide storage for ashes for no charge. As, under the new regulations, the local government pays for the cremations for the peasants, more people are now beginning to understand and accept the new funeral regulations. The widespread use of cremation has finally terminated the traditional use of cemeteries. As noted earlier, this has also dramatically influenced the use-frequency of ancestral temples. The 2011 investigation showed that for centuries there had been a series of burial ceremonies observed in the principal temple and the shrines. When inhumation was still widely practiced in the past, tradition required that people had to combine their burial practices with the use of the ancestral offering facilities. In those days, by the light of an oil lamp, the soul of the deceased could still be guided from the grave site back to the temple in which the ancestors resided. This observance upheld ties between the temple and the cemeteries. At certain points, the people of the settlement, not necessarily the near relatives of the dead, would gather in the temple to make offerings to the newly deceased, mourn him/her and reflect on his/her deeds when alive. This link between the grave and the temple was finally cut in 2003 when cremation began to be implemented throughout the whole area. Now, as local people are encouraged to take their dead to crematoria in towns, the use of ancestral temples has been even more curtailed to the ordinary offering ceremonies held in the course of the year. This decrease in use-frequency has led to a *de facto* abandonment of the temple for most of the year.[63] During the 2010 investigation, I had

Fig. 35 The *tang* structure in a new house.

a brief conversation with Enhan, the former village head, who was then in his fifties. He was brought up in the Yongsheng-lou of Hekeng village and had grown up with the traditional burial practices. He lamented the end of the commemorative gatherings in the principal ancestral temple. In his eyes and in those of many other local residents of the Zhang lineage he supposed, this commemorative gathering was something more than just a big occasion for mourning, it was also an opportunity for reflection. He remembered that the local people would usually get together in the principal ancestral temple to recall the whole life of the deceased. Interestingly in the course of this commemoration, a person might acquire a posthumous reputation. The reflection on a person's life could in itself also set a good example to the villagers, particularly the young people. Whether or not his remark on the new policy was accurate, it is undeniable that, as a result of the separation between the deceased and the living, place-attachment has already diminished since the early twenty-first century.

In any consideration of the natural environment, it is important to remember that it is always possible to differentiate the constituent parts of a landscape even further into two main categories. One is the functioning part, that is, the buildings and public

Fujian Province. Under this plan, Nanjing and Pinghe counties were required by the provincial government to achieve an 85 percent cremation rate by 2005.

63. Nevertheless, it should be stressed that the ways in which the temples are now used are still very similar in many respects to the ways they had been used in the past; in other words, they, as well as shrines, altars and burials, are still regarded as the representation of a common past, and hence the most important part of their nostalgia by the local people.

facilities in a settlement landscape. The other is the symbolic part. Among all the constituent parts enshrined in a settlement landscape, views with symbolic significance have almost without exception been created to convey some special significance to the local community members. More often than not, these structures and buildings are of a religious nature, including the *fengshui* (*kanyu*) building and the patterns of structural arrangement, the *fengshui* cemetery location patterns, paddy-field burials (*tianzhong mu*), shrines (*she*) and altars (*tan*), ancestral halls (*tang*) and temples (*miao*). They have all been created for the purpose of seeing, practicing and sensing (Tilley, 2010) the intimate relationship between humans and nature, between the living and the deceased and among the living. They provide the places in which mundane social relationships can be practiced and manipulated.[64] Besides the huge ritual buildings, these panoramic views are also a very apt choice for representing the local people's past. Unfortunately, they are not seen in this light by the local site managers and planners.

3.3.2 Depopulation and the Desire to Leave or Relocate

Ever since the late 1990s, large segments of the local population, especially adult males and females, have begun to move to the urban areas of Nanjing county, Zhangzhou and Xiamen cities, to find jobs.[65] Most of them are known as *nongmin gong*, peasant workers or migrant workers, and they constitute the overwhelming majority of the urban labor force working in service industries, small businesses or other kinds of relatively unskilled jobs, for instance, in construction and the transport services, clothing manufacturing and assembly-line jobs. The 2011 investigation revealed that nearly 70 percent of the population in each Hekeng settlement has moved away. Like migratory birds, most of them still move regularly between their hometown and the urban area in which they work. However, they only choose to go back home at some special times in the year. Apart from irregular, unexpected events such as the death of a family member, they only return for the Spring Festival holidays and popular local ceremonies such as *zuo dafu* (Fig. 36), or the 'grand blessings', the most important local Hakka festival in the hilly region.[66] The now rather solitary, deserted settlements only begin to bustle with life again at these times. After the long hollowing-out process to which it has been subjected, the settlements' remote past can only be occasionally remembered when the adult workers come back to hold ceremonies at the principal ancestral temple and the shrines less than twice a year. Compared with the 'old' days, interpersonal relationships between fellow villagers have now become more attenuated. A dispersed settlement population is simply not in a position to maintain religious architecture and facilities adequately. Owing in a large part to this inevitable social process, the past of the settlements is slowly but surely becoming increasingly fragmented and vague. In villages like Hekeng, some of the interviewees[67] even expressed their desire to leave the settlement forever if they could obtain a stable, permanent position in an urban area. The outside world dangles a very powerful lure for them.

According to the updated demographic statistics in 2014, there are now about 1,600 people registered as permanent residents of Hekeng village. When all the peasant workers do come back from the urban areas, the settlements are so overcrowded that five to eight people might have to 'pile' themselves up into the

64. Halls, temples, cemeteries are all places in which rituals are performed. Cogently, these places might say less about the deceased ancestors, with the exception of their names, than about their descendants, the heirs to their property and about how these people wish to assert their own social status in the settlement society.

65. In villages such as Hekeng, the population is fluid. These peasant workers occasionally come back to the valley for vacations or festivals, but these are not their most important motivation. The rural-urban labor movement has also caused the huge upsurge in the local population over the past 30 years. A situation also not unheard of in the past. Because of a severe lack of arable land resources, the river valley has always only been able to support part of the local population. At any given period, some of the population would have always had to uproot themselves and move to other places. This is the reason the Hakka people are commonly known as 'the people on the move'.

66. The most important leading roles in these ceremonies are those of the Protector and the Lord of the People. In Hekeng, people usually conduct a series of rituals at this particular point in the year.

67. Interviews with Zhang Enhan, Zhan Mintai and Zhang Wenzhu in 2011 and 2013.

Fig. 36 The *Zuo dafu* ceremony in Nanou.

same shabby room that measures only 6 to 8 square meters. Sometimes they even have to resort to the long-disused Yongsheng-lou *tulou* as a temporary hotel to accommodate this surplus population.[68] The traditional housing capacity is quite limited. Nowadays on such important occasions, the old shelters are not enough to satisfy the basic housing requirements. This calls to mind another looming problem: Most of these migrant workers will still definitely return home from urban areas after their retirement. Therefore, there is actually growing gap between the increasing population and the limited residential spaces the settlement has been able to provide so far. As demonstrated in Chapter 1, in a natural response to demographic developments, the landscape should have begun to metabolize again. Should this have been the case, a large proportion of the buildings would have been replaced by more modern counterparts but, since the late 1990s, any such plans have been greatly delayed by the rural-urban population movement. The depopulation of Hekeng village for most of the year, a problem common to many other settlements in southern Fujian, is only an apparent alleviation of housing pressures, and is not a true reflection of the situation.

Although most adult people have opted to work outside the village, they still have the ownership of over two-thirds of the rooms in the *tulou* buildings. Their most often heard complaint is that the old buildings are no longer appropriate for residential use. People under forty years old, are apparently 'unprepared' to lead a rural life when they return home. Years of work in urban areas has disassociated them from life in Hekeng. They enjoy, and hence prefer, the modern atmosphere and better living conditions in the cities. None of the people interviewed believes the rooms in the *tulou* buildings are comfortable. The majority of the young people between twenty and thirty have spent most of their childhood and early adulthood with their parents who work as first-generation peasant workers in the urban areas of Fujian. They no longer even have the knowledge of how to cultivate the land. The historical economic basis for *tulou* residence has gone forever, and the *tulou* rooms are no longer suited to being used in the traditional way. For most of the young people in the Hekeng settlements, these rooms only represent the possibility of some compensation for being reused as tourist attractions. At the present moment, the *tulou* buildings in the Hekeng River Valley could still function properly if there was enough maintenance and repairs were carried out regularly. The fly in the ointment is that fewer and fewer local people think of these shabby shelters as their home. The new generation peasant workers still and will continue to possess the ownership of the shelter property, but no matter how authentic the heritage might be according to the WHC principles, it is no longer the home of Hakka people in the sense that it once was for over the past 500 years. As noted earlier, the lineage identity of the Hakka people is specifically reflected in their use of ancestor worship shrines and facilities. However, as indicated in Chapter 2, the Shiying-tang or principal ancestral temple has only been rarely used for a long time. The stone pillars proclaiming the glories of the Zhang lineage in Hekeng have now even been moved from their original plinths to be employed for other unknown uses. Ceremonies have degenerated into a mere formality. The sense of place is blurring and weakening. The recent history

68. Personal communication from the Hekeng village head, Ms. Zhang Wenzhu.

from the late 1990s to the present has witnessed not only the collapse of the agricultural economy, the depopulation of the settlements, and the disuse of both residential and ceremonial spaces for most of the year, but also, importantly, the devaluation of the built environment in local people's minds and hearts. In short, it is no longer as important as it was in the past.

The value of the agricultural economy in the Hekeng River Valley has fallen dramatically over the past ten years or so. As the 2011 investigation revealed, permanent residents in the settlements now even have to buy rice, pork and other foodstuffs from local food companies. Economically speaking, the settlements are by no means as purely 'rural' as they once were. Most of the local residents have become a sort of commuter between home and the urban areas in which they work. There is some justice in the claim that the settlements have been reduced to being the labor pools of the urban centers. As calculated in previous chapters, the acreage *per capita* in Hekeng is only about 0.2 *mu*. This figure is much lower than the baseline, namely: 0.5 *mu*/person level required to support an average person under traditional farming conditions. As said, the present local residents have to rely fully on the urban centers as their stable source of income. The destruction of the modern buildings and some old houses inside the World Heritage site area has exacerbated the decrease in the residential space available to these peasant commuters. Rapid deterioration in living conditions has made Hekeng a pretty unpalatable place and concomitantly undermined local people's confidence in their future. They can no longer summon up any heartfelt affection for it.

3.4 PLACE DETACHMENT AND HERITAGE RESISTANCE

The erosion of the sense of place in Hekeng over the past ten years that is the outcome of inescapable socioeconomic factors has been referred to already. The swamping of the village in regulations, as suggested in Chapter 2, also heavily affected local people's lives. Drowning in bureaucracy, Hekeng has become a place that is hard to love. The local people still retain the ownership for their properties but they are being disassociated from their dwellings that they feel that no longer offer them the proper amenities they think they should have. A strong sense of placelessness has begun to overwhelm them. If the truth be told, their attachment to the place had already been seriously undermined long before it was declared a heritage site. The crucial question is can such a sentimental loss be compensated by the creation of a cultural heritage? Should the answer to this be negative, or if the local people are no longer interested in their own past, what can the heritage representation provide? A rootless past?

As Bell (2010) comments, 'Heritage implies notions of inheritance and identity – it is the things we want to keep, protect and manage to pass on to future generations. It also helps shape, strengthen and express who we are as a community (at whichever level that is expressed).' In fact, the ideal lying behind these ideas is that the best solution would be if the heirs to that heritage, the protectors of that heritage and the beneficiaries of that heritage were all one and the same group of people. Although this comment of mine might be criticized as very narrow-minded, I am still convinced that the unification of the three roles in heritage practice could help solve many problems. In Chapter 2, I raised several questions about cultural heritage rights. Local people are the legal heirs to their ancestral inheritance and hence they are the proper persons to maintain these properties. The crux of the matter is that they are not necessarily the beneficiaries of such legacies. Unrealistic compensation, overregulation, limited ticket income, economic recessions and worsening housing conditions have all conspired to make the local people conceive an aversion to their own heritage and hence reject it. Quite apart from significant difficulties, their relationship with the heritage has been undermined even more by their loss of skills in building and maintenance techniques. In theory, as the heirs to the legacy, their maintenance skills are the prerequisite for inheriting the properties. Unfortunately, largely owing to the rising sense of placelessness and the radical changes in lifestyle in recent years, the younger generation rarely shows any interest in acquiring this knowledge.

The last huge round *tulou* building in the Hekeng River Valley was built in the early 1980s. Most of the twentieth and some twenty-first generation male villagers did participate in the post-1960s *tulou* construction work, and are therefore familiar with the construction techniques. In 2011, interviews with a twenty-first generation Hekeng village artisan did elicit more stories about building techniques. He sometimes helped other residents with their repair work, and was invited by the local government to restore round *tulou* buildings in anticipation of the 2007 nomination. His dismal story was that the younger generation preferred to leave the hilly region, and no one wanted to learn the traditional building and repair techniques. This gave rise to the dilemma, noted earlier: that just at the moment local government thought to shift the daily care and conservation duties to the residents, the acquisition of the basic knowledge of building and maintenance techniques is being rapidly lost among the local people. Unquestionably, the Hakka do think that a building could function well and its preservation be guaranteed, but only if there are enough residents still living in it. Their reasoning is clear. Those who live inside it could take care of the *tulou*/courtyard dwelling by substituting new building components for old. They are perfectly aware that, in the past, the regular use of the wooden apartments guaranteed good ventilation. Long-term human occupation of the dwelling and rooms kept mice, swallows and other vermin at bay; even the depredations of termites could be effectively detected and dealt with promptly. The local people are convinced that use and constant repair are the only appropriate ways to keep the buildings in good condition. Today's high vacancy rate in the *tulou* buildings has caused a number of preservation problems. This difficulty is compounded by the fact that fewer and fewer people know how to fix the structures properly. Techniques are important, not least because they are a tangible sign of the affection of the local people for their buildings. Now, sinking under the unrealistic demands of heritage management, the local people are teetering on the point of being lost taking their techniques with them. Sowing a great lack of foresight, these skills are viewed by local authorities as a minor matter, no more than a few cosmetic techniques for the embellishment of the buildings. Some have recognized the problem. In recent years, ICCROM has developed and promoted a people-centered conservation approach,[69] in which the living dimensions are viewed as being as important as the material fabric, and heritage is viewed as the living part of the community. The perceptive rationale behind this approach is that the values of heritage are intrinsically those recognized by the heirs to that heritage, and the tensions between this heritage and its heirs are probably the major and most immediate factor that triggers irreversible demolition. The most challenging task facing this approach is to make the local community aware of these values and accept their existence. In fact, the term 'living' in this context is synonymous with 'using' for, when it is all said and done, only use can keep a heritage alive. Lately, ICCROM has been implementing this approach in its heritage conservation and management practice, but, as the Hekeng case shows, tension between local communities and 'their' heritage is not derived from just one single cause, various socioeconomic reasons can affect it. Born in the heritage place, local people are very knowledgeable about their legacies. In the last few decades, the Hakka people, with the help of academic professionals, have even 'invented' the legend of the Hakka *tulou*. Although most of the local people have no trouble in making a clear statement of what their basic values are, they still reject the heritage in one way or another. Heritage, as viewed by many local people, is an obstacle that stands in the way of their right to progress and hence is a major obstacle against which to struggle and overcome. O'Brien and Li (2006) called this a 'rightful resistance'.

3.5 HERITAGE-MAKING PROCESSES

As described in the previous chapter, between 2006 and 2012, Hekeng was successfully transformed into what is actually an architectural museum, in which visitors have the opportunity to appreciate specimens of *tulou*. As the process of museumization took hold over the village, it was not hard to see why the local people's place attachment to their home weakened. The river valley had been re-created as a world of buildings, not a place in which the Zhang lineage members could make their home. The story of how

69. *Promoting People-Centered Approaches to Conservation: Living Heritage.* http://www.iccrom.org/priority-areas/living-heritage/.

the Hekeng villagers were even 'hired' (by paying them19 *yuan*) by the local government as caretakers of the WH site has been recounted. From 2006 to 2012, the making of Hekeng into the WH site drove the wedge between the local people and their worsening living environment even deeper. As far as the local people were concerned, improving their relationship with their heritage would be an uphill battle; they were simply not interested in engaging in conservation and protection. Their negativity was exacerbated by the fact that the local government did not treat them as the true owners of the cultural heritage. Therefore, when an image of the past was being conjured up, the local people's voice was finally stifled.

3.5.1 Different Values, Different Monuments and Different Pasts

Heritage lives only when people use it. Without use it is reduced to a museum housing exhibits for outsiders. In a rural society, the value of a property usually derives from inheritance and use. Both this chapter and the last have explored the point that, in the past, by maintaining their properties, the local people continued to use and hence sustained the value of the *tulou* buildings. It is fair to say that use values do indeed lie at the heart of all heritage values, and the attitudes of local people towards maintenance work reveal how much they recognize these use values. Sometimes the conflicts between local people and outsiders originate from differences in their opinions about these values. In principle, all Outstanding Universal Values are either cultural or natural values. The nub of the matter lies in the fact that neither the *Convention* nor the *Operational Guidelines* recognizes any type of use values as a basic component of OUV. Crucially the OUV are the values that represent the past of humankind, hence the values of heritage representation. What is uppermost in the minds of the local people is the use values of their 'land'. A place used as a museum is totally different to a place used as settlement.

With only the sketchiest consultation with the local residents, the construction of the Hekeng 'museum' began in 2006. As said earlier, in its efforts to museumize Hekeng, the local government overregulated the settlements. As might be expected, this museumization (museumification) of heritage places has been a hot topic of debate. Di Giovine (2009) has defined, museumification[70] as a 'transition from a living city to that of an idealized representation of itself, wherein everything is considered not for its use but for its value as a potential museum artifact'. When creating its living heritage discourse, ICCROM has used 'continuity' as a key concept by which to characterize living heritage. It has recognized that the isolation of heritage from local communities is the inexorable consequence of the museumification process that many Western management systems had set in motion. Philippot (1996) describes the viewpoint of a Western notion like 'panorama', that, as explained by ICCROM, tends to 'draw a line between the past, present and future'. In many Asian cases (Dellios, 2002), the use of a village heritage by the 'outsiders' usually involves a museumization process. In the Hekeng case, the term 'outsiders' refer to the *tulou* users from outside the Hekeng River Valley. Certainly some of them are Hakka people, but even so they are not the members of local communities. The outsiders who have taken part in the museumification process include local policy makers on behalf of the local and central governments, site planners, local cultural resource managers, tourism developers,[71] conservators and national and international cultural heritage organizations, like the WHC, and their chief concern is to make a particular site into a public attraction will capture the imagination of a wider public. Heritage organizations also undertake these sorts of projects. Kolb's theory about 'theming as narrowing space' is extremely relevant to the present discussion. He believes theming disciplines space,[72] and he goes on to argue that it is a kind of simplification.[73] In 2007, a total of

70. The term museumification has been adopted in many literature sources (Duane, 1999; Ashworth, 1998; Huxtable, 1997; Berdahl, 1999). The end result of this process is a shift in the meanings, behaviors and experiences that people might experience in relation to a place or subject (Gobster, 2007).

71. The concomitant of museumization primarily consists of the commodification process.

72. Themed places can be inhabited in a more complex manner than they suggest. They already have internal distances; these need to be emphasized. The attraction of themed places requires a border, a place of seduction and encounter created by their disconnection from everyday affairs. The place might strive to hide the discontinuity, but its attraction depends on that gap (Kolb, 2007).

73. Theming restricts a place's natural connectivity to a nar-

forty-six earthen *tulou* buildings were nominated either as individual architectural specimens or as clusters (for instance, Hekeng) that met the basic requirements of the Outstanding Universal Values principles.[74] The OUV are a set of criteria that are supposed to provide a theoretical basis for managing the past in a globalizing world (Yan, 2014). Experts and the local residents might both talk about 'memory', but conceive of completely different meanings of the same word. What the international heritage regime is demanding is actually the representation of a local people's past in honor of humankind. As I have just mentioned, the local Hakka people had their own 'monumental culture', characterized by the use of genealogies, graves and epitaphs, shrines, temples and halls. This culture was embodied in the use of burials in conjunction with temples, single use of grave memorials and the glorious symbolism in the principal temple. It was also possible to discern the use of shrines, halls and temples as a three-layered memorial system, cutting through the boundaries of homesteads and households. All these spatial elements constituted a particular way of sharing collective memory. To state the matter succinctly, they had their own method for remembering the past. What the international heritage regime wants to claim is surely an important part of the Hakka memory, because the houses are the places in which the local people were brought up, generation after generation. However, what the local people formally recognize as their past is usually hidden in the abovementioned memorials and their oral history. It is absolutely essential that we are aware of the fact that the rural monumental architectures are used only by the local communities themselves. Crucially, they are places in which to have a dialogue with the ancestors and the past. Obviously, most of these places are imbued with a high degree of privacy. This past differs from the OUV past in that it is definitely not a past that can be shared with outsiders. In comparison with chosen memory, the Hakka people's monumental space might have been much more activated in the past. Obviously, temples, shrines, cemeteries, theatrical venues and many other cultural landscapes are intrinsically very performative. Symbolism was their prime function. Unfortunately what the local people remember as their past cannot be regarded as part of the WH memory. Even more seriously, the representation of the WH past actually diminishes the local people's past, and with it the local people themselves. In a similar vein, what are assumed by the specialists to be very important architectural specimens of the human past are, to some extent, not regarded as monuments representing that past by local communities. Therefore, the local people also diminish the monumental representation of their houses.

This is an appropriate point to introduce the value of religious architecture. Values are the reasons that this type of architecture is important and therefore they ensure that it is preserved. The burning question is: To whom is it important? Is something important to A to the same extent as something important to B? Use of land creates value, but use of land also means quite different things, sometimes even opposing uses, to insiders and outsiders. In many cases, the outsiders can only make the land socially or economically valuable (to themselves) by transferring their 'values' into a visualized form. Values serve as a theoretical basis on which cultural heritage selection can proceed; that is, the decision about which buildings or remains can be regarded as a cultural heritage and therefore preserved and exhibited. The values of a site, like typological time, are usually divided into many subcategories ranging over scientific significance, esthetic significance, historical significance and so forth. In one or several of these categories, if a site can represent the most important characteristics of that kind, it will be given a high evaluation. It is the quality of being representative of a certain kind of character that makes a site or building important or valuable. Searching for representations of values is a pursuit rather similar to looking for specimens for 'museums'. In other words, site museumization in itself is a value typology, indeed a process rather similar to what Fabian (1983) called 'objectification'. It selects specimens for 'theme parks' by deploying

row channel. The doubling of the self-consciousness of a themed place subordinates the many modes of self-reference to one dominant obvious self-presentation. A theme focuses the place's constitutive relations on a single, usually simplified prior identity. (*ibid*)

74. Inscribed for criteria III, IV, V.

value-comparison strategies. Representation indicates not only the choice and exhibiting of the highly valued, but also, in the background, the ignoring or even removing of the devalued. Making comparisons between the carriers of values on a typological basis lies at the core of the first steps leading toward museumization. This raises the question: Can the Shiying-tang principal temple in Hekeng and the Deyuan-tang temple in Taxia, for instance, actually be compared to each other, given the fact the latter is much better preserved and has more important architectural traits than the former? As far as outsiders are concerned, the answer has to be positive; indeed were it not so the whole value typology might collapse. By contrast, for the insiders in the local communities, the answer is negative. The 'outsiders' are simultaneously comparing the values of different sites/buildings in different locations as well as the worth of buildings that are actually in the same river valleys.

Any comparison between different ancestor temples located in different river valleys is meaningless to insiders. Each lineage has only one principal temple; therefore, the temple of lineage A definitely cannot be compared to that belonging to lineage B. An evaluation based on architectural typology is therefore invalid in the realms of meaning defined by the consanguineous boundaries. A comparison between a number of different buildings located in the same river valleys on the basis of an architectural typology is equally incomprehensible to insiders, who judge the importance of each building and structure by its use; each building is important only if it is a properly functioning entity. By their use of these buildings, the insiders confirm the meanings of the whole built environment. Big *tulou* buildings and small *yizixing tulou* both serve in the residential system of a settlement but with different functions, therefore they are not comparable. The essential truth of the matter is that insiders and outsiders have totally different value systems. The outsiders exploit cultural resources by museumizing the built environment. Unfortunately as they set about their task they tend to be rather set on following a particular path whose direction has been determined by their own backgrounds and hence their own preconceptions. Consequently, they do not stop to think about the sorts of values that the architecture might represent to people from another cultural tradition. These values are not arbitrary but are solidly founded on a set of typological strategies based on 'permutations' that include pairs of socioculturally meaningful events. Unrestricted by these considerations, the outsiders blithely forge ahead and eventually create, what is in their eyes at least, a 'heritage'.

3.5.2 The Museumization of a Dying/Moribund Place

Memory, whether personal or collective, is highly selective (Hall, 1999). Anyon (1991) has also pointed out: 'While the protection of the past appears to be a simple concept, both the "past" and the nature of its "protection" are culturally defined.' To be more exact, as demonstrated in Chapter 2, in China it is usually the local cultural authorities who evaluate heritage and decide what to preserve. In their deliberations, they can, if they wish, also make use of the OUV principles for theming spaces with heritage interests. The OUV rules are, by nature, a typology of values that could provide good reasons to support a nomination but it is the States Parties themselves that define what the heritage is and determine what to nominate. In short, in practice, it is a basic right of a State Party to select anything it believes to be important on the grounds of the solid reasons provided by the WHC. In other words, the regulations set by the WHC are not supposed to offer direct guidance in the process of heritage selection by any State Party. To a large extent, the applicant itself is the first evaluator who interprets what 'authenticity' is and what 'integrity' means in specific heritage contexts. The applicant itself has to choose appropriate strategies for making selections. One big stumbling-block is that, on the county level, heritage designation is sometimes carried out very casually. What the site managers choose to follow in practice is nothing less than a dichotomous typology, a theming device.

Fabian (1983) talks about three types of temporal frameworks. The most relevant one here is 'typological time' that is deeply rooted in the cognitive dichotomy of human society, not necessarily just Western society. Anthropologists are used to classifying basic social facts into a polarized framework, or, as Fabian describes the situation, 'permutations' that include pairs of socio-culturally meaningful events.[75] In a very political discourse (such as the context of imperialism or colonization), epistemological dichotomy analysis does help to understand the flexible yet dogmatic use of 'time' in anthropological discipline as a political instrument of Western power. However, Fabian's theory is pertinent to the present discussion, not only because of his critiques of the allochronic position the discipline has decided to take, but because his theory suggests a possibility that the epistemological dichotomy is in itself a very powerful theoretical tool by which to generate views of and, consequently, to affect the management of spaces.

A dichotomous taxonomy defines the nature of the things: male or female, agricultural or industrial, authentic or inauthentic and so on. Sometimes, however, it goes much further to define the nature of a place, for instance, preliterate *versus* illiterate, traditional *versus* modern, old *versus* new, early *versus* late and central *versus* peripheral. By analogy, when outsiders decide to use Hakka heritage, the first step they feel they need to take is to put the 'historical totality' into the temporal-spatial framework with which they are familiar and can easily follow. In a Fabian sense, museumization is taking a typological point of view. When they put museumization into practice, the first action they want to do is to deconstruct the existing time-system and transfer or reduce it to an easily manageable typological time system. To achieve a typological time-framework, it is essential to place the land features including the buildings and structures into a number of typological dichotomies, for instance, traditional or modern (or simply old and new), authentic or inauthentic, representative or unrepresentative, magnificent or humble, past or contemporary, core or peripheral. What actually does have a negative impact on cultural resources is not these views of the past, but the ensuing selection processes that proceed from such dichotomies.

In the Hekeng case, authenticity has been reduced to, or even replaced by, the concepts of 'traditional' and 'real Hakka'. One preoccupation is that the 'real' Hakka heritage consists primarily of rammed-earthen *tulou* buildings and, as mentioned in Chapter 1, the local Hakka people themselves have now also embraced the 'Hakka *tulou*' reputation for the past twenty years. The upshot is that most of the modern-looking buildings are not regarded as 'real' Hakka. Therefore, as said in the last chapter, in preparation for the 2007 WH nomination, buildings with putative non-Hakka characteristics were removed from the preservation list. Architecturally speaking, three types of *tulou* buildings have conventionally been regarded as 'real' Hakka: the square, the round and the *wufeng* types of building (Huang, 1987). Undeniably, they do make up the majority of edifices in each vernacular settlement. Nevertheless, as said, that does not tell the whole story of the dwelling system in a settlement. Throughout their settlement history the local people have had to alleviate their housing shortage by resorting to supplementary architectures in other convenient forms. These structures are actually small-sized *lou* in a simplified shape — the *yizixing tulou*. One *idée fixe* is that, as these buildings are very simple in style devoid of the intricacies of the magnificent edifices, they cannot *represent* genuine 'Hakkaness'. Therefore, a number of these buildings were demolished by the local site managers in 2007. They simply made the judgment that the *yizixing tulou* did not fit the scene. They were not viewed as the sort of architecture that represented the quintessence of Hakka architectural arts. The aftermath of their decision is that, what people can view in the river valley today is only the 'quintessence' and a 'petrified' landscape of the 'real Hakka'. In fact, the whole gamut of permutations is by no means restricted to, as Fabian describes, 'temporal distancing devices' whose use also extends to a kind of 'spatial selecting device' in the creation of heritage themes. Epistemological dichotomies provide labels to denote a time sequence that seems different from 'now'. A heritage park is transformed or selected into a realm of the past, and anything irrelevant to that 'then' is ruthlessly expunged from the museum inventory. To achieve this goal, the outsiders' approach is to adopt sensible spatial dimensions to indicate a visible time depth. Historical time and

75. Also noteworthy, speaking about how the environments inform people about in which kind of domain or setting they are, the conceptual taxonomic terms are formed in pairs (Rapoport, 1990:56).

historical space benefit each other. A past is in itself a time concept defined by the visible boundaries of the site; what can be observed as 'past' has been staged inside the site boundaries. The chosen buildings and structures inside these boundaries constitute the contents of that past. All these spatial characteristics have been employed to create a temporal distance. To cut a long story short, museumization is a process of reordering a set of land features. When they set about introducing dichotomous concepts, the local site managers commence by rephrasing such doctrines and regulations in the WH transnational documents as the authenticity and integrity rules. In the process these rules are transformed into many 'either-or' questions. Through their actions, the outsider-managers localize and pinpoint the sort of selecting standards that they have no difficulty following in management practice. They finally reach a series of manipulable principles in terms of requirements for materials, dates, authenticity, integrity and representativeness; all linking the concepts of 'the real Hakka', authentic and representative. However, cultural heritage selection criteria are usually flexible and can even be manipulated (Yan, 2014). It is, after all, the site managers who eventually determine which architecture should or should not be preserved by following the localized selection methods. In fact, their choices have not been clear cut. The temporal distance between the present and past is therefore not as objective as it is supposed to be: instead, it is a controllable scenario of which only selected aspects are shown.

By contrast, as I described earlier in this chapter, when we examine the time phrases that were used by the Hakka people before 1949, we are immediately aware that they had their own time frameworks, in which each lineage member could find his or her position along the timeline constituted by generations, highlighting the continuity of the community and kinship relations. As will be discussed in later chapters, the built environment in river valleys such as that of the Hekeng, particularly the buildings and structures, represents a continuous demographic process. This lies at the very heart of its heritage value. Very importantly, although it might not be appropriate to put heritage buildings and structures displaying a very strong demographic and cultural continuity into an oversimplified authentic/inauthentic or traditional/modern dichotomy, these categorizations have nevertheless been warmly embraced by most museumization processes.

The problem has not been ignored. Over a hundred years ago, the Madrid Conference (1904) adopted useful resolutions by which to divide 'monuments' into two categories, namely: dead monuments and living monuments. ICCROM has said that[76] the debate about these distinctions continued throughout the whole of the twentieth century (Emerick 2003; Marshall, 1923; Paranavitana,1945; Philippot, 1996). The divide between dead and living monuments accurately pinpoints the dilemma of conservation in different heritage contexts. In most cases, we need to understand the real relationship between the local people and their heritage. However, the phrase 'still in use' has a broad scope when it comes to the 'modal verbs' that can be used in the same heritage-use discourses. Local people might still inhabit and use their properties, but are uneasy bedfellows and therefore might be unwilling to continue this sort of coexistence. In the Hekeng case, coincidence or not, the museumization happened at a critical time at which the local people's place attachment had already been seriously undermined. Their heritage is not yet dead but it is dying. Depopulation, poor housing conditions, an unstable economy, worsening interpersonal relationships and the inconvenience caused by the heritage-making all culminated in the *de facto* divorce of the local residents from their place. Every dead monument must have experienced a similar divorce as a final stage before its death. Under such circumstances, museumization might be seen as a sort of revitalization, but the preservation of the old buildings sometimes also means the perpetuation of the disputes they have caused so far. If a new place like the Hekeng 'museum' is generated by the revitalization of a dying place, what kind of new relationship can be created between the residents and this 'new' place? Continuity is not the whole answer.

76. http://www.iccrom.org/wp-content/uploads/PCA_Annexe-1.pdf.

3.6 A PLACE OF PLACELESSNESS

In this chapter, I have explored the manifold problems linked to the preservation and representation of the Hekeng people's past. Local site managers and the cultural authorities have museumized the residential part of the Hekeng built environment in order to theme the whole place. A past thus represented is not the past enshrined in local people's minds. To continue Relph's discussion on sense of place, insideness and placeness, I have focused on the local people's use of buildings and structures. In fact, all sense of losing an insideness is rooted in the obstacles to property use, use rights and profits deriving from such use. As has been discussed in Chapter 2 and this chapter, a museumized place is quite different from a settlement place in that a museumized place is created for the reception of visitors. This makes economic values such as tourist revenues, paramount to all other practical uses that are the foremost purpose of a settlement place. Some might argue that an agricultural settlement in the traditional sense (Fei, 1963) is quite different from urban centers, market towns[77] and administrative centers because the role of a settlement is confined to agricultural production and a self-sufficient economy, and the land dominated by this sort of economy is invariably fragmented. This impression is incorrect. As I mentioned briefly in Chapter 1, the rural settlements in neighboring Yongding county all abandoned rice cultivation and turned to a tobacco economy in the early Qing dynasty. These 'once-and-for-all' land-use transformations have recurred here and there throughout historical Chinese rural areas. Although farming is usually seen as the economic basis of traditional Chinese settlements, the people in these settlements have never refused to take the chance to rely on other more profitable economic pursuits. Therefore, I see no difference between these economic transformations that happened in the past and the museumization process that occurred between 2006 and 2012 in land-use respects, provided that the local peasants are able to hold firmly to their rights to the land. Under Chinese law, more specifically the *National Land Management Law* (*Tudi Guanlifa*) and the general provisions of the *Civil Law* (*Minfa Tongze*), the land in Chinese rural areas belongs to the 'collectivities' of villages and townships. Apart from these legal specifications, from a rural planning viewpoint the fields reserved for agricultural use (*jiben nongtian*) may not be used for other purposes. Moreover, it is theoretically impossible to come across any recent radical change in agricultural land-use functions in the Chinese rural areas, such as the tobacco movement in the Qing dynasty. Under the Chinese *wenwu baohu* system, land in the heritage sites under national protection is more often than not multifunctional. Most heritage sites, especially archaeological sites, are composed of agricultural fields and land for dwelling construction (*zhaijidi*) and how they can be used generally falls under two laws. Without the intrusion of externalities or the involvement of theming orientations, the Chinese *wenwu baohu danwei* is usually sufficient to accommodate the basic land-uses of the local people but no radical changes can be introduced. This means, as a WH site, the land inside the Hekeng site area could still be used as *jiben nongtian* and *zhaijidi*, indicating that no *de facto* changes in land-use functions have ever taken place there. As a result, the local people are unable to come up with any changes in land-use to be used as evidence in any claim they might make for heritage compensation. In other words, what they could claim as a loss covers only the demolition of their new houses, but not the use-right transfer as a World Heritage site; this is conventionally known as 'unpriced' (Licciardi and Amirtahmasebi, 2012).

77. Faure (2005), Zhou (2007), Oxfeld (2010), Lagerwey and Faure (2014) have studied the commercialization of Chinese rural agriculture, particularly the rise of rural commercial activities characterized by small market townships, contracts and ritual practices in southern China since the Ming dynasty. In southern China, the majority of the small towns that developed into the local commercial and trade centers were distributed in the important river valleys among the hills and the coastal areas. The most advanced commercial towns, as the above researches reported, might have initially developed from small markets shared by several nearby lineage villages, and gradually become a prosperous commercial center governed by the prominent, powerful lineage segments of these villages. Some of them located along the Ting River corridor and in the New Territories even had strong walls and moats. Medium and small market places, such as the Qujiang Market, were usually walled and sometimes had security guards. It should be noted that most of these small towns and markets were established spontaneously by the local people and therefore managed autonomously by them. They might not have served as official markets administrated by the local government.

3.6.1 The Use of Agricultural Fields (*Nongyongdi*)

To ensure the circulation of agricultural land use-rights and to 'stabilize the rural land contractual relationship, as well as for abiding by the principle of fair negotiation, in accordance with law, free will and onerousness', the *Law of the People's Republic of China on the Contracting of Rural Land* (*Zhonghua Renmin Gongheguo Tudi Chengbaofa*) and the *Measures for the Administration of the Circulation of Rural Land Contracted Management Right* (*Nongcun Tudi Chengbao-Jingyingquan Guanli Banfa*) are already in place to regulate 'acts of circulation of rural land contracted management right' and the rural land resource functions. I have selected a few articles particularly relevant to the discussion in this thesis:

Article 33 The following principles shall be abided by in the circulation of right to operate the contracted land: (a) Exercising equal consultation, voluntarism, paying compensation; no organizations or individuals shall force the contract-undertaking party to circulate the contracted land or prevent him from do so; (b) The nature of the ownership of the contracted land and its use for agriculture shall not be altered; (c) The term of the circulated contract shall not exceed the surplus of the duration of the contract already concluded; (d) The party to whom the land is transferred shall have the operation capability; and (e) Under the same conditions members of the economic organizations of the said collective shall be entitled the priority. (*Zhonghua Renmin Gongheguo Tudi Chengbaofa*)

Article 3 The agricultural use of any contracted land shall not be altered owing to the circulation of rural land contracted management right, the term of circulation may not exceed the remaining time limit of the contract term, and the lawful rights and interests of the interested parties and the rural collective economic organizations may not be impaired. (*Nongcun Tudi Chengbao-Jingyingquan Guanli Banfa*)

Article 6 A contractor shall have the right to determine of its/his own will concerning whether the contracted land shall be circulated, and determine the objects and ways of circulation. No entity or individual may force or obstruct the contractor to circulate its/his contracted land according to the law. (*Nongcun Tudi Chengbao-Jingyingquan Guanli Banfa*)

Article 7 The income from the circulation of the rural land contracted management right shall be owned by the contractor, no organization or individual may seize, retain or withhold it. (*Nongcun Tudi Chengbao-Jingyingquan Guanli Banfa*)

Article 9 The assignee of the circulation of rural land contracted management right may be the contracting farmer, or may be any other organization or individual that is allowed to undertake agricultural production and management according to the relevant laws and provisions. Under the same conditions, a member of the same collective economic organization shall have the priority. The assignee shall have the agricultural management capacity. (*Nongcun Tudi Chengbao-Jingyingquan Guanli Banfa*)

Article 12 An assignee shall protect the land according to the provisions of the relevant laws and regulations, no assignee may alter the agriculture use of the circulated land. (*Nongcun Tudi Chengbao-Jingyingquan Guanli Banfa*)

An examination of the articles cited above allows us to draw some brief conclusions about the Hekeng affair, as follows: (a) Agricultural land such as flat fields, terraced fields and hillside fields are the property of the collective landowners, not individuals. (b) The basic agricultural functions of such fields cannot be altered after the use-right is transferred to others. (c) The individuals or organizations who accept the use-right transfer cannot use the land for non-agricultural purposes and are obliged to share the benefits with the people who have made the transfer under the agreed terms. However, in China conventional cultural heritage preservation and conservation strategies require the designation of a buffer zone or *jianzhu kongzhi didai* (literally, construction controlling area) in rural areas that usually includes a large area surrounding the property. In the Hekeng case, the buffer zone covers nearly all the terraced fields and hillside areas. Not to put too fine a point on it, this land has been seized and designated an area of separation between the property and outside impacts. Therefore, new non-agricultural functions have already been imposed on these agricultural fields, although he local people are still supposed to be able to cultivate and use the fields in no violation of the heritage preservation requirements.

3.6.2 The Use of *Zhaijidi*

'Homestead' in a Western social context refers to 'a house and the surrounding area of land, usually used as a farm'. In China the story is different. Owing to the division of the ownership of a house (personal or household property) and the piece of land on which the house is built, a 'homestead' in rural China might refer solely to the area of the construction site. Under the terms of the *Property Law*, the transfer of the use-right of *zhaijidi* in rural China should be done in compliance with the following rules: (a) the transfer should be authorized by the collective economic organization (for example, hamlets and villages) that owns the land; (b) the assignee who receives a use-right transfer should belong to the same collective as the transferor; (c) the assignee should not have any real-estate and land for house construction. In short, the law excludes the possibility that any urban individuals and organizations can obtain the use-rights to rural *zhaijidi*. In Hekeng, in the post-1950s period all the *tulou* buildings have been constructed on the *zhaijidi* owned by the village collectives. Consequently, under the principles of jurisprudence, it should be impossible for any 'outsiders' to rent and use the *zhaijidi* for any heritage protection purposes, given the fact that all such *tulou* buildings are located on land designated as such. In other words, under these fundamental laws, heritage preservation is not considered one of the primary forms of land-use in rural China, or perhaps it would be better to say that in these land laws nothing has been clearly set out with reference to the legitimacy of this heritage use of *zhaijidi*. Unfortunately, it is conceivable that *zhaijidi* in a WH site such as Hekeng might share a large overlap with the so-called core zone, indicating a *de facto* land-use by the 'outsiders' who do not belong to 'the same collective economic organization' as required by the fundamental laws.

Apart from these problems, under *Zhonghua Renmin Gongheguo Tudi Guanlifa* (Article 63), 'use-rights to the land owned by the collectives may not be transferred for the construction of buildings and structures that have no relation to agricultural use.' Therefore, all the tourist facilities established in a settlement (for example, Tianluokeng) designated for heritage use should be considered illegal. Strictly speaking, the local cultural authorities, the local government and tourism developers are all outsiders who do not have the legal right to purchase or implement the use-right to collectively-owned land, if we view heritage use or protection use as a *de facto* way of using rural land. As has been argued previously, all the legal activities pertaining to heritage preservation and conservation in such rural social contexts are technically illegal under the provisions of the Chinese land laws.

3.6.3 The Use of Rural Houses

Unlike the *jiben nongtian* and *zhaijidi*, rural houses, under the terms of these fundamental Chinese laws, are the property of the local rural residents. Under the provisions of the fundamental laws, as personal property these houses may legally be purchased, transferred and rented. Without explaining the heritage-use-related issues explicitly to the local people, the local cultural authorities simply began to use the local *tulou* houses as tourist attractions in the ten villages in which forty-six *tulou* houses had been registered on the WHL. This raises the legal point: In what lawful way or ways pertaining to rural house-use can we classify such a transformative use of the local people's homes as touristic attractions: purchasing, transferring or renting? It is impossible to find an answer to this question in either the fundamental laws or the heritage bylaws. What is certain is that, through their division of the whole settlement area into the core and buffer zones, outsiders have used the insiders' houses. Some might argue that the property actually used by the local government in this heritage-making process is restricted to the houses of local peasants and the latter are still free to cultivate and use their arable fields as they have always done. All well and good on paper, but the truth of the matter might be very different. The vexed question is how can the heritage-makers use the residential area without designating a buffer zone, a feature that seems to be a prerequisite for gaining a World Heritage listing? As previously stated, the crux of the matter is that the buffer zone is actually constituted by the agricultural fields. The truth is that the heritage-making process has involved all the land in the local settlements. Without transgressing any existing land-use orders and regulations in the Chinese land laws, the local government has managed to transform all the collectively owned fields into a kind of architectural museum and, adding insult to injury, the size of the budget for the compensation of the local people was also reduced to the minimum. Although they might derive some monetary benefit from this transformation, the peasants have no direct legal claim on the local government by which they could demand a fair share of this benefit. Any claim for compensation for the partial loss of land-use rights is therefore invalid in legal terms.

In this chapter, I have proposed a picture of two coexisting worlds in the Hekeng River Valley. One is obviously the world of a rural settlement in which people live their lives. The other is a world of heritage imposed by the local government. The second world has been created to be a representation of the first but at the expense of the first world that was created for living in and for use. People who inhabited this world had their own ways of using the whole built environment to create, remember and respect their past. As insiders, they had their own sense of the place, a feeling that was based on the interaction with the built environment and the temporal-spatial geography governing that place. The representation of the Hekeng place, in a Relph's sense, preserves only part of the physical settings of the Hekeng place. What the local people recognize as their past is not the theme of this representation. In the first world, the local residents have gradually lost their sense of place, in the wake of depopulation, economic recessions, a worsening environment, shortage of income and poor housing conditions. In the heritage world, however, playing a role they do not acknowledge, they are caretakers, supporting actors and actresses and authenticity evidence-providers. The flaws in the land legislation prevent them from making a reasonable profit from making land-use right transfers. Bereft of the past and with little hope of the future, they have little or no chance of making any place-attachment to the heritage world. The heritage place is still and ever will be a place of placelessness.

4. Heritage Site: a Place of Cultural Resource Game

In the first three chapters I have discussed the interpretation of the site formation process in Hekeng from three perspectives: that of a landscape biography, that of the dilemma of the local people confronted with the implementation of a plethora of laws and regulations and that of the placelessness revealed in the Hekeng heritage representation and use. In this final chapter, I shall expand on some of the views on heritage management in current Chinese cultural resource competition discourses. To carry out the exercise the metaphor of a game is used for the competitive struggle for cultural resources in rural China, particularly that arising from the use of peasants' vernacular buildings and land. Before pursuing the metaphor in greater depth, a few definitions are called for. What is a game? A game produces winners and losers. Can all the participants win simultaneously, or can there at least be no losers? The answer to the first is no, but 'no losers' is possible, but only if an equilibrium balancing the players' demands can eventually be achieved. The draw has always been part of chess, but, what is that equilibrium? Why should all the participants intend to reach equilibrium? How can such equilibrium be reached?

4.1 BRAND AWARENESS, BUREAUCRATIC RECIPROCITY AND LAND DISPUTES

In the case of this thesis, the game discussed is a bundle of requirements placed on the peasants' properties and lands. I use the term 'game' in the sense that each player's result is determined not only by his own efforts but also by the strategies all other participants in the same game have planned and deployed as they play it. At present, Chinese cultural heritage protection work is still largely a 'state-sponsored' and 'state-led' (*zhengfu zhudao*) cultural resource enterprise, a situation that has been clearly written into the *Chinese Cultural Heritage Law* (amended in 2002). However, as some of its officials have always complained, the SACH is still an underdog trailing behind all the other Chinese government departments. In its attempt to deal with the situations I have explained in the previous two chapters, the role of the SACH has been reduced to that a financial supporter in Chinese cultural heritage management. In other words, as it lacks any executive power over land resource management, it has been forced to rely completely on the cooperation of the local governments (especially the cultural management departments) in order to achieve its primary goals.

As briefly mentioned in Chapter 2, the overall preservation plan of a site (*zongti baohu guihua*) can only be fully implemented legislatively on condition that it has been first endorsed and then promulgated by the provincial People's Congress. In practice, the local government officials are invariably the people who actually determine whether or not to issue the site preservation and management plans that have already been produced by the relevant qualified planning organizations and to decree to what extent the cultural resources can be protected and used. This is the situation on paper. My 2014 investigations at Chinese archaeological sites of great significance (*dayizhi*) showed that, in the past twenty years, site plans of over 30 percent[78] of such important sites have not been formally proclaimed by the Chinese local provincial governments and the Congress (Wang and Wang, 2015), suggesting perhaps a rather uncoordinated and incoherent heritage management style on a national scale. In fact, local governments are selective in their issuance and implementation of the site plans implemented by the SACH on behalf of the central government.

The weakness of the SACH is also reflected in its conservative attitude toward applications to local

78. In 2015, the Institute of Archaeology CASS agreed to undertake a project funded by the SACH to make a plan for the preservation and management of the Chinese archaeological sites of great significances from 2016 to 2021. In the review of the site management situation between 2010 and 2015, it was estimated that nearly 40% of sites are now being or will be transformed into urban parks.

cultural authorities for the use of some sites as heritage parks. To be fair, since 2009, the SACH has initiated a new program, the 'National Archaeological Site Park Program', drawing on the experience of the US National Park Service system. Over the past six years or so, twelve archaeological sites have been registered, and twenty-three important sites put on the tentative list. Under the rules set by the SACH, these sites will be transformed into urban cultural spaces (*chengshi wenhua kongjian*). This new program immediately caught the interest of local governments at provincial and county levels. Many were itching to have a try. Nevertheless, with some reason fearful of uncontrollable damage to the sites, later the SACH nearly called a halt to the park program. This unenviable situation is a clear illustration that the tricky relationship between the SACH and local governments in China is the indelible backdrop to all the games being played out in the field of heritage use. However awkward this relationship might be, it is not the only fly in the ointment. Contradictions between the fundamental land management laws and heritage management regulations are easy to pinpoint and these all offer the opportunity to introduce different strategies by which to escape the unwanted results and obligations arising from the use of peasants' fields and houses as cultural sites. As mentioned in previous chapters, the local government and local cultural authorities usually play a vital role in Chinese heritage designation and preservation. The SACH has to rely fully on their support to enforce the national laws and regulations on cultural heritage protection, especially in efforts to solve disputes about land expropriation. In this sense, the SACH enters into a reciprocal relationship with the local government.

It has to be said that they are sometimes uneasy bedfellows. SACH officials are very concerned about the registered cultural resources directly administered by the local government. They are worried about the local government's veiled attitudes toward heritage protection. If they put a firm hand on the tiller and expose the local government authorities' negligence in the performance of their duties to the public, the local officials might be even more chary about the truth. Nor is the position of the local government officials an enviable one. They have to balance the relationship between economic development and cultural resource protection. Their position is exacerbated because they need the reputation of the cultural resources to enhance the brand awareness of their city.

In the 2000s, the buzz word among many Chinese city governments was *chengshi mingpian* (literally, a city business card). The term usually refers to 'those special local products, typical sceneries and landmarks, which can represent the image of the city'. Generally speaking, a local government has two sources from which to obtain this sort of reputation. Clearly the first is the SACH that has the power to register local cultural resources on the national heritage list. The other one is the Ministry of Housing and Urban-Rural Development of the PRC (*Zhonghua Renmin Gongheguo Zhufang ji Chengxiang Jianshebu*), that has the power to select what are known as 'renowned cities, towns and villages' (*lishi wenhua mingcheng, mingzhen, mingcun*). That said, the biggest stumbling-block to these arrangements is that local governments usually do not want to abide strictly by the heritage restrictions set down in the cultural resource planning endorsed by the SACH and the MHUD. Particularly, as a customer who is paying for the planning service, local governments usually like to immerse themselves thoroughly in the site planning process. Sometimes, they might even put direct pressure on the planners so that the site planning will follow their directions or at least make some compromise to suit their requirements. It is usually the local cultural department (*difang wenhua bumen*) as part of the local county or provincial governments that plays the role of a buffer between the SACH, the planners and the local government officials. The local government officials might ask the staff of cultural department to convey their ideas, advice and implications to the site planners. This is most likely to occur after the local government officials have already decided how to use the land in the vicinity of the site area. It is not unknown for them to hire tourism design companies to draw up tourism development plans even before they begin to consider any cultural resource preservation issues. When this happens, the site planners can find themselves required to make the cultural resource preservation plan on condition that it should not significantly violate the tourism plan that has preceded it.

If and when this state of affairs crops up, the cultural department staff can be made to feel very embarrassed. They are on the horns of a dilemma. Although they work for the local governments, their job is to take care of the cultural resources of the state. Consequently, despite the fact that this department is answerable to the SACH, the money for its expenditure comes from the local government. Sandwiched between the SACH and the local government officials with little room to maneuver, cultural departments usually have no choice but to make their own tradeoffs. Nor do their problems end there. The local cultural departments are also usually required to assess the officials' requirements for local economic development fully and pinpoint the discrepancies in different, even opposing, understandings of land-use in relation to specific cultural resources. A good example of this dilemma is presented by the site of the Mausoleum of the First Emperor Qin Shihuang located in the rural area in the east of Lintong county. In 2012, the Shaanxi provincial government initiated the 'Qin-Han Boulevard' construction project. Under this construction plan, the new boulevard extending 4.25 kilometers from east to west would traverse the Xi'an Economic Development zone, the Western Han dynasty capital site, the Weiyang new apartment block, the Chan-Ba Ecological District, the Xi'an International Trade and Business Center and the Lintong new urban center. Therefore this new thoroughfare would pass through the most important cultural resource distribution area of Xi'an, above all the fringe area of the Mausoleum of Qin Shihuang. In 2013, the Institute of Archaeology CASS in conjunction with the Architectural School of Tsinghua University began work on a heritage park, with the burial garden section of the Mausoleum as its theme. The site planners suggested that, in view of the damage the proposed boulevard might entail and the need to preserve the historical views of the landscape, it would be much better to reroute the traffic to the northern area. However, in the ensuing discussions between the planners and the head of local cultural authorities on behalf of the provincial government, the head began to persuade the planners to change their minds. He not only insisted on constructing the road as initially planned, but did his best to have the planners add a new tunnel to the site area and a new service building to the core zone. In this case, the local cultural department had to change its role. Under pressure from the local government officials, the cultural department felt as if it has to help enforce new planning strategies and hence failed to hold its position. This incident has shown that, in this instance at least, the local cultural department could not have adopted its own independent stance. By and large it would be fair to say that, should a discrepancy arise in opinions about cultural resource preservation, the most likely scenario is that this department will support the local government.

Furthermore, in many Chinese county governments,[79] the cultural resource department is ultimately incorporated into the 'county cultural bureau' (*xian wenhuaju*), the body usually in complete charge of local tourism, cultural advertisement dissemination, television program production, county museums and local cultural resource. As a constituent part of the bureau, it needs to put its interests first. In 2015, the Institute of Archaeology, CASS, took on the task of drawing up an overall preservation plan for the Majiayao prehistoric site located in the southern rural area of Lintao county. In early 2016, the provincial government commenced the process of making an application for funding from the World Bank. The emphasis of the project was not directed solely to economic development; it is also an attempt to manage the utilization of cultural resources. Initially it was hoped to find the local government enough money to finance the initiation of the use of its cultural heritage so as to make a profit. In accordance with the requirements of the provincial government officials, the county officials asked the staff of cultural department to complete the application report. Conventionally and for the sake of the cultural heritage itself, the overall preservation plan should have priority over any other initiatives for the use of the land for cultural or non-cultural purposes. In order to carry out the theming of the place, the cultural department staff made efforts to persuade the site planners to add more information about the use of the site as a park, hopeful that this

79. The counties I know in which this is the case include Zou county in Shandong province, Lintao county in Gansu province, Qionglai county in Sichuan province and Nanjing county in Fujian province.

move might increase the budget produced to apply for funding from the World Bank. In a nutshell, all the initiatives actually came from the local government, but it is always the cultural department staff who talked to the site planners on its behalf; albeit their negotiations were not always effective.

These two examples make it perfectly clear that there are potentially three influential bureaucratic groups involved in playing the game, namely: the SACH, the local governments and the local cultural management departments. They each have some power to influence decision-making processes, and therefore they can be said to form the basic framework of the Chinese cultural heritage regime. If one more factor should be added to this regime, it is the cultural resource planners. Heritage site planning usually refers to taking control of land use in some specific areas with heritage values in order to preserve and protect the property.

In China, the majority of site planners are professionals in architectural history, urban planning or urban design. Some are urban landscape architects or garden designers. As professionals in modern urban and rural built environment planning, in the first place their duty is to assist in the development of the local society. Lacking knowledge of the cultural resource being planned (particularly the archaeological sites) yet coveting the handsome rewards on offer, as a rule they tend to reorganize heritage planning as a zoning process that necessarily precedes the creation of urban or rural cultural spaces; an exercise at which they can be exceedingly efficient. If the truth be told, they are likely to be supported by the local government that would be much happier to see the emergence of a heritage park in place of an age-old patchwork of arable fields and farmhouses. This clash of interests sometimes leads to the expulsion of the CRM staff who do understand the heritage sites and can become an obstacle to constructing a heritage park if they believe that fundamental knowledge about the heritage site is not enough to support theming. At this point it is important to emphasize that the fledgling Chinese heritage planning profession still needs to seek out the way to involve all kinds of CRM people in the site planning process. If it does not succeed in this goal, heritage might turn out to be nothing more than part of a new landscape park and this can be a disaster.

Reducing heritage site planning to park theming or urban space-creating processes at the very least necessarily results in the oversimplification of the place represented; at worst it can even damage it,[80] as I have discussed in Chapters 2 and 3. The situation at the moment is that, by and large, planning companies in China usually focus on how a piece of cultural heritage can be utilized, not its protection. Intrinsically they are the new space creators working for the governments that pay them with taxpayers' money. Their situation is rather similar to that of the local cultural departments in that neither has an independent stance of its own about the preservation and use of a specific heritage site. So, who can represent the interests of the cultural resource itself (Wang, 2010)?

The answer to this is far from simple. It does seem that all these problems might ultimately derive from the attitude of local governments toward heritage preservation, particularly on the provincial and county levels. As the *China Statistical Yearbook* says, the urban population rose from191,400,000 in 1980 to 731,110,000 in 2013, and the urbanization rate increased enormously from 19.4 to 53.73 percent during this period (Bao and Peng, 2016). Since the 2000s, rapid urbanization and economic development have constantly demanded more land. In the face of the very real problem of serious land shortage, local government officials have to trivialize cultural heritage preservation problems. In the Chinese government system, when an official's performance is evaluated, heritage preservation usually does not feature on the list. Conversely, an official's contribution to local economic development is conventionally accorded a high significance and a high score is essential to get a promotion. When push comes to shove, heritage has become a kind of superfluous matter in the present bureaucratic competition. Below I would like to give my view of the Chinese cultural heritage management system.

Managing all Chinese cultural heritage places is conventionally thought of as the basic role and

80. A typical example is the Daming Palace site.

responsibility of the Chinese State Administration of Cultural Heritage (SACH). Correspondingly, there is usually one major department in each provincial and county government (*difang wenwuju*) that is assigned to take care of the cultural resources throughout the whole province or the whole county. From an administrative point of view, the SACH and the *difang wenwuju* share no hierarchical relations and no common interests. The SACH, working as a department of the Chinese Ministry of Culture (*Zhongguo Wenhuabu*), is answerable only to that Ministry, whereas each *difang wenwuju* is committed to working for the local government to which it is affiliated. Although it is the leading Chinese cultural resource manager, the SACH itself has no administrative capacity to govern the cultural resources throughout the country. However, it does have the power to allocate the funds that are necessary for the *difang wenwuju* to continue their work. In the eyes of the local government officials, the existence of local cultural department constitutes their basic eligibility to apply for funding opportunities from the SACH. In this scenario, it is easy to see that local government officials can and do make good use of all kinds of political resources. The heritage game penetrates the boundary between the Chinese cultural resource management system and the administrative system but, in most cases, it is the local government that plays a vital role in the practical aspects of the Chinese cultural heritage management.

4.2 THE GAME PLAYERS, THEIR BARGAINING CHIPS AND THEIR ROLES

To take Hekeng as an example, there are probably five game players participating in the heritage resource game, each of them wanting to use of the local people's land in some way.

4.2.1 The SACH

In 2015 the SACH formally issued the *Guidelines in the Maintenance of Ancient Architectures* (*Gujianzhu Baoyang Weihu Guicheng*). This manual is applicable to the architecture registered on the list of the *Quanguo zhongdian wenwu baohu danwei*, or the cultural heritage under the national protection. Crucially the bulk of these consist not of vernacular buildings but of *guanshi jianzhu* (official buildings). Nevertheless, in 2012, the SACH, in conjunction with MHUD and the Ministry of Finance (*caizhengbu*), initiated a complete survey of traditional Chinese villages. The outcome seems amazing: there are about 12,000 of these villages remaining throughout China.

The SACH has decreed that the time criteria for designating a traditional village is that a proposed settlement should have been initially established before the Republican period, that is, before AD 1911. There is a good chance that this inventory might still contain omissions, one particular example being villages established in the Republican period such as the Qujiang Market near the Hekeng River Valley mentioned earlier. As one of the most important sites of memory of the Zhang lineage, it contains a huge market block and is an example of refined architecture in the early-modern style. Although the Hekeng *tulou* cluster has already been registered on the Cultural Heritage under Provincial Protection List and also on the WHL, other *tulou* settlements such as Nanou, Taxia and Shiqiao have so far not been paid much attention. There have been other startling omissions. The old residence of the only imperial-exam degree-holder (*Jinshi*) in this hilly area, a member of the local gentry, Zhang Jinba, is even not counted on the County Cultural Heritage List. Double-checking with the MHUD List of Historically and Culturally Well-known Villages, it turns out that only the Tianluokeng *tulou* village in this area is registered, and is also a WH site. This would seem to indicate that neither the SACH nor the MHUD seems to carry much weight in this hilly region in the vicinity of Shuyang township. As the nomination of the Hekeng and the Tianluokeng World Heritage candidates was fully based on the existing designation of the two villages, it would appear that their present WH site statuses are probably just an upgraded version of a Well-known village (Tianluokeng) and a Provincial-level significant site (Hekeng). This inconsistency raises the question: If only two settlement places have been placed under the strict restrictions of the international and national laws and regulations, why is most of the landscape in this hilly area so well preserved? The first answer, according to Fletcher (2007), is that a built environment might have to be maintained not because it is useful but because of the considerable cost of removing or renovating it.

The second, as noted in Chapter 2, is that the local government has actually issued many regulations to protect the historical built environment in the lower reaches of the Jiulong Stream.

Basically, the SACH has exerted its influence on two aspects of this hilly region famous for its *tulou* buildings. First and foremost, the SACH helped the Nanjing local government successfully gain the WH title. Secondly, once this was in the grasp of the local government, it supported the former in the hiring of professionals to do the site planning, an exercise that put the final nail in the coffin of the museumization process of the settlement place. Of overwhelming importance to the SACH is the final result: China has successfully gained two more World Heritage titles. What do the SACH officials themselves think about the WH application? At a conference of the International Council of Museums (ICOM), the-now Vice Director of the SACH, Song Xinchao, commented, 'The World Heritage application aims to promote the people's awareness of the importance of cultural heritage and heritage protection'.[81] Nevertheless, Song was also voiced his worries about the nomination, 'Although the World Heritage status might present the local societies with good economic opportunities, the heritage itself might sometimes become a money-spinner (*yaoqianshu*[82]) of the local governments; and overexploitation of the local cultural resource might cause many problems'.[83] In 2013, the SACH issued the *Regulations on the World Cultural Heritage Nomination* (tentative) (*Shijie Wenhua Yichan Shenbao Shenhe Guanli Guiding*).[84] In this short document, it is suggested that: 'Application work should be carried out in a diligent and thrifty manner. When making a WH application, the local government applicants should try their best to spare the budget as much as possible,[85] avoid over-relocation and solve disputes about land expropriation properly' (SACH, 2013).[86]

81. http://news.xinhuanet.com/politics/2010-11/14/c_12772125.htm.

82. Literally 'money-tree'.

83. http://news.xinhuanet.com/politics/2010-11/14/c_12772125.htm.

84. http://www.lawinfochina.com/display.aspx?lib=law&id=8911&CGid=.

85. According to the *People's Daily* (December, 28th, 2010), to apply for a WH title can cost a lot. The Luoyang government spent 0.1 billion *yuan* RMB on preparing the nomination of the Longmen Grottoes. This money was used to remove intrusive architectures outside the southern gate. Similarly, the Sichuan government paid 0.22 billion *yuan* RMB to remove extraneous buildings, when nominating the Dujiangyan landscape as WH. The WH nomination of the Mount Wuyi landscape and the Eastern Mausoleum of the Qing dynasty each cost nearly 0.1 billion *yuan* RMB. A report on August 14 2010 on the *New China* web journal states that the China Danxia nomination cost nearly 0.12 billion *yuan* RMB. Over half of the money has been spent on the demolition of houses. As one of the local cultural resource managers Peng Hua said, although WH application is very costly, only a very small sum of money is actually spent on site planning, holding symposiums and international consultancy. Similar information was stated by Yan (2014): 'As some recall, during the first wave of nomination, the decision was not about which *tulou* buildings should be selected, but about which counties would participate. Pinghe county, in which the Shengwu-lou was located, was originally considered as a candidate. However, having estimated that the basic expenses for the drafting and translation of nomination files might cost RMB500,000 (US$60,000), Pinghe county government decided it was not worth spending that much on the project and the county eventually withdrew the nomination.'

86. Right now China has become the second largest WH State Party. In fact, there have been many debates about the World Heritage applications in China. Most of the negative remarks have been made in newspapers and magazines. People have begun to think about both the positive and negative aspects of WH nomination (Zhao, 2015; Zhang and Li, 2014; Tang, 2013; Li and Kuang, 2011). Sometimes, as Zhao (2015) has pointed out, with an eye to potential commercial prospects a local government can be extremely enthusiastic about applying for a WH title. In one of her articles, Zhao reports an extreme case involving the registration of the Xingjiao Temple as a WH site. The Xingjiao Temple is most famous as the burial place of the Tang dynasty Tripitaka Buddhist Monk Xuanzang. Despite the abbot's strong objections, the local Xi'an government insisted on placing the temple on the WH nomination list. After some hesitation, the local government finally took action and issued the *Regulations on the Management of the Xingjiao Temple*. Thereby, the government took the total management control of the temple and expelled the abbot by cancelling his Buddhist identity. In 2013, commissioned experts from the ICOMOS went there to evaluate the proposed heritage site. In 2014, the Silk Road (including the temple as an important site on the route) of China was finally registered on the WHL. In this case, the SACH preferred not to comment on the local government's behavior. On the one hand, the SACH was also very keen to ensure the successful registration of the Silk Road on the WHL. On the other hand, as a cultural resource management department of the central government, it had no right to intervene the domestic administrative affairs of the local government. Unfortunately, in the Xingjiao Temple affair, the SACH chose to collude with the local government. As Zhao remarks, what the local government wanted was the huge economic benefits the commercialized temple could attract; while what the SACH wanted was to achieve its WH goal.

These paragraphs just cited make it crystal clear that the SACH officials are fully aware of the problems confronting local government applicants. However, the regulations it issues are actually no more than suggestions for the local governments. Nobody is quite sure how many of these suggestions they will adopt. Most of the SACH staff see themselves as advisors and professional guides (*yewu zhidao*) to the local cultural authorities. Now the situation is becoming more acute. In the past two decades or so, cultural resource preservation in most local areas has been required to give way to economic development (*jingji jianshe*). Nearly every member of the local cultural departments I have ever met has complained of their feelings of impotence. And I was sometimes aware of a kind of tension between the SACH and the local government authorities. Therefore the problem that the SACH has no executive power over the local governments remains but, despite this we should not underestimate the real influence of the SACH in the management of local cultural resources, given the fact it is the supreme body in the hierarchy of the Chinese cultural heritage administration. The bargaining chips that the SACH holds to influence other WH game players are double-sided: (1) as the representative of the State Party, it controls the only diplomatic channel through which WH applications can be made; (2) as the only national-level cultural heritage administrator, it has the right to allocate funds for site planning and conservation.

4.2.2 The WHC

The principal concern of the WHC is the future of the past. In the tangible heritage world, the baseline of the WHC is primarily represented in its conservative attitude toward the physical part of heritage, above all the preservation and use of cultural heritage. The division between the 'dead' and the 'dying' had long been ignored. Now the winds of change are blowing and, as a counterweight, since the 2000s 'living heritage' has been emerging globally as a recurring theme in heritage management area. The ICCROM has finally put forward a people-centered approach to redress balance between developmental needs and the long-existing Western museumification methodology. Going by the case studies on the ICCROM website, the Advisory Body has been trying to help the local people continue to use their built environment in traditional ways. To a large extent, they are assisting them to continue their traditional ways of life. Although certainly most of this sort of heritage is located in underdeveloped areas, the premise of this approach should be whether the local people still want to or have to use the 'objects' that have been labeled a treasure of the humankind. Unsurprisingly, there is no possibility of urging any people to use their buildings and structures for heritage protection purposes only, unless this use can bring them economic profits. Bearing this dichotomy in mind, I see a basic difference between the Fujian *tulou* heritage and other built heritages of small minority groups. The unwillingness of the local people to use the *tulou* heritage as residences is quite obvious in the southern Fujian *tulou* cases. This despite the fact that, as peasants, they have the capability both financially and technically to renovate and improve their outdated built environment fully. So far, throughout the whole process of museumization of the built environment, the WHC regulations have been closely adhered to by Chinese experts and the SACH. They have adopted WHC concepts defining authenticity and integrity as their basic doctrines and as an excuse to intervene or even terminate the metabolization process of the built environment. For its part, the WHC and its Advisory Bodies is in a position to set the rules from a value comparison and competition point of view, because it needs to be sure that the elements that are important are still 'there'. Nevertheless, unquestionably it is the State Party government that ultimately decides to translate a heritage site into the realm of museumization and the role of the WHC and its Advisory Bodies is simply to take the nominated values as real and conduct regular reviews to convince themselves that the nominated features are still there and they do not need to play any real part in the heritage selection process. Nevertheless, basic concerns should be raised about the relationship between the museumized and the original local inhabitants. Specifically this concern should not be about whether or not the local people are still continuing to use the buildings or structures registered, but whether or not they are able to obtain benefits from the museumized places. In this instance, the continuity of a living heritage is totally different from that of the museumized place in that it is the latter that is based primarily on the exclusion of non-cultural-heritage uses. As I have discussed in Chapters 2 and 3, in most cases the use-right to a place is almost entirely transferred to the local government, but, if the profit-sharing issue is not incorporated into the existing heritage review system, a process that could result in a delisting, the WHC and its Advisory Bodies could be construed as accomplices of the local government.

Actually, what the WHC holds as bargaining chips in the WH game is no more than the power of enlisting or delisting. Interestingly, the reason for making a choice to delist is usually the fact that the State Party has failed to fulfill its obligations toward the conservation of the registered property as defined by the *World Heritage Convention*. To date, two heritage sites have been removed from the WHL. The first delisting event that occurred in 2007 was the deletion of the Arabian Oryx Sanctuary from the WHL. This decision was based on two facts.[87] The first was Oman's own decision to reduce the size of the protected area by 90 percent. The second reason was a sharp decrease in the population in the site area from 450 to only sixty-five. Two years later, in 2009, the WHC decided to remove Germany's Dresden Elbe Valley from the WHC on account of the 'building of a four-lane bridge in the heart of the cultural landscape which meant that the property failed to keep its OUVs'.[88] So far, it seems that a violation of the OUV principles is the only condition that can lead to a delisting. Although only two delistings have ever been announced by the WHC, quite a substantial number of delisting warnings have been issued. Before 2002, the WHC had warned the SACH of delisting risks. It was worried about several mixed World Heritage sites, including Mount Huang and Mount Tai. The WHC warned the SACH that the commercialization of the landscapes could pose a threat to the OUVs. In all these cases, the WHC was only concerned about the loss of the OUV characteristics. However, it stands to reason that the continuity of a WH site can also rely heavily on the local inhabitants' willingness to live with the sites and the compensation for the economic loss they have incurred during the WH application process. There is an inherent danger that revenue-sharing in a post-registration context could result in disputes about heritage use and sometimes even the demolition of the heritage sites, particularly in China's rural areas. Therefore, to ensure the security of the WH sites, the WHC should take fully into consideration the relationship between the local people and the local government, a delicate state of affairs that can be seriously upset by revenue-sharing issues. Nevertheless, so far a bad relationship between the local residents and the local government has not constituted a reason for which the WHC can refuse to register a site or a WH site can be delisted.

4.2.3 The Local Government and the *Tulou* Companies

As noted in the Preface, the bulk of the development in urban areas in China is based on the exploitation of rural resources. Certainly, one cause of this situation has arisen in part at least from the long-term advantages enjoyed and the leading role played by the urban centers (*xian*) throughout most of Chinese imperial history. The centuries-old dominance of urban centers has been reinforced to an even greater degree by urban capital since the Republican period. In that period, Chinese rural society began to compete to serve the urban centers. Since the 1990s, capital has again quickly become centralized in Chinese urban areas. Urban development needs resources that can only be obtained from the country's vast rural areas, the principal source of labor, energy, farm produce, mines and so on. Less obviously, rural scenery and landscapes are also resources pursued by urban tourist interests. The overexploitation of rural resources has already caused many social problems. Apart from rural depopulation and the collapse of the rural agricultural economy, the most significant result is the loss of economic ability. Relying heavily on urban job opportunities, the rural areas of China have been reduced to the 'rear service suppliers' of local urban centers. In a large number of rural settlements in Anhui, Jiangxi, Sichuan, Hubei, Henan, Guangxi, Chongqing and Guizhou, the major sources of migrant workers, the previously self-sufficient rural economy has almost disappeared, and with its eclipse has come the disuse/suspension/abandonment/demolition of a considerable part of the 'traditional' rural built environment. No longer

87. http://whc.unesco.org/en/news/362/.
88. http://whc.unesco.org/en/news/522/.

a home, a workplace, a traditional countryside, as I have elaborated at length in Chapter 3, the previous settlements have become 'placeless'. In the first decade of the twenty-first century, *tulou* tourism embarked on its heyday. As it flourished, the local county governments began to get involved in the regulation process. Their involvement leads inexorably to the question: How have the local government authorities that represent urban interests managed the rural heritage world?[89]

Again taking the *tulou* villages as examples, in 2007, 410,000 tourists[90] came to visit the Nanjing *tulou* villages. In 2009, this had risen by more than 100,000 to 518,000. In 2010, the settlements of Yongding alone attracted around 710,000 tourists. It is estimated by the local government that Yongding county on its own generated a total tourist income of 0.3 billion *yuan* RMB in 2007,[91] and in 2010 the figure had soared to 1.82 billion.[92] As said, both the local governments and their cultural departments can play a very important role in heritage games. In 2011, the Nanjing *tulou* received no fewer than 1,390,000 visitors and produced 0.4 billion *yuan* RMB in income.[93] The next year, 2012, the Nanjing *tulou* villages received nearly 250,000 visitors during the National Day holidays alone, yielding 0.1 billion *yuan* RMB income.[94] In 2013, Nanjing *tulou* villages received 1.52 million visitors, creating 0.6 billion yuan RMB income.[95] Two years later, in 2015, Nanjing *tulou* villages received roughly double this total attracting 3.35 million people, who produced a 2 billion *yuan* RMB income.[96] Obviously the Nanjing tourism-generated income has increased sharply over the past five years. Although it is impossible to know the exact proportion this income has accounted for in the entire earnings derived from local tourism, it is conceivable that the local government has received quite a comfortable income from the tourism taxes. As a paper published online[97] in 2015, entitled 'The Problems of *Tulou* Tourism Resource Exploitation and the Countermeasures', has pointed out, the local governments usually use *tulou* companies to manage the *tulou* buildings in a highly commercial way. In stark contrast, the *tulou* residents are assigned only a minor role in the tourism development process and earn very little income from the use of their heritage. This despite the fact

89. A small question pertinent to the present discussion is: Where is the border between the urban world and the rural world? 'Rural' in Chinese political terms does not refer to fields occupied by some autonomous settlements (although autonomous lineage villages have existed from time to time in Chinese rural history), but should be seen in juxtaposition to the word 'urban'. In the traditional Chinese political administration, the county was usually called a '*xian cheng*'. *Cheng*, usually refers to the enclosures surrounding the urban area. In short, the first border between the two worlds was just the enclosures. Consequently, in each county area, there is indeed a border separating the rural and the urban. In other words, each county governs and manages its own rural areas. There are also many townships (*xiang* or *zhen*) scattered in between the *xian* and villages. Historically, the majority of these towns developed from local agricultural produce distribution centers. A *xian* in Imperial China, as reflected in the Qin dynasty bamboo inscriptions excavated at Shuihudi, usually served as key administrative node, governing the whole Chinese rural areas that provided the empire with agricultural goods, a labor force and taxation. Chinese rural areas were intrinsically the resource pools of the country. In the historical written records so far as I have access to them, since the Republican period, some small settlements in the Fuzhou region had already become the labor pool that supplied the nearby county administrative seats with all kinds of services; and in these places, agriculture might have already dwindled to a minor income source. A full awareness of the importance of the rural cultural resources is by no means a modern invention in China. Apart from the records in ancient Chinese geographers' works, for centuries Chinese county and prefectural gazetteer writing since the Ming dynasty has referred to rural landscapes and settlements as the pride of the county and evidence of its long civilized history since even preliterate times. In China, the earliest modern use of rural cultural resources by the urbanites can be traced back to the 1970s. The first tourist attractions were used as sanatoriums for the recuperation of Chinese cadres and foreign guests of the governments. As Zhang (2003) has pointed out, the earliest tourist attractions such as Sijiqing, Dazhai, Xiaojinzhuang and the Chongming Island were 'half political and half touristic'. Using rural cultural and natural resources as tourist destinations only began in the 1990s, particularly after the five-day work week had been widely implemented in China.

90. http://www.docin.com/p-786273107.html.

91. The Chinese Tourism Planning Academy. 2008. *Yongding Tulou Settlement Tourism Design*. Unpublished.

92. http://lykj.tsk.libsou.com/info/22268.jspx.

93. http://travel.ce.cn/jd/201212/03/t20121203_23901589.shtml.

94. http://news.163.com/12/1018/11/8E3JD17800014JB6.html.

95. http://www.fjnj.gov.cn/view.asp?id=10432.

96. http://www.fjnj.gov.cn/view.asp?id=28803.

97. http://m.xuehuile.com/blog/ab1dcf63cb6b4668a879d20ff70a18c5.html.

that, using cultural heritage authenticity and integrity as an excuse, the *tulou* companies usually require the *tulou* residents to leave the buildings 'intact'. This commercialization has been a hotbed of numerous disputes among the local *tulou* residents.

So far, the largest *tulou* tourism company in Fujian is the Fujian Kejia *Tulou* Culture Tourism Company. The company was founded in 2007 and is a state enterprise. As the company's prospectus[98] shows, the Yongding county government controls the interests of the company. In the Chinese context, '*konggu*' (literally controlling shares) refers to a situation in which a shareholder controls at least over 50 percent of the company's shares or interests. This removes any shadow of doubt that the local government is indeed the largest shareholder in the *tulou* resource exploitation activities. The prospectus also says that the company with the chief business of the company is sightseeing, tourism resource exploitation, scenery facility construction, tourism real-estate development, arts and crafts production and sales, investment, property management and so forth. The company, actually fully controlled by the county government, owns the exclusive right to exploit all the *tulou* cultural resources in the county area. However, a little probing has shown that tourism companies are by no means a new thing in the hilly region and that most of the tourist capital comes from the county urban areas.

The local people living in the four river valleys investigated in 2011 had no tourism companies of their own. Outsiders were allowed by the local government to establish travel agencies such as the one at Taxia in these settlements. Optimistically, these agencies might still offer the local people some economic opportunities, since the tourists brought there by the tourist guides might buy some souvenirs. Although the travel agencies do not pay the local people, they are required to pay taxes to the county government, thereby benefiting it financially. The only real worry hanging over their heads is the possibility of any change in the landscape panoramas. This anxiety is a reminder of what McCannell (1973) has said about the 'staged authenticity' of touristic attractions. He even states that the settings are actually contrived by providing 'the real thing' as free as air. Actually, what these companies care about is not the true 'authenticity' of the architecture, they are only interested in the fact that that has been authenticated as 'real' by the WHC. Ironically, only the authenticity that is 'staged' has become a touristic resource. Who has actually put it on the stage? The answer is that, after the WHC and other advisory organizations have carried out the authentication job at the sites, these places are prioritized by the government over most other sites of local significance. This situation provides just what the tourism companies want: a good reputation. The World Heritage treasures, in the name of humankind, are cared for by governments on all levels. They spend the taxpayers' income on the maintenance fees, carrying out site planning and whatever else is needed to preserve the architectural traits that ensure the buildings and structures continue to remain on the WHL, thereby maintaining their good reputation. Tourism companies do not need to pay a thing, even though they are indeed the real touristic resource developers. This has lowered their costs considerably. However, if the company is in fact run by the local government as the Yongding case shows, it is an indication that the local government is spending the taxpayers' money on maintaining a cultural resource that can reap them high rewards. Although investment from outside area might be welcomed, the major economic interests should be assigned to the government. Obviously the local government plays important roles in the following aspects:

- Through the implementation of the heritage laws and local regulations on heritage protection (Chapter 2), the local government is fully controlling the 'past' of the local people. At the WH sites, it has museumized the places (Chapter 3). At non-WH settlement places, it has still seized every chance to control the metabolization of the local built environment (Chapter 3).

- The local government has established cultural resource exploitation companies. Without any recourse to proper legal procedures, some settlement sites have already been used by the local government as tourist attractions. The whole process of the transformation of (tangible)

98. http://www.hakkatulou.com/about/xianqingjianjie.html.

space and (intangible) rights has been discussed in detail in Chapters 2 and 3. Unfortunately, by paraphrasing the doctrines set out in cultural heritage laws and regulations to suit its own purposes, it has become the arbiter of what is right and wrong (Chapter 3). Hence, heritage laws and regulations have to some extent become the legal basis supporting its demands on local cultural resources.

- Apart from assuming control of the cultural resources, the local government has also been demanding more land on which to build basic tourist facilities, such as hotels, restaurants, parking lots and so on. To improve hygiene and sanitary conditions for tourists, the local government and tourism companies have set limits on land-use in buffer zone areas (Chapter 2). By transforming the settlements into Hakka culture villages, the local government has in effect seized and monopolized the right to cultural resource exploitation.

Although the local government is obviously the real owner of the cultural resource exploitation vehicles, government officials and employees themselves have no rightful claim to the tourist incomes. Why therefore without any pecuniary incentive did they feel they had to play such a role in controlling the local cultural resource? There seems to be no direct, uncomplicated answer. Nonetheless, it is still possible for us to pick up some hints from the KPI government assessment criteria. Liu (2008) has suggested that efficiency in attracting investments, taxations, GDP, development of township-owned enterprises (*xiangzhen qiye*) is the most important indicator in assessing the capability of a county government. Liu's analyses were based on his investigations in 120 villages and sixty townships distributed over six provinces of China and, given the spread of the investigation, it is feasible that the result is both representative and reliable. In my view, the result, plus what I have personally experienced in rural China, does reflect the basic fact that economic efficiency is conventionally prioritized in the bureaucratic performance appraisal system. Double-checking with the official websites of the Nanjing County Government and the Yongding County Government, this view is confirmed by their statement of annual conclusions. Subject to the high pressure of the annual performance appraisal, local government officials have to prove their capacity for self-sustainability and their efficiency in managing the local resources. The upshot is that, in the heritage game, local governments play a decisive role in heritage management and utilization. They are the policy makers, the game players and also the embodiment of the urban power that competes with the local people for the exploitation of their cultural resources. It is noteworthy that in his criticism of the nomination of Fujian *tulou* World Heritage, Yan (2014) has pointed out that the nomination of this site was bureaucratically managed to within an inch of its life, and was in fact decided solely by a small number of county officials on the basis of their personal understanding (often misunderstanding) of World Heritage. Apart from potential economic benefits, the local government officials are also highly motivated by the lure of international prestige and the attraction of international tourists (Graburn, 2016).

4.2.4 Site Planners and Conservators

A site planner in the Chinese heritage protection context usually refers to a person or a team with expertise in heritage land zoning and making heritage preservation and management plans. A conservator usually refers to a person who can prolong the lifespan of archaeological sites, heritage buildings or moveable objects with cultural values. Sometimes they are the same group of professionals. In China, with few exceptions, site planners and conservators come from two sources. They can be the staff of state-sponsored (*shiye danwei*) scientific research institutions (*keyan jigou*) or sometimes they are just ordinary companies with a heritage protection qualification approved by the SACH. However, the boundary between the two kinds of practitioners is becoming blurred. The SACH usually allocates the funds for making protection plans and undertaking the conservation to the local governments. All the planners with the relevant qualifications are eligible to attend the bidding procedures for the protection of a specific heritage site organized by the local government (*zhengfu zhaobiao*). Hence in this instance, the site planners and conservators are in fact hired by the local governments to carry out heritage site planning and conservation jobs. At the same time, the local government might, as noted earlier, hire other people or relevant companies to make plans for exploiting the local cultural resources. Tourism planning, whose aim is to provide entertainment and diversion, is usually less concerned about the future security of the cultural resources. Indeed, local governments usually like to get tourism planning over and done with before the heritage pressure has been properly dealt with. Mixed land-use intentions and improperly arranged working procedures can give rise to conflicts between tourism planners and CR planners.[99] As discussed earlier, site planners and conservators might sometimes have to compromise on the preservation area or conservation approaches. Having said this, planners and conservators are both very important elements in heritage management in China. A baseline is that any further plan in terms of heritage use can only be ratified by the SACH on condition that the preservation plan has already been approved by experts it has commissioned. This might be the only bargaining chip the planners and conservators, whose position can be precarious, can use to curb the negative impacts of local government plans. After all, as they have been hired by the local governments to fulfill the tasks, their first duty is to serve the interests of the local governments and not upset the apple-cart.

4.2.5 The Local People

What role can the local people play in the heritage game? As I have stated, the local people are in fact the owners of the *tulou* houses, but are not necessarily the *de facto* beneficiaries of the cultural heritage. In its description of the relationship between cultural heritage and local communities, the *Aoi An Protocols for the Best Conservation Practice in Asia* says: 'Asian cultural landscapes are frequently inhabited and or cultivated by local populations; it is important that many of the tasks of conservation be given to these communities, with appropriate training and supervision, in order that they can consolidate their own heritage.' Noble though these intentions may be, it seems that in reality the local people's role is doomed to be limited to meeting preservation and conservation obligations, without asking what benefits they might get from their imposed duties. The *International Charter on Cultural Tourism* (1999)[100] only mentions that cultural tourism should benefit the host communities in passing. As the *Operational Guidelines* and many other relevant international policies have required, the local people should be invited to participate in the protection and conservation of their heritage. The crux of the problem is that also in the abovementioned transnational doctrines, the local residents in rural areas of Asia are usually described as backward, economically underdeveloped and, above all, with neither the motivation nor the techniques to conserve the buildings and objects with heritage values to a standard required by the national or international heritage regimes, and therefore they need help from experts. Although, on occasion the transnational regimes might indeed believe that it is the obligation of the experts in some places to enable the local people to become fully aware of the importance of 'their' heritage, the local government on the spot might just as easily take the earlier mentioned dogmatic and patronizing view as a scientific doctrine and order the experts to write innocuous remarks, both positive and negative, on the local cultural resource management work. Nevertheless, for the local government, the involvement of these experts who are supposed to promote the local people's awareness of heritage importance is quite a necessary corollary to building up the impression that the local government is standing shoulder to shoulder with the knowledge authorities. If the experts work purely for the purpose of preserving the heritage values, the local government might foster the hope that the heritage that has been judged by knowledge authorities to be authentic, complete and important can be used as evidence of the great past of the county that they govern, and therefore be transposed

---

99. In 2015, the Institute of Archaeology CASS helped the Qinghe local county government in Xinjiang Autonomous Region draw up a plan for preserving the stone circle religious sites in the Altai Mountains. However, before taking this step it had already asked a company to come up with a tourism plan. In the plan produced, the tourism planner had already decided to construct service facilities inside the site area. Apart from this, it also proposed a road along a nearby hillside that could disfigure the whole landscape.

100. http://www.icomos.org/charters/tourism_e.pdf.

into a kind administrative cultural capital that attracts more investment. Furthermore, as demonstrated in the Yongding company case, on a more ignoble note it might also want to exploit these cultural resources to improve its financial status. Nonetheless, albeit for different purposes, a local government and the experts might find themselves in the same boat. In the very first stage of the heritage game, the local people are to a large extent placed in opposition to their own inheritance. Sometimes, the local people can be unsure about whether the so-called buffer zone has been established for protecting the heritage or just for restricting them. In most cases, experts and local officials might both talk about the heritage continuity (*chuancheng*) but, despite their fine words, they cannot change their ingrained perception that the local people are both the property owners and the social group that might inflict direct negative impacts on the heritage.

This preamble leads to the first batch of questions that need to be asked: Who is eligible to maintain the property of the local people? Who has the power to authorize all kinds of experts to plan, re-plan, conserve and restore the buildings of the local peasants? The answer to both is surely the 'local governments'. This conclusion is made perfectly plain in Yan's article (2013), in which he refers to the power these bodies exercise: 'By manipulating particular forms of knowledge, authorities are able to claim legitimacy for their rule. Foucault's thesis on knowledge/power is evident in heritage conservation. Armed with the knowledge of heritage defined by the authorized heritage discourse, technical experts and governmental agencies are empowered to assert their superiority to identify and define innate values of heritage. In addition, the knowledge/power nexus is strongly associated with governmentality.'

In other words, when creating a backward image of the local rural population, the local government has adopted authenticity and integrity rules as the tools it can use to lever open the door of the local heritage world and local governments are adept at using the 'authorized heritage discourse' (Smith, 2006) to control the local cultural resources. However, there is no shadow of doubt that no transnational regulations exists that says that a local government or the company it controls has the exclusive right to exploit/develop the local people's ancestral inheritance (Chapter 2).

What capabilities do the local peasants have to possess if they are to play the heritage game, and do they already have these capabilities under their belt? What advantages and disadvantages do the local people have when playing the heritage game? Turning first to the advantageous aspects: first and foremost the local people are the heirs to the *tulou* houses and any other ancestral inheritance. Obviously the most fundamental right they have to defend is: the right to be compensated from the use of 'their' heritage. Furthermore, let it be understood that, unlike the situations foreseen in the transnational documents, the local people in the southern Fujian hilly region are well equipped with a knowledge of home maintenance. Although the younger generations are not keen to learn house-building and maintenance techniques, there are still many middle-aged and elderly people who are actively involved in house construction and helping others with maintenance work. Turning now at the disadvantageous aspects, the first that strikes the eye is that, although they are the owners of their houses, the local people do not have the ownership of the land on which their dwellings are built. The land of a settlement is usually owned by a collective economic organization (*jingji jiti zuzhi*). This makes it impossible for any single individual to influence the use of the entire space of the settlement by purchasing or selling land. Nonetheless, there is a real danger that this concept of collective ownership could put excessive power in the hands of the local cadres, who might subsequently decide in the name of the Village Committee the use of some parts of the land. In Chapter 3, I have discussed the case of the Fujian *tulou* settlements. On the basis of its collective ownership, the *de facto* use-right of the entire settlement space was in effect completely transferred to heritage and tourism use, even though the people still live there and could continue their cultivation undisturbed. Ownership issues do not stop here. They also affect the ordinary villagers who already rent some parts of the collectively owned land for tourism use. As Liu *et al.* (2015) have reported, in one central Fujian village, young people rented the land of the township and built a B & B hotel, *Jizhi Shanzhuang*, for the reception of tourists. Several years later, they had become rich and the assets they built up are now worth tens of thousands of RMB *yuan*. The earlier small hotel has become a garden resort. They have even developed a museum of lion culture. However, the land that is now used as a resort was in fact designated agricultural land by law. If it is still recognized as agricultural land or another type of land still related to agricultural uses, this asset development is illegal. If it is recognized as land for non-agriculture uses, land bidding procedures will have to be reinitiated, and the young people might lose out on the bidding. Should this happen, the set-back will dampen the peasants' enthusiasm for developing their own tourism business. This case, taken in conjunction with the previous analysis, aptly demonstrates the major problems with which an ordinary peasant can be confronted should he want to use the collectively owned land to develop his own small business. Compared to the difficulties in land circulation affecting single rural individuals, it is much easier for the local government that governs the rural economic units on all levels to redefine the land-use functions. In my own experiences, the local government can choose to circulate some land for other agricultural or non-agriculture purposes. Especially, when a local government is seeking out opportunities to attract investment from the outside, it might give the developers and investors preferential treatment, the right to use the land at little charge in particular. Obviously, the *tulou* tourism cases must have involved redefinitions of the land-use functions, that single *tulou* residents must have seen as an almost impossible mountain to climb. In fact, it must have loomed as a nigh on impossible undertaking because, proposing a necessary change in the use function of a specific land is usually a task assigned to the county land resource bureau. The local government can and does decide changes in land-use functions and once the decision has been made, it asks the bureau to report the changes to upper higher authorities for approval. At the other end of the spectrum, single rural individuals are almost inevitably deprived of these administrative advantages. For all these reasons, I view the touristic use of Yongding rural settlement lands over the past ten years as a kind of centralized government operation. In the Yongding *tulou* cases, the most outstanding feature has been the competition for *tulou* resource between the Yongding county government and the local rural residents.

No big company like that in Yongding has ever been established by the Nanjing county government. Compared to the Yongding county's *tulou* operation, the use of *tulou* resources in the rural area of Nanjing county is very decentralized. The Tianluokeng World Heritage site is a good example of this sort of discrepancy. In 2010, the local government decided to use part of the ticket income to reward the local *tulou* residents[101] (Tan and Zhang, 2010). Once this decision had been made it launched plans to design a new commercial street for the local people. Its purpose was to mitigate the tourist pressure in the core zone area and to provide the *tulou* residents with a better place in which to do business. For obvious reasons, it is not possible to estimate the monthly income of a local household. However, it is clear that, owing in a large part to the loose control over the Tianluokeng *tulou* resource, the local people might sincerely desire to embrace their *tulou* buildings and be highly motivated to protect them. The situation in Tianluokeng forms a sharp contrast to that in Yongding and, although they both involve the same sort of settlement, they are literally miles apart.

4.3 HERITAGE SITE AS A PLACE OF CULTURAL RESOURCE GAME

Heritage tourism is in fact a newly developed area in China's economy, one that only began in the late 1990s. Since time immemorial, the urban-rural dichotomy between a walled urban county seat and its rural areas has been a fact-of-life in Chinese history. However, now the winds of change are blowing and over the past twenty years, owing to long-term resource extraction by the urban centers, in many respects China's rural areas have been exhibiting symptoms of exhaustion. All their important natural and social resources have for centuries served the interests of China's urban areas. Aware of this divide and wanting to narrow the gap between the

101. http://paper.people.com.cn/zgjjzk/html/2010-01/25/content_436770.htm.

industrialized urban areas and the agricultural rural areas, at the Fourth Plenary Session of the Sixteenth Central Committee of the Communist Party of China (September 16, 2004), the central government put forward the idea that, 'industry should foster agriculture and cities should support rural areas'. Likewise, the Politburo meeting of the Communist Party held on April 30, 2015, re-emphasized that the stance that the *Property Law* should protect private enterprises has not changed and, furthermore, apart from the property rights of private entrepreneurs, the property of each household and the interests of each individual citizen should also be protected by that law. Also at this meeting, the Politburo Standing Committee reviewed the social development over the past several years and took special note of the widening gap between China's urban and rural areas. Its deliberations led it to reach the succinct conclusion that the government authorities should immediately stop competing with the people for profits and that any types of resource plundering and serious resource extraction should be suspended. In my view this meeting marks a very important milestone in China's political history. Although it skimmed around touching on any sensitive land ownership topics, it did highlight the importance of legislation and the spirit of the contract. It clearly reflects that the central government is already fully aware of the fact that public power has long been abusive in its exploitation of the resources of the people. Not to put too fine a point on it, the immediate urban threats competing with the local peasants for their cultural resources might even be being posed by the nearby county government authorities.

As I have discussed in this chapter, heritage in present-day China has become a crucial cultural resource. The SACH (2009) has ordained that in the first place heritage parks, museums and other themed cultural spaces in the urban areas should serve the needs of the city-dwellers. Urban development and redevelopment have given rise to a number of Chinese heritage parks, such as the Daming Palace Site Park, the Sui and Tang Luoyang City Site Park and the Jinsha Site Park in Chengdu. All these site parks have been established as part of an urban redevelopment. At least in the examples mentioned we can see a clear relationship between the site and its users. They, together with other kinds of parks and museums, constitute the major public cultural spaces of urban China, particularly in large such provincial capital cities as Xi'an, Luoyang, Beijing and Nanjing (capital of Jiangsu province). In other words, they are, first and foremost, the public cultural resource of the city-dwellers. In 2012, the Ministry of Housing and Urban-Rural Development (MHUD) issued the *Code for Classification of Urban Land-use and Planning Standards of Development Land* (GB 50137-2011) (*Chengshi Yongdi Fenlei yu Guihua Jianshe Yongdi Biaozhun*).[102] These urban heritage parks can be divided into at least two categories of land-use function, namely: G1. park and green land and A7. cultural relics and historical sites, including archaeological sites, ancient burials, ancient architecture, grottoes-temples, modern buildings from the contemporary past, memorials and monuments that commemorate China's revolutions. In their category as the major land resource for providing public services, either the cultural departments (*wenwuju*) or the bureaus of parks and forestry (*yuanlinju*) can assume the care of these public service land resources on behalf of the government. Indubitably this land is owned by the state, and used by the government on behalf of the Chinese people. The ownership, use-right, duties of the managers relating to the use of heritage parks in urban areas are all very clear. Unlike this cut-and-dried situation in urban China, no cultural resource category is clearly defined in the *Rural Land-use and Planning Guidelines* (*Nongcun Yongdi Guihua Fenlei Zhinan*) issued by the MHUD in 2014.[103] Actually this reveals that the critical fact that cultural reserves cannot be viewed as a basic land-use function in rural China. In the past sixty years or so, China's rural areas have been considered as the 'rear service suppliers' of urban areas by the government. Therefore, any land-use functions beyond agricultural purposes are very likely dismissed as superfluous. Heritage land-use undoubtedly does not fit in with this stereotype. The problem is compounded because the flexibility of what land-use patterns there are in the countryside does not allow for any immutable expectations.

102. www.mohurd.gov.cn/wjfb/201407/W020140716110637.doc.

103. http://www.mohurd.gov.cn/zcfg/jsbwj_0/jsbwjczghyjs/201407/t20140716_218493.html.

Furthermore, as they have not been classified as essential land-use patterns, the obligations and rights of the users, managers and *de facto* collective owners of cultural spaces in rural areas are usually rather ambiguous. In all the laws relating to rural land management, it is emphasized that the land in China's rural areas belongs to the economic collective organizations (*jingji jiti zuzhi*, abbreviated to *jiti*) not the individuals. This has determined that the local cultural resource in whatever form on the peasants' land is also largely affected or even, in many cases, directly managed by the collective organizations not the individuals. As noted previously, a peasant can claim the ownership of his house but not the land on which he has built it, but it is the *jiti* that has the power to decide how to manage and use each field it administers. The separation of ownership and use-right, as I have demonstrated in previous chapters, provides the collective cadres and county officials with an opportunity to transfer the use-right, indeed the whole historical settlement area to the cultural development companies such as the one run by Yongding county in one fell swoop. Theoretically, this transfer effectively evades the contradictions between ownership and use-right. Although, as they still do have some direct influence on land-use patterns, peasants can continue to cultivate their land and live in their homes, the whole settlement landscape has already effectively been transformed into a tourist attraction in the name of heritage protection. Therefore, without breaching the peasants' land-use-right to the bulk of their land, the local power-holders impose additional land-use functions on 'their' land. I would argue that the rural cultural resource in terms of vernacular or tradition buildings is first and foremost the property of the local people. In an analysis of the case studies of culture villages in Malaysia, Dellios (2002) points out:

> *Museumification is a process whilst originating in the museum is not confined by it. In the interpretive medium of museumification, everything is a potential 'artifact'—entire villages, or abstractions such as 'ethnicity' and 'nation', or human beings. Yet, reality cannot be represented: museumification distorts inverts and subverts meanings.*

In these cases, all the local people's lives, farming activities, festival performances and so forth have already been subsumed into the village theme representation (a cultural and touristic resource), that fills the coffers of the tourist companies. These inconsistencies are not limited to the Fujian culture villages, but are myriad, particularly in the areas of China's minorities. Rural cultural resource, as the analyses of many scholars have shown (Sun, 2005), usually refers not only to the tangible heritage but also the intangible, running the gamut from the fine arts, performing arts, oral traditions, crafts, local flavors, special farm produce, ceremonies, costumes and even languages (Zheng, 2014). In the eyes of the cultural resource development companies, the high value of rural cultural resources lies in the fact that they are quite different from the urban cultures, particularly the metropolitan cultures. This also explains why we almost invariably come across mentions of authenticity and integrity in the statements of the local officials. In this instance, they are not talking about the key concepts of the UNESCO but are referring to a kind of cultural diversity that can be used for making money. In this heritage game, the local people are viewed as nothing more nor less than cultural goods providers and the situation is not improving. In recent years, local governments in China have been paying more attention to what is referred to as the 'cultural industry' (*wenhua chanye*). Local government officials usually live in hope that more attractions can be found in their rural areas. They think highly of the cultural resource planners, because these people are able to identify even more local cultural resources that will add to the value of their area. This begs the question: If the explicit aim of an urban heritage site is to be of service to society and its development (Dellios, 2002), who do the cultural villages ultimately serve? In a heritage game, if a local government is the final winner, who are the ultimate losers?

In an urban context, the heritage space is usually created separately from any other kinds of spaces, for example, residential areas or commercial streets. In 2012, the MHUD issued *Current Regulations on Urban Parks and Woods*. In this document, the MHUD defines urban parks, green fields and all kinds of public cultural facilities as public properties. It states that it is the duty of the local government with the assistance of a slice of its income to support and finance the development of these public spaces. Although in these urban cases, there is a clearly defined governmental duty in terms of resource maintenance, out in the countryside it is a different matter. In a rural settlement, it is assumed that the entire physical setting has to be included in the cultural representation if an appropriate atmosphere in which to showcase a culture different to that of the urban centers is to be created. This expectation results in a 100 percent spatial overlap between a settlement's today and its past. I would argue that, if the local government has used the local people's property in whatever form to generate tourist income, the property itself should be legally regarded as cultural property or a cultural resource, regardless of whether or not it is a WH site. The majority of the present-day problems affecting the use of peasants' property as a cultural resource seem to derive from unfair rules of the game and the inadequate protection of peasants' interests.

4.4 DUTIES, RIGHTS AND COMPENSATIONS IN THE HERITAGE GAME

It seems that, although local people are consistently linked to their roles in heritage preservation and building maintenance, little has been said how they can benefit from the use of their inheritance. In fact, this right has not been fully considered in Chinese legislation. In 2013, the-then Director of the SACH, Li Xiaojie, told the reporters from the *People's Daily* that articles specifying compensation issues would be incorporated into the existing heritage laws. This move had been prompted by some scholars in China who had proposed that the law should be concerned with to providing compensation opportunities to the local people who 'may be negatively influenced by the public authorities when executing their obligations in the name of laws' (Si, 2005). In 2016, the State Council issued an important policy document, *Guidelines for Improving Cultural Heritage Management* (*Guowuyuan guanyu Jinyibu Jiaqiang Wenwu Gongzo de Zhidao Yijian*).[104] This document also points out the necessity of compensation: 'It is necessary to legislate on compensation issues arising from the preservation of cultural heritage. The proposed articles should protect a citizen's or an organization's right to gain reasonable compensation for any loss resulting from cultural heritage preservation.'

Talking about the cultural resource owned by individuals, the spokesman representing the SACH, Zhu Xiaodong, said (Deng, 2016):[105]

> *Privately-owned buildings and structures account for a high proportion of China's cultural heritage resource. Some of them are even designated as preservation sites. However, because they are owned by individuals not by the public, the owners of such buildings and structures are not eligible to apply for any financial support from the governments. However, their personal or household properties have already been recognized as the goals of heritage protection. Central and local governments can only provide funds for preserving and conserving state-owned built heritage. For all such reasons, built heritage owned by individuals are usually exposed to the threats; many of them are really dilapidated, damaged or even totally demolished. We (the SACH) are now going to establish a grant through donations and other possible means to protect such privately-owned built heritage.*

These statements seem to hint that that the rationale of the SACH is to seek funding sources for designated[106] yet privately owned built heritage. However, the truth is that only a very small number of privately owned buildings and structures have been designated as preservation sites. To take *tulou* buildings as an example, there are over 3,000 *tulou* buildings dispersed throughout southwestern Fujian, but only thirty-five single buildings have been designated as preservation sites. Most of the undesignated, privately owned buildings exhibiting typical cultural values are also very likely cultural resources heavily exploited by the urban centers. When thinking about this problem, we should be fully aware of the fact that a privately owned built heritage is well-protected does not automatically

104. http://www.gov.cn/zhengce/content/2016-03/08/content_5050721.htm.

105. http://news.cri.cn/20160401/ddc97dc3-98ce-1f1d-7680-f38fe20b65bb.html.

106. Designated as preservation sites on county, provincial and state level.

lead to the protection of the residents' economic and cultural rights. Nevertheless, there are two possibilities in which payment compensation is absolutely necessary. The first of these, as Zhu has commented, is when the local people's life has been negatively affected by preservation activities. That is to say, they have had to sacrifice part of their own interests in order to preserve the heritage for the public. Suchlike situations have been recognized by the SACH since 2015 and so far have mainly concerned the demolition of houses in the core and buffer zones and a limitation set on the mass and height of personal buildings in the buffer zones, a directive that involves the partial loss of a person's right to construct. I have discussed this situation specifically in the Hekeng case in Chapters 2 and 3, but applies to most designated personal built heritage. The second possibility is that their inheritance is used by someone else in order to make money. In other words, the use-right to the settlement land has been transferred to other individuals or organizations. Quite unequivocally, the owners of the built heritage should have the right to share the income resulting from the use of their personal properties and this entitlement is applicable to both designated and undesignated[107] private built heritage. In both situations, the private owners of the built heritage should be compensated in some way. At the moment it can be argued that the designated built heritage owned by the local people still accounts for only a very limited proportion of the total, as most of the houses with high cultural values are still unprotected. As I discussed in the Preface, nothing is destined to be preserved and protected. Lacking preservation funding, that seems to be the magic wand to 'rejuvenate' the old buildings, no one, including the SACH, is able to stop the metabolization processes on such undesignated yet highly-valued vernacular built inheritance, that includes nearly 95 percent of the *tulou* buildings. When it is all said and done, spontaneous metabolization has been an ongoing process throughout the history of any settlement anyway and will never stop until the settlement lands have been fully redeveloped and modernized. Under these circumstances, the preservation of the buildings as specimens, their use as tourist attractions and the improvement of the adaptability of the old architecture to modern use constitute the only three reasons that will underpin the continued existence of undesignated *tulou* or other types of vernacular buildings for the future. Each of these reasons can generate or involve some essential duties and rights.

4.4.1 The Preservation of Old Architecture as Specimens for the Public

The three basic game players in this situation include the state (the SACH), the owners of built heritage and the local government.

As discussed in Chapters 2 and 3, the first step in the preservation of old buildings and structures owned by the local residents as heritage places involves a transfer of land-use-right. Unfortunately, as noted earlier, in contrast to the procedures in urban situations, preservation of the built heritage in rural China is not one of the essential legitimate land-use functions, and to some extent is even still partially incompatible with the existing laws and regulations on land-use in rural China. This presents

107. My own experience has taught me that the majority of vernacular buildings and structures in a traditional settlement are usually still in a state of metabolic process. These architectures are of esthetic value and usually constitute the settings of the built environment of settlements, but they are also undeniably the dwellings of the local people and can rarely be transformed into any type of public space. By their very nature, they are private spaces. Having not been designated a heritage of the country, they are not, even in theory, the subject to CRM practice (Chapter 3). Importantly the number of such architectures is huge. On the grounds of private ownership and funding, they cannot be easily designated as heritage attractions and this means that the major proportion of the past is still at large within the grasp of CRM practitioners. I would argue that in most vernacular settlement heritage at present, these architectures constitute the most important part. They serve as a heritage pool and can provide heritage attractions for designation and registration. However, the loss of the traditional traits of these private buildings and structures as they succumb to metabolic degradation or physical destruction could lead directly to the loss of the potential objects we want to protect. (Largely attributable to the declining settlement economy and the loss of traditional wood carving, matting and construction skills, the restoration work done by the local communities themselves is usually of very poor quality. In fact, the metabolic process of these architectures only leads to 'decaying'). Therefore, it should be a very important task of the CR managers, on behalf of the local government, to negotiate with the local people and persuade them to control the changes in a manageable way.

the SACH that assumes the major responsibility for looking after World Heritage in rural China with some problems. The knottiest of these is how should we define the relationship between the state and the heritage house residents? Interviews with the local people reveal that they have always believed that it was the state (*guojia* or *gongjia*) that was planning to use their houses. Occasionally they have also referred to the local government as representative of the state. Therefore, in the eyes of a local resident, both the SACH and the local government might stand for the state, from which they can ask for compensation. On the part of the state, I find it very interesting that no one in the SACH or in academic conservation circles views heritage preservation as a kind of land-use. In the past sixty years or so, one widespread idea has been that it should be viewed as a peasant's duty and honor to protect any heritage so designated by the state. An ambiguous relationship between the state and the built heritage owners, largely founded on morality, has replaced the *de facto* legal relationships based on a clear definition in the rights and duties between the state and the rural property owners. Under the terms of the *General Principles of the Civil Law* (1986) (*Minfa Tongze*), legal relations refer to the relationship of duty and rights between legal subjects (individuals or entities). Undoubtedly, *tulou* houses and any other type of personal property in architectural form constitute the 'legal objects' defined by the *Civil Law*. Two essential facts have also served to build up the relationship between the legal subjects, namely: the house owners, and the legal objects, namely: the *tulou* houses. Firstly, the local *tulou* residents, for example, own and use the buildings. Secondly, their regular or irregular maintenance activities have helped to preserve the built heritage designated by the SACH, given the fact that the aim of this body acting on behalf of the central government is to preserve World Heritage for the future generations. Therefore, it is undeniable that, as the *de facto* legal subject, the SACH, has already benefited from the local WH *tulou* residents. Even without any form of contract or agreement between the two subject sides, it is still possible to determine that the factual relationship concerning the use of *tulou* houses between them are still legal relations. Under the *Civil Law*, both the SACH and local government, or even local cultural authorities, can represent the interests of the state. Consequently, preservation use should be determined as a factual use activity that has already occurred on WH heritage sites. Consequently, it should be the local government or the SACH that compensates the *de facto* loss of the heritage owners that is the outcome of heritage preservation, new zoning activities and museumification.

Secondly, apart from preservation, local people's maintenance obligations should also constitute a reasonable nexus linking the state and the local *tulou* residents. As analyzed in Chapters 2 and 3, unlike other vernacular buildings in courtyard forms, the *tulou* buildings are generally well protected by their outer walls, but the metabolic rate of the more exposed superstructures of these shelters is actually fairly similar to that of courtyard buildings. As stable vernacular buildings, they do not need to be renovated regularly, but day-to-day maintenance and the substitution of elements of the superstructures like tiles and rafters might be very necessary. Traditionally,[108] local artisans are the most suitable persons to take charge of conserving their own architecture. Their former role in the settlements was not simply to restore but to prolong the lifespan of the architecture. Safeguarding the residences has always been important in the past. The local builders constructed, repaired, protected and sometimes rebuilt. They were an indispensible part of the 'life' of the *tulou* buildings. As noted earlier in Chapter 3, most of the twentieth-generation male settlement

108. According to the oral history widespread among the settlements of Shuyang township, during the Qing dynasty when round *tulou* architectures gained popularity in the rural areas of Nanjing, the early artisans who helped to build these round *tulou* buildings were invited separately from Yongding, Shanghang and Dabu. In the *Nanjingxian diming lu*, or *An Atlas of Nanjing County*, artisans from Yongding already had a good reputation for their skill in ramming earth, Shanghang craftsmen were adept at masonry work and Dabu workmen were invited to tile the roofs. This evidence implies the round *tulou* construction projects in rural areas of Shuyang township (in which Hekeng is located) were probably funded by the clans/lineages but directed and undertaken by the artisans invited from the abovementioned places. Yongding has been well known for huge round *tulou* buildings since the late 17th century (early Qing dynasty). It is therefore not a surprise that the majority of artisans were invited from Yongding county. Their contribution was the standardization of the round *tulou* building construction procedures to a large extent.

members had participated in the construction of the round *tulou* buildings between the late 1940s and the early 1980s. Over the past thirty years, the techniques, particularly such complicated procedures as 'ramming earth using two-headed sticks' and 'firing bamboo nails into sands', have teetered on the verge of dying out. Ceremonies practiced before, during and after the construction of *tulou* buildings are now also rarely performed. In the past ten years, the local craftsmen were hired only once by the local government, namely: to repair buildings for the 2007 WHL nomination, and were paid a very low salary for their work. Despite their major role in scientific preservation treatments, conservators only seem to take steps to conserve the *tulou* buildings when they are so seriously damaged it threatens to lead to the loss of OUV attributes. The long and the short of it is that the bulk of the practical work in building maintenance is done by the local people themselves and their efforts have already undeniably helped the SACH and the local government preserve the *tulou* heritage. On balance, it should be the state's role to pay the local people for their maintenance services. Basically, the SACH and the local government acting on behalf of the state should purchase the land use-right from the local peasants to make the area a better place for preserving the cultural heritage for future generations.

4.4.2 The Use of Old Architecture as Tourist Attractions

The situation described above mainly involves the local residents, the local government and tourist resource development companies. As demonstrated in Chapter 3, WH sites can bring in large profits. These benefits are not limited to ticket income. In the Yongding case it is obvious that Yongding county also built up its reputation as 'the home of Hakka *tulou* mansions' by using the WH and the non-WH *tulou* settlements as a kind of 'cultural goods' and as an advertisement for the country, potentially attracting more outside investment. Likewise, the tourist resource development companies also share these sorts of economic benefits with the local governments.

In urban China, the best-known land resource development company in recent years has been the Qujiang Development Group based in Xi'an. As noted earlier, the Qujiang Group has accumulated a huge amount of money by developing the tenured land at the outskirts of Xi'an city. It usually prefers places in rural areas in which a famous historical site is located nearby. Its attitude demonstrates the truth of assumption that the high reputation of a place can also lead directly to an increase in the value of real-estate built in the adjacent area. It sums up its development methods in the slogan 'the Qujiang model'. Obviously, if they are used like this, cultural landscapes are a good excuse to raise the price of real-estate. Embracing the same sort of philosophy, the county-led Yongding tourist resource development company has also sought to manage not only its *tulou* attractions but also much of the surrounding land resources to construct hotels, resorts and villas. Besides the income it derives from its use of the peasants' land, it has branched out into new brands of cultural goods, such as Hakka cuisine. Consequently, capital accumulation has now been taken a step farther and is being boosted by using the cultural heritage in diverse ways. Be that as it may, there is no way around the fact that all such additional values are actually attached to the existence of *tulou* settlements. As the principal beneficiary of local cultural resource development, the company has undeniably used the local people's assets in many ways. I would argue that in this case a *tulou* should also be viewed as a kind of intangible asset.[109] If my assertion is correct, who is eligible to use such an intangible asset (*wuxing zichan*), that is, the *tulou* name, fame, brand, architectural design and many other local products with a potential intellectual copyright? By transferring the use-right to the rural land, the local government working hand-in-glove with the company it runs has also obtained the use-right to the intangible assets of the local residents. Under **Article 31** of *Enterprise Accounting Standards*

109. An intangible asset in the West is an asset that is not physical in nature. Corporate intellectual property (items such as patents, trademarks, copyrights, business methodologies), goodwill and brand recognition are all common intangible assets in today's marketplace. An intangible asset can be classified as either indefinite or definite depending on the specifics of that asset. A company brand name is considered to be an indefinite asset, as it stays with the company as long as the company continues operations. (http://www.businessdictionary.com/definition/intangible-asset.html.)

(issued in 2006 and amended in 2014), intangible assets in China refer to patents, special non-patent techniques, trademarks, copyrights, land-use-right and business reputation. In short, an intangible is something indefinable yet profitable. Under **Article 8** of *A Notice on the Issuance of the Annotation of the 'Items of Sales Tax* (draft) (*Guojia Shuiwuju Guanyu Yinfa Yingyeshui Shuimu Zhushi de Tongzhi*)'[110] (State Administration of Taxation), a transfer of an intangible asset is the transfer of the ownership or use-right to the immaterial assets. This document also lays down that a transfer of a land-use-right is to permit the transferee enterprise to develop, use and manage a piece of land. As has been emphasized throughout this thesis, although the land in rural China belongs to economic collective organizations, it is usually the local county government (for example, *xian guotu ziyuanju*, or *xian tudiju*, county bureau of land resource management) that exercises full control of the use-right to the land in county territory. Hence, in order to gain the use-right of a certain area of county land, a tourist resource development company only need to persuade the officials of local government to transfer the use-right to the land it wants to it. As noted previously, 'attracting investment' (*zhaoshang yinzi*) is usually a desideratum in a local government annual performance appraisal. As discussed in Chapters 2 and 3, the 'overall tourist resource development' in the rural area of Yongding county had partially transferred the land use-right of the local people to the company, in the process also grabbing the right to use many local people's intangible assets at no cost. All that has been left for the local villagers is usually the chance to run stalls inside their *tulou* houses or on the newly built commercial street away from the settlement (Zhang, 2007). The situation reminds us of the basic principle of PPG 16 implemented in the UK. In short, it should be the persons who obtain the benefits that who pay for the preservation of the heritage. In other words, if local people's houses are used as tourist attractions, compensation should include first and foremost the following: a rent for using local people's houses as tourist attractions (ticket-income sharing); expenditure for maintaining and conserving the cultural resource (calculated in consultation with the local people and conservation experts); reimbursement for the loss of industry, farm produce and deteriorating housing conditions for receiving visitors (Zhang, 2014); rent for using images of the *tulou*, related Hakka cultural expressions or any other intangible assets in tourism advertisements; compensation for using the land (previously occupied or used by local people) to built tourism facilities, hotels, parking lots and so forth; cost of supporting local people to renovate and use adaptively or reuse their houses (see below); cost for population relocation (if applicable).

110. http://www.doc88.com/p-775863691705.html.

Owing largely to the separation of land ownership and use-right in rural China, tourism compensation is usually very controversial. Both the local governments and tourist resource development companies desire to maximize their own interests in the heritage game at the price of reducing the budget for reimbursing the local residents. The *Zhonghua Renmin Gongheguo Tudi Chengbaofa* (Law on the Contracting of Rural Land of the People's Republic of China) decrees that the village committee has the right to sign a contract with developers from outside the collective on behalf of the villagers for the transference of the use-right of piece of land under the following conditions:

Article 47 In the event that rural land is contracted through other means, members of the economic organizations of the collectives of the land shall enjoy priority to operation right under the same conditions.

Article 48 If the contract-letting party contracting its land to units or individuals that do not belong the economic organization of the said collectives, the contract shall have met in advance the consent of at least two-thirds of the members of the village assembly or of the representatives of villagers, and the contract shall be submitted to the people's government of the township (town) for approval. In the case that land is contracted to units or individuals that do not belong to the economic organization of the said collectives, the contract-taking party's credit and operation capability shall be examined before the establishment of the contract.

These articles indicate: (a) in principle the local people do take precedence in the exploitation of the cultural resources; and (b) by law, any decision on a land-use transfer should be made in full consultation with the local villagers first. There should have been some kind of contractual relationship drawn up between the Yongding villagers and the tourist resource development company. Furthermore, this contract should have been signed by the committees of the villages involved and the company. A double check with the model contract on line, this document usually specifies the following points: the area of land, new land-use functions, duration of agreement, rental, and rights and duties. The good news is that it is possible for the local people to protect their own rights through contracts and negotiation with the developers from outside. However, I do not think any contract signed between local people and a company has already included these seven points to be used in the calculation of compensation.

4.4.3 Improvement of the Adaptability of the Old Structures to Modern Use

'All too often our conservation and adaptive reuse projects compromise aspects of authenticity of a heritage property, such as its original use (e.g., the conversion of a religious building into pubs and restaurants), spatial layout (*e.g.* the construction of high-rise buildings inside a low-rise historic precinct) or traditional materials (*e.g.* replacing traditional lime-based with cement-based renders). These interventions usually have negative impacts on the spirit of place.' (*Aoi An Protocols: for Best Conservation Practice in Asia*)

'Wherever possible, existing historic building stock should be conserved, upgraded and reused in sympathetic ways. The focus should be on assisting residents of properties to continue residential use. Continued residential use may not always be feasible or desirable, and former housing stock may need to be adapted for commercial or community use. This must not be done at the cost of displacement of populations and homogenization or commercialization of originally diverse precincts.' (*Aoi An Protocols: for Best Conservation Practice in Asia*)

'Rehabilitation: The modification, including adaptive re-use, of resources to meet various functional requirements such as safety, property protection and access while preserving the historic character of the structure.' (*Aoi An Protocols: for Best Conservation Practice in Asia*)

The articles cited above make it abundantly clear that adaptation and rehabilitation are both viewed as important strategies by which to encourage local people to continue to live inside their old buildings and thereby retain the authenticity of architecture. Who should pay for such renovations and who should look after the projects?

As demonstrated in Chapter 2, a renovation that would meet present-day standard of living requirements might involve the use of new materials, changes in structures and new additions to existing room fixtures. Once again, it should be the residents who benefit from the use of the buildings involved. In 2016, the SACH announced that the individuals or entities who are planning to maintain or renovate the heritage houses need no longer require a qualification certificate, unless the architecture in question has been designated as a national preservation building. I would argue that this event could be an indication that: (a) more peasant workers will participate in the maintenance of designated buildings; (b) the authenticity principle might give way to the consideration of amenities; (c) designated personal or household property might receive more finance from non-governmental sources; (d) private capital might play an more influential role in the conservation and use of vernacular buildings with historical and cultural values, especially that architecture the SACH is not able to look after; (e) under the aegis of the tourism economy, adaptive use or re-use will become very popular in these rural villages.

The rural villages of China endowed with cultural resources have been transformed into places of heritage game competition over the past ten years. The SACH, WHC, local governments, tourism developers and local residents are the players involved in this complex game. In the Shaanxi, Yongding and Hekeng cases, each has tried to preserve its own interests in the use of local people's land resources. Sometimes they have coalesced, sometimes conflicted, sometimes contrived with the latter. The foregoing analysis reveals quite explicitly that China's laws and regulations on land ownership in rural areas tend to favor the local collectives and governments on whatever level. Nevertheless, it is unfair to ascribe all the local people's difficulties to the local government. In view of the fact that the tourist revenue might account for a high proportion of the county financial income, it is conceivable that the government might choose to spend some of it on improving the local environment and other necessary management costs.

In the long run, a kind of equilibrium can be reached between all the game players. If this desirable state of affairs it to be achieved, three conditions are extremely relevant to the future use of the peasants' heritage. Firstly, it will be necessary to regulate the rights and duties connected to the use of local people's houses and land. This should be enshrined in great detail in the form of contract between the local people and developers. Secondly, it will require that the local government stop being shareholders in any touristic resource development project and participate only as an independent overseer making sure that each game player can fulfill his obligations by following the letter of the contract scrupulously. Thirdly, it is quite natural that building maintenance and conservation companies should play a very positive role in preserving the undesignated or underfinanced past, if tourism development can provide enough financial support. In my view, in response to the central government's call for a contractual spirit, the SACH is loosening its control on the built heritage in rural China. Although a number of historical and cultural villages have been designated by the SACH and MHUD, the preservation and protection of such a village heritage might now rely fully on the local government's financial support. The underlying reason is that the number of state-sponsored conservation institutes is quite limited. Lacking manpower and financial support, the SACH can only look after the most important heritage buildings and structures. The metaphor 'heritage game' that has haunted this chapter is actually a reference to the complicated relationships between the stakeholders. In the future, a new built heritage management system might need be initiated by ensuring the creation of a more reasonable relationship between the four stakeholders, namely: the local residents, the local government and *tulou* companies, the SACH and professional planners and conservators. An agreement between them seems to offer the best chance of them being able to reach a practical equilibrium of interests.

5. Suggestions

In Chapter 4, I defined five fundamental stakeholders that are the contestants in the heritage games played out in association with the use of local Hakka people's houses and lands in southern Fujian, namely: the local communities, the SACH (on behalf of the state), the WHC, local government (the state), tourism resource developers plus site planners and conservators. As mentioned previously, the majority of the present-day problems to do with built-heritage preservation and use in southwestern Fujian have arisen principally from the lack of specification and inconsistency in the laws and regulations governing the management of rural land resource. In this chapter, I shall offer these game players some recommendations.

5.1 SUGGESTIONS FOR MANAGING THE HEKENG TULOU HERITAGE SITE

The results of my 2014 research in the local communities suggest the possibility that more people will leave behind their old valley home for a new settlement nearby.[111] The most obvious effect of this demographic change is that it could conceivably pose a considerable threat to the museumized built-environment as the latter would be deprived of regular maintenance. Faced with a seriously depopulated and highly museumized settlement, more often than not the site managers will soon keenly feel their investors breathing down their necks. As the latter live in hope of a sound reward on their investment, the voice of experience warns that this might be the most risky moment at which to make wrong decisions, especially any to do with the construction of tourism service buildings and facilities. Before matters spin out of hand in this small river valley, I would like to offer the local communities and the site managers the following suggestions.

5.1.1 Agreement among Stakeholders

An agreement among the stakeholders in the form of a contract as noted above will prove extremely important to the local residents in the protection of their own heritage rights. Not only might it determine the roles of the stakeholders in the upcoming management of the valley heritage, it could also help in establishing the logic of heritage use in a mutually beneficial way (see below).

5.1.2 Landscape Biography as Site Interpretation

Sadly so far the local site managers have not been fully aware of the importance of site interpretation to any future management work in this region. Information that can be used to write the complete landscape biography of settlement in this region is usually fragmented and quite limited. The danger that looms largest is that different researchers from different academic backgrounds could all descend upon the place, bringing with them a host of diverse critical tasks. The crux of the problem is that what each and every one is pursuing cannot be used to piece together a relatively complete scenario pertinent to any specific individual settlement. The core of the difficulty lies in the methodologies they have embraced and applied in their research; these reveal no more than a sample of what there is to find and the subsequent fragmentation will certainly not be a good guarantee of achieving a holistic view of any individual settlement. Architectural specialists might want to understand the significance of a type of building in the whole building pedigree of this region, but are not interested in the specific meanings that make them significant to the local people. A site interpreter should be fully aware that the basic standpoint from which a heritage can be understood is always 'a place', namely: a river valley containing the lineage settlement(s) defined not just architecturally or spatially but also anthropologically. It is impossible to understand the habitation process without being well informed about the daily needs, habits, activities and place attachment of the local communities. This dichotomy indicates an essential contradiction between the logic of making a heritage inventory and the writing of a landscape biography.

111. Interview with Zhang Wenzhu in 2014.

5.1.3 Hekeng for Reference Use

As noted earlier, the Hekeng people's lives have already suffered a heavy negative influence from the heritage-making process that the local government has been championing since 2006. This has sharply differentiated the three settlements from any of the others distributed in the vicinities of Shiqiao, Nanou and Taxia, whose pasts have not yet been themed or museumized. The Hekeng River Valley is now in the process of being transformed into a sort of *tulou* park and the local residents are still being seriously affected by the repercussions of this move. Of all the forty-six *tulou* buildings registered on the WHL, the position of the thirteen *tulou* buildings located in Hekeng itself is quite different in that the architectures registered there include all the extant *tulou* houses of the Zhang lineage in this valley. Hence, the *de facto* architectural museumization space overlaps with the entire living area of the valley. Leaving aside the moral issue of whether this is bodes good or ill, it does provide an opportunity to understand what the short- and long-term impacts of a museumization might have on the local society and the heritage itself when the protection area, the museumization area, the area proposed for touristic use and the *de facto* settlement area roughly overlap with one another. Full-coverage museumization is found only in Hekeng. Whether or not the relocation of its people will eventually turn out to be a success, the complete spatial transformation from a village into a heritage attraction should be considered a valid experiment. As I have elaborated in Chapter 3, the nomination of the Hakka *tulou* heritage was a process of building selection. Therefore, in some settlements, only one *tulou* building has been registered on the WHL. Compared to the three Hekeng settlements, life in these undisturbed settlements is rarely disturbed by such social processes as nomination, registration and museumization and consequently the touristic use of their buildings is relatively light. In the long run of Hekeng heritage use, there might well be failures and lessons from which other settlements with low spatial transformation rates can learn for the future. Bearing this thought in mind, I would suggest that a long-term monitoring of the impacts of both the Hekeng heritage and its relocation process should be set in motion so that more useful information can be collected. This will be beneficial in determining the extent to which similar museumization should be carried out in other river valleys.

5.1.4 Economic Diversity

In Hekeng, as elsewhere in rural China since the 1990s, labor export has been a major income source of the local people and there is still a long way to go before any village such as Hekeng can rely heavily on an advanced local tourism economy. As an outcome of the growth of the migrant labor economy, it should be noted that some fields are now left uncultivated, a state of affairs principally attributable to depopulation. As noted earlier, the fields are fairly fragmented not only in 'ownership' but also in distribution. Nevertheless, it would be much better if the local communities were still able to make good use of these fields as part of their annual income source. It might be rewarding for them to turn to such traditional Hakka farming industries as tea production, bamboo plantations and basket-making, and so forth. However, this depends on a number of factors, chief among them the scale of the businesses, the availability and size of the labor force, the advantageous scale effects and so on. Importantly, although it should not be forgotten that these seemingly small businesses do in fact contain a sizable amount of intangible heritage information, the most important goal is to preserve economic diversity. The latter can stem from a multitude of capabilities for making use of the settlement fields to make a living.

5.2 PROCESSUAL INTEGRITY AS AN OPPORTUNITY TO REVITALIZE HAKKA HISTORICAL SPACES

I suggest that the relevant heritage organizations should consider the use of 'processual integrity' as a means to embrace a holistic view of the Hakka population processes on different spatial levels. My chief concern is that the importance of a heritage like that of the Hakka built environment should be understood as a reflection of the Hakka population processes, not just as a static representation of the buildings and structures themselves. Who migrated to these river valleys and by which river or mountain routes? Who created these settlements and buildings? Routes, valleys, settlements, buildings and structures are a record of the ways that a clan, a lineage, a lineage segment, a family and an individual used the land resource and hence the ways by which they made their livings and survived over time. As demonstrated in Chapters 1 and 4, in the past the use of land on diverse scales also assisted the Hakka in the creation of their own lineage and cultural identities. When they trace their history far back to the apical ancestors, they link themselves to an origin in a faraway land by way of a route that links a series of places. Places, settings and architectures are records of how populations moved and lived in the past. Since demographic processes constitute the major reasons for which each building was constructed, the built environment should be interpreted by linking buildings and structures to social groups or individuals with clear-cut lineage and cultural identities; they are about people.

The concept of 'integrity' is actually not very well expressed in the 1972 *World Heritage Convention*. Nevertheless, it has been continued to be used as the basis for defining the size, scope and boundaries of heritage sites and, consequently, the precise physical goals of preservation. As mentioned previously, the *Convention* and *Operational Guidelines* both fall short in that neither provides much guidance on how much of a built environment we should protect in order to preserve the integrity of the collective memory that this built environment is supposed to represent. The summary of the meeting of the International Expert Workshop on Integrity and Authenticity of World Heritage Cultural Landscapes, 11-12 December 2007, in Aranjuez, Spain, reveals that the participants had already begun to note that, 'integrity is illustrated for each natural criterion and not for cultural criteria...the current use of integrity and authenticity need to be defined in their application to specific criteria; and that these are not yet clearly defined for the nomination processes, technical review and evaluation, on-going site management and monitoring processes.' Although the concept of integrity is still rather vague, the WHC does continue to require it. 'All properties nominated for inscription on the World Heritage List shall satisfy the conditions of integrity', according to the *Operational Guidelines for the Implementation of the World Heritage Convention* (WHC. 13/01 July 2013).

The *Guidelines* define the term integrity as 'a measure of the wholeness and intactness of the natural and/ or cultural heritage and its attributes'. The most up-to-date version of the *Guidelines* (2015) suggests that, in order to examine conditions of integrity properly, one should assess the extent to which the property: a) includes all the elements necessary to express its outstanding universal value; b) is of a size adequate to ensure the complete representation of the features and processes that convey that property's significance; c) is suffering from the adverse effects of development and/or neglect. Of the three basic requirements, the second point is the most relevant to the present discussion. By its very definition given by the WHC, 'integrity' should answer the question: To what degree does the proposed protected area literally represent the 'original' historical place in size, area, views and composition?

5.2.1 Built-Environment Integrity and Population Development

When we speak of the integrity of a historical building, for example, we mean how complete it is or to what extent does the extant structure still represent the original blueprint. In this case, the spatial context or scale is the entire volume of a complete individual architecture in which a fixed number of wooden and earthen building components once existed. Although the context might not be highlighted or even clarified, it does denote the genuine existence of wood and earthen structures inside a three-dimensional space. This is the context or reference against which we speak of a building either having or lacking in 'integrity'. Integrity of architecture can involve a comparison with its previous situation when it was built or still in active use. Hence, it is often difficult to differentiate integrity assessment from authenticity assessment because, if a building can be completely preserved, it could be highly authentic. If we speak of integrity on a higher spatial scale, for instance, the residential area or the cemetery of a settlement, we are talking about the architectural position, arrangement, orientation and interrelationships between individual components. The targets we use to make these comparison have also been borrowed from the past. Unquestionably, the integrity of a residential area can also be viewed as part of its authenticity and a similar logic can also be applied to settlement and the landscape scales. Authenticity in terms of spatial attributes can only be understood by making comparison with those previous to it. A change in a built environment is intrinsically a geographical process. These changes have occurred both vertically and horizontally. Horizontal changes in a settlement context have usually been settlement expansions and intra-valley resettlements within the same river valley, whereas vertical changes have usually involved the metabolic processes of buildings and structures. Horizontal and vertical changes, as demonstrated in Chapter 1, represent the evolutionary process of a built environment in response to demographic developments; sometimes even population overgrowth. Vertical changes also reflect local people's desires for architectural renovation, restoration, adaptation, reconstruction and redevelopment throughout a lineage's history. As the Hekeng case in Chapter 1 shows, these processes were usually triggered by demographic changes.

5.2.2 Processual Integrity

As mentioned in Chapter 1, a complete cycle of demographic process exhibited in a space usually consists of four steps, namely: settlement and habitation; family and lineage segment spinoffs and settlement expansion; intra-valley resettlement; and trans-valley resettlement (move). These four steps have usually been the prelude to significant modifications to the built environment. The history of the Zhang surname's move to and early settlement in Hekeng is reflected in the remains (if any) of early occupation and construction. In river valleys such as that of the Hekeng, for centuries land has been used repeatedly and, as discussed previously, as metabolic changes have taken their toll, the evidence of early land-use has gradually disappeared. Nowhere is this more noticeable that in those places later known as the *tulou* settlements. The Zhang lineage's relocation to Hekeng in the late-fifteenth century could have marked the beginning of a long period of construction and land exploitation, reflected in the continuous use of non-*tulou* residences that were characterized by frequent architectural metabolic changes and a host of different kinds of maintenance activities. The sad fact is that evidence of early land-use and non-*tulou* architectural construction was usually completely destroyed during later *tulou* construction when the whole settlement began to expand rapidly. The construction of new houses in ordinary Chinese rural settlements is often linked to family splitting. In *tulou* settlements, the ownership of *tulou* apartments among families is not evenly distributed. Marriage in poor families could result in a loss of residence for unmarried siblings. A surge in population and concomitant lineage segment spinoffs could eventually trigger the construction of temporary shelters or even new *tulou* buildings in answer to residential shortages. Intra-valley resettlements, such as Yuantang and Xizhuba, have also been an important strategy by which to deal with sharp population increases. The final step in a population process cycle is inter-valley resettlement. In contrast to the other four steps, inter-valley resettlement might have happened from time to time after the establishment of the settlement. Usually, it is impossible to observe traces of it from any physical evidence in the valley, even though it is clear that there has been a correlation between the population process and the evolutionary process of the built environment. I call this correlation built-heritage processual integrity. The question of to what extent the extant local built environment can represent historical population processes lies at the core of processual integrity. As far as the Hakka people are concerned, population once flowed and continues to flow from river valley to river valley. Therefore, the river valley should be regarded as the most suitable unit or measure for the assessment of processual integrity.

Processual integrity is also correlated to variation in kinship distance. In many river valleys, the creation of most houses is recorded in genealogical materials, in written records such as inscriptions on the wooden/stone plaques, or in local people's memories. By scrupulous use of this information, especially in the place in which the head of each generation and core families had lived, the whole demographic process can be reconstructed. As mentioned in Chapter 3, the relationships between *tulou* buildings also signify the kinship relations between the major lineage segments. The population has flowed from settlement to settlement within a river valley, then from *tulou* to *tulou* and finally into other valleys. These population processes are reflected in the evolution of the built environment. The case study in Chapter 1 has demonstrated this kind of process with particular reference to the relationships between demographic process and the evolution of the built environment in Hekeng.

5.2.3 Processual Integrity on Different Spatial Scales

Tim Ingold (2000) has explored the 'dwelling perspective' of human society. This concept highlights the influence of the currents of residents' activities and the 'specific relational contexts of their practical engagement with their surroundings'. For Ingold (2011), 'to dwell' or 'to inhabit' is the basic form of living or life. The whole built environment provides a spectrum of the ways that people get themselves fully 'immersed' in their surroundings. As Ingold suggests, by and large, there are two kinds of population processes, that are both very important to the present study: one is inhabitation; the other is occupation. Ingold (2011) postulates that the former is 'lineal' and the latter is 'areal'. He uses the two concepts together to illustrate how humans move from place to place. Venturing even farther, he identifies two types of what he calls 'trails', that is, the network of transport and meshwork of wayfaring. In fact, on the whole the population processes of the Hakka actually combine the two types of trails. On the one hand, they had to keep moving on and on and inhabit new valleys. On the other hand, they had to settle down in order to lead a stable life. These are just the two sides of the same coin that are inseparable from one another. As discussed in Chapter 3, a river valley is roughly equal to a 'place' in Ingold's theory. Throughout history, each place has served both as a destination and a new point of departure, aptly illustrated in Chapter 1. Like the wave-particle duality of light, the river valley figures as a stable place in which cultural and population development can take place; however, conversely under resource pressures it triggers new demographic relocations. Consequently, every river valley in itself also plays a role in coordinating regional population processes. Changes in lineage population size also play an important role in reshaping the built environment of each river valley, as demonstrated in Chapter 1. Therefore, I see the river valleys widely distributed throughout the Fujian hilly areas as a combination of meshwork and network. On the meshwork side, the Hakka people and their culture just kept on moving into every possible passage, tributary and river valley. On the network side, each river valley is and has been a destination linked to many other similar ones by mountain paths and river corridors. Inside such small areas among the hills, the Hakka and Minnan settled down and gradually expanded their own territories. They then began to establish relationships with the environment they had occupied by using the land strategically.

For such settlements as Hekeng, Shiqiao, Taxia and Nanou, it is possible to interpret the demographic process by using the historical records. This interpretation should be viewed as the basis for designating heritage values, as it combines socioeconomic aspects with the architectural aspects. The evolution of the built environment has mainly been prompted by demographic developments. What we should strive to preserve is the possibility for future generations to see and understand the social process known as the Hakka Exodus that has taken place on different spatial scales. If this is to be done properly, it requires the construction of links between lineage groups, settlement places and migration routes.

On a regional scale: The Hakka migrations could not have been accomplished in a short time. The river valleys of western and southern Fujian, linked by tortuous mountain or river routes, constitute a series of spatial evidence that reflects the population moves over time. Any migration was organized and undertaken by a specific clan, lineage, lineage segment or family, whose leaders at that time were usually clearly recorded in the genealogies compiled by their descendants at the new settlements. This multi-level population diverting system has been described in Chapter 1. A river valley such as that of the Hekeng only served as the final receiving location in this process. Although Hekeng was settled only by people of the Zhang surname group, there are also many other river valleys, listed in Chapter 1, that were the reception areas of multiple surname groups that had arrived at different periods. These river valleys have experienced demographic deposits on many occasions. It would not be possible for us to work out the social significance of these migration routes and valleys, unless we are able to link these historical spaces to the specific surname groups recorded in genealogies or oral history. The historical migrations moved along a plethora of paths that are related to different specific surname groups, whose populations were successively or intermittently deposited in the same or different river valleys along their own migration routes.

On a landscape scale: Chapter 1 was devoted to illustrating both the demographic and architectural processes that have occurred in the Hekeng River Valley. It demonstrates the possibility that a single surname lineage settlement could certainly have evolved into a large lineage village in the space of the past 500 years. Remarkably the built environment in the Hekeng River Valley is so well preserved that we are able to explore the settlement changes over nearly the entire length of the valley (except for the pre-*tulou* period). As evident from Chapter 1, important demographic changes are reflected in the different rhythms at which the built environment evolved. Hakka built-heritage preservation on the river-valley scale concerns the intensive use of the valley land resource in the history of a specific surname lineage as it responded to the challenges of population growth within the boundaries of the river valley. Processual integrity on this spatial level can only be assessed by double-checking the written/oral records and the land-use evidence. The majority of the important settlement historical events that should be reflected in the heritage include sharp population changes, major adjustments to land-use strategies and subsistence patterns, intra-valley resettlements and changes in relations between the new settlements and the old ones that can be traced by examining religious and monumental aspects and so forth.

On a settlement scale: There is usually more than one settlement in a river valley. What Chapter 1 tries to reconstruct is only one of the many possibilities. As that chapter explains, whether or not all the settlements in the same valley belonged to the same surname lineage group, they usually exhibited a kind of competing relationship. This means that each settlement can have its own core interests, that are embodied in a series of *zuchan* (literally, ancestral property) in the form of *tulou* apartments, fields or forests. Processual integrity on the settlement level has to do with such social activities (also demographic processes) as zoning (respectively for residential, ceremonial, funerary, subsistence or other uses in relation to demographic development), construction, expansion and redevelopment, once again shown in Chapter 1. In the case of *tulou* settlements, there is usually more than one major *tulou* shelter in each settlement. Traditionally, each *tulou* formed a residential camp housing families belonging to the same lineage segment (*fang*). As mentioned in Chapter 3, this suggests an intergenerational hierarchy in which all the major residential buildings could find their positions. However, there are exceptions. In oral history, room borrowings have long been remarked upon not just confined to the same *tulou* building, but also occurring between different buildings, as an answer to residential shortages resulting from unevenly distributed apartment ownership. On the whole, processual integrity should clearly represent the population process and the relationship between different architectural units.

On an architectural scale: Processual integrity is principally concerned with the architectural metabolization process. Changes in terms of renovation, restoration, repair, substitution and so forth are important indicators of the residents' needs and intentions. As discussed earlier, it should be these spontaneous changes that have marked the authenticity of the architecture. From a demographic point of view, it would be very important to know who had been or are the major users of historical buildings, and the major demographic changes in such buildings as recorded or implicated in the genealogies or other relevant oral or written sources.

By and large, the current *World Heritage Convention* and the *Operational Guidelines* are the continuation of the *Venice Charter* and other international protocols developed in the early period of international heritage management. All these documents strictly follow architectural conservation principles that focus on the materiality of heritage, and they 'define and value heritage primarily for its static representation of aesthetics and monumentality'

(Yan, 2014). In essential respects, these principles reflect a viewpoint that has long underpinned transnational cultural heritage designation, nomination, registration and utilization. Although, the WHL might collect large numbers of specimens transmitted down from a 'common' past, practically speaking, static architectural values often obscure the processual integrity the extant heritage might still be able to convey. In the Hakka *tulou* cases, it is impossible to find any useful information in the relevant WHL registration materials that sheds any light on the identity of the local people who live and lived inside the buildings. Social and demographic processes have been almost totally neglected. This trend can also be found in the site interpretations of most Hakka heritage attractions. When the architectural values are overstated and the six criteria for OUV registration are followed too closely, the site interpretation is very often reduced to a cluster of abstract esthetic values. As illustrated in Chapter 1, what genealogies and oral history can tell about a building is much more than a reiteration of abstract values but, unfortunately, this information is not yet considered to represent the most essential significance of the heritage by the local site managers. My argument is that the Hakka people's long-term migrations and their cycles of settlement and resettlement among the river valleys in western and southern Fujian make up the fundamental context against which any Hakka buildings had been created. As analyzed above, spaces on different scales can be linked to different demographic events or changes that have been of great significance in the formation of the Hakka people's collective and cultural identities. If this line of thinking is accepted, respecting and preserving of these identities should also be regarded as one of the goals of historical preservation.

5.3 AMENDMENTS TO LAWS AND REGULATIONS LEGITIMIZING PRESERVATION LAND-USE IN RURAL CHINA

As discussed in Chapters 3 and 4, cultural resources designated *wenwu baohu danwei* (cultural heritage preservation sites) are protected by the *Chinese Cultural Heritage Law*. However, so far legislation in China has not made historical preservation a legal requirement in the rural land resource management system. The upshot of this omission is rather serious. If heritage preservation is not formally legalized as a basic form of rural land-use, it is an impossible task to define the legal relationship between local residents and the state in concrete terms. Another hurdle not as yet surmounted is that the term 'public lands' in China has still not been clearly defined in law. Unlike the US system, in which a public domain (land) can belong in terms of cultural heritage preservation, no unequivocal cultural resource statistics have been reported by the SACH or any other important departments of the central government. Obviously the time has come for the state to take a stand and establish a clear legal framework and a system of annual statistics in order to establish a proper legal record of which lands contain important cultural heritage resources. In examples of the built heritage owned by local residents, the lands are unquestionably owned by the collectives, but the houses on these lands are the property of the peasants. Therefore, the houses can only be considered public cultural resources under one condition and one condition only, namely that: the state, on behalf of the Chinese public, redeems or rents the use-right to such houses so that they can be preserved and conserved in the public interest. Any amendment to the articles in the *Land Resources Management Law of the PRC* (*Zhonghua Renmin Gongheguo Tudi Guanlifa*) should include three fundamental requirements: (a) the *Management Law* should view cultural resource preservation as one of the primary land-use functions in rural China; (b) any designation of the local people's real-estate as preservation sites should be based on an agreement between the local residents and the SACH (or local governments if applicable) representing the state, declaring the wishes of the property owners, any rental payments or reimbursements that might be involved and the rights and duties on the two sides in matters concerning maintenance and revenue; (c) a designation of local people's property as a national treasure also needs to include an explicit statement of the status of the ownership of the land on which the property designated is located; if there is no need to transform it into some form of public land as in the urban areas, rents or reimbursements should be paid to the collective landowners; should there be a necessity to change its status into a state-owned public domain, an agreement regulating the change in land ownership and reimbursement should also be signed between the collective owners and the government.

5.4 AGREEMENT ON REGULATING THE RIGHTS AND DUTIES BETWEEN TOURISM DEVELOPERS AND THE LOCAL COLLECTIVE AND INDIVIDUAL STAKEHOLDERS

Any single tourism developer that wants to develop the local people's houses or even an entire settlement as a tourist attraction should sign a contract, specifying the rights and duties on both sides, directly with the property owners as has been suggested in Chapter 4. The developer should also be required by law to sign an agreement with the collective owner of the land, for example, the local village committee on behalf of the villagers, that clearly sets out the duties and rights on both sides, as suggested in the *Zhonghua Renmin Gongheguo Nongcun Tudi Chengbaofa*.

5.5 SAFEGUARDING THE HERITAGE IN USE

On a provincial level, the SACH and cultural heritage administrations should be in full charge of the security of designated cultural resources, and therefore should be entitled to examine all the sorts of business contracts enumerated in 5.3 and 5.4 specifying the use of such resources in great detail. As a safeguard to the designated cultural resource, along with site preservation, conservation and management plans, the SACH or provincial administrations should also meticulously examine tourism plans that propose the exploitation of a designated built heritage as a scenic attraction.

5.6 AMENDMENTS TO WH ENLISTING AND DELISTING CRITERIA

I would like to suggest that any contract or agreement with legal force should be required by the WHC as important references in making a decision about registering a living heritage on the WHL. The suggestion for the appending of such legal documents to WH application materials is founded on the consideration that a harmonious relationship between major stakeholders concerning the balance of their own interests should be viewed as a good omen for perfect heritage preservation. Conversely, a bad relationship between the major stakeholders, as could be reflected in the absence of requested agreement materials, might be viewed as serious matter for thought that might lead to a refusal to register the nominated sites on WHL. Likewise, the discrediting of tourism developers for reneging on promises in contracts that might happen to be observed when site reviews are being carried out should also be regarded as important evidence that could lead to a delisting decision.

5.7 SYSTEMIZATION OF HISTORICAL VILLAGE MANAGEMENT AND CULTURAL RESOURCE STRATIFICATION

In any discussion of heritage site planning, one widely accepted notion is that, as a significant preservation strategy, the first responsibility of any plans should be to secure the cultural heritage. However, it is also extremely important that any planning should also take the development of the local rural society into serious consideration, particularly local residents' demands for land. As noted previously, there are nearly 3,000 *tulou* buildings dispersed throughout the large and small river valleys in southwestern Fujian. As important evidence of the local people's past and, in particular, of a very special kind of architectural style that differs from all the other folk buildings and structures of Han nationality, *tulou* buildings should undoubtedly be nurtured by the state. Nevertheless, impoverished as they are in land resources, the local residents might well be in desperate need of more space to develop their settlement economy and construct new architecture rather than preserving old buildings. As demonstrated in Chapter 2, *tulou* buildings have a low adaptability to new modern use, a factor that has led to either their complete demolition or less drastic structural modification. A new wave of metabolization throughout the hilly areas is now inevitable. Therefore this is a critical moment to come up with plans to adjust preservation strategies to deal with these inexorable changes. One possible method that that has much to recommend it is to stratify the *tulou* cultural resources more specifically into three basic categories: theme parks or living museums, culture villages and development areas. The three categories are not mutually exclusive.

A *tulou* theme park could provide the general public with opportunities to experience *tulou* architectural specimens that have been fully repaired and conserved in a way scrupulously adhering to WH and national standards. As the quintessential Fujian built heritage, the number of these *tulou* museum villages should be pretty restricted; few enough to be at least easily monitored by the SACH. Because they are used as a representation of national pride, the SACH on behalf of central government should not only fully support the preservation and conservation of the built heritage but assist the local government in reimbursing the local people with enough income to provide them with basic living expenses. Although tourism development is necessary to such museumized places, the basic income of the residents who own apartments in these *tulou* museums should come from the governments on different levels. As I have said previously, it should be the government that plays the leading role in transforming these *tulou* houses and the concomitant settlement landscape into a living museum. Very probably Hekeng and Tianluokeng represent the most important and typical traditional Hakka settlements. Therefore the SACH should assign them the status of national cultural reserves or include them in some other type of registration system equivalent to the national site parks in urban areas, even though it might be impossible for the government to purchase all the settlement land for preservation use. Under the direct, strict control of the SACH to safeguard the most representative traditional architectural attributes, tourism in these heritage sites, although the *de facto* major income source, should be kept within manageable bounds. Since the museumization approach can indubitably have a negative impact on these villages and as any kind of development is totally prohibited, the people in these settlements should be provided with an opportunity to relocate themselves to other suitable places. Above all, it should be emphasized that it is the responsibility of both the national cultural authorities and the local governments to finance relocation fully, if the local people agree to move to new places.

A *tulou* culture village would be a designation that refers to those settlements with important as yet undesignated *tulou* buildings. Although there are no formal statistics about the number of these villages, it can be said with certainty that they do constitute a large proportion of China's *tulou* villages. In the cultural heritage laws, it is absolutely necessary to recognize the legal status of those houses with a specific cultural value in these villages, as household and individual properties. Should the heritage designation be pursued any farther, the best suggestion for carrying this out in an orderly fashion might be to follow the steps listed in section 5.3. Furthermore, any tourism resource development in these villages should be based on contracts between the villagers and the developers, as argued in section 5.4. In this sort of negotiation, a local county government should limit its role to overseeing and coordinating the ongoing projects. It should not play the part of a *de facto* shareholder in the projects. Although these villages have no or only quite limited numbers of designated traditional houses, the sustainability of tourism use is still a matter for the SACH. As has been discussed in Chapters 2 and 4, formerly the traditional built environment in southwestern Fujian was actually maintained by the local government that promulgated diverse policies and regulations governing the regulation of the environment. Pragmatically, as times have changed, private capital is now needed in these villages in order to form a beneficial circle constituted by tourism, adaptive maintenance of architecture and sustainable use of agricultural land and traditional industries. Obviously, in the modern social context, the *tulou* cultural resources of a settlement can only be sustained if they can be made to be of some use. Should they prove to be financially unproductive, people are definitely going to choose to build new residences in a more modern style. Therefore, if the SACH wants to prolong the lifespan of these folk buildings, it should do more to encourage and promote the use of the *tulou* heritage set in its traditional surroundings and landscapes.

The third category is that of the *tulou* settlements to be redeveloped. As mentioned in the Preface, the need to develop is usually underestimated. In the *tulou* settlements in which the traditional building arrangements and the appearance of landscape have already both been changed dramatically, the local people should be allowed to alter their antiquated *tulou* houses and make them into modern new buildings. In this event, the local people should be encouraged to demolish their *tulou* castles if they have the economic capability to embark on a new residential pattern. Despite the radical changes this would involve, it is essential that the development of these settlements can also be incorporated into whole *tulou* management scenario of Fujian province. Some of these villages could also be developed into sites for the relocation of the displaced population from other places, especially fully museumized ones.

5.8 ARCHITECTURAL MAINTENANCE GUIDANCE

As soon as possible, the SACH and the Fujian provincial cultural heritage administration should issue regulations governing the basic requirements for *tulou* renovation and adaptation, preferably in the form of an illustrated guide. There should be a clear division between an area that is preserved intact and an area that might be altered, modified or redeveloped in response to updated needs in many aspects. Local people, especially the local conservator-artisans, should be able to understand clearly what can and what cannot be done. Design standards should also explicitly set be out. If the river valley is designated to be used as a unified landscape or scenic setting, inevitably new service buildings will need to be erected in it or its near vicinity. Again, in this instance clear requirements should be laid down to regulate the forms and structures these new buildings might take. I would argue that there is still a possibility to accommodate some of the local population in these new modern service buildings to make up for the loss of their residences caused by the destruction of the 'new' buildings since 2006. Importantly, these new service buildings could take the form of a simplified version of a rammed earthen building. This could also provide a testing field for local artisans who have been neglected for a very long time, even by local society, indeed since the erection of the last round *tulou* buildings in the early 1980s. The goal of the new tests should be to arrive at a suitable combination of the traditional rammed-earthen and wooden construction techniques and a more up-to-date inner structure. As they are already regarded as part of the traditional built environment of a Hakka settlement, these adapted buildings would be easily compatible with the magnificent *tulou* buildings in style and façade, but much more comfortable to live in.

5.9 A SHORT CONCLUSION

In conclusion, like most Chinese rural settlements, the *tulou* settlements widely scattered throughout the rural areas of Fujian province, are now suffering the negative consequences of the overgrowth of the local urban centers. Rural mountain ranges cover nearly over 75 percent of the total area of Fujian province. Large numbers of historical settlements and towns are distributed in the river valleys between the mountain ranges. Since the Ming and Qing dynasties, time and again outsiders have 'discovered' and 'rediscovered' the splendid architectural world hidden deep in the mountains. For many centuries, rural society had been isolated from the outside world. Confronted by the harsh challenges thrown at them by nature, throughout history in order to survive each male and female Hakka settlement member has been required to be an expert in every aspect of life, ranging from sowing, harvesting, animal husbandry, hunting, paper-manufacturing and earth-ramming to bargaining prices with outsiders. They have piously worshipped their ancestors and their gods and, in the course of their habitation, they have developed a series of *fengshui* philosophies. Yes, they do things differently there but it is also an incontrovertible fact that they have been changing all the time. In each generation, there has always been someone who has left the river valley to search for a new life beyond the mountains. When they became rich in other places in China or even abroad, they made donations to the settlements of their birth, and helped to renovate the local built environment. During the Republican period, they even assisted their relatives to construct Western-style buildings. Theirs is a rather complicated rural world that is impossible to represent as a homogeneous whole. Nevertheless, we have to understand that it is still their own choice if they want to make themselves resemble outsiders more closely. Therefore, what we as either site managers or conservators have the right to do is not by stretch of the imagination to freeze all of that past into a museum specimen. Unfortunately, the intangible part of a culture can be its most fragile part — that is, in comparison to material aspects, easily overridden by the decisions of CR managers. This is a disaster as the intangible can actually represent a life capability, a lifestyle or a habitat that has been central to the culture since antiquity. We as outsiders can do no more than catch a glimpse of this central quality of traditional culture when we see an experienced local peasant aged over fifty wielding a heavy ramming stick in the air to show his little grandson how his grandfather built a huge *tulou* in the past.

Appendix

THE RISE OF FUJIAN EARTHEN FORTS IN THE SIXTEENTH AND SEVENTEENTH CENTURY, CHENG, BAO, LOU AND ZHAI

1. Eastern Fujian: the *Mingshenzong shilu,* the *Wanli sanshinian*, or the *Chronicles of the Ming Dynasty*, Shenzong Emperor, the thirty-first Year of the Wanli reign (1603): 'When Xu Kui administrated Leling county, an intensification of the social chaos resulted in an official decree that ordered the moat be deepened and that the walled enclosures in the county be strengthened. Moreover, the county magistrate also required the peasants who lived in the rural areas of the county to prepare against pillaging by constructing strong walls around their dwellings. It was required that the walls be built higher than the eaves. Gates in these walled enclosures were no more than narrow openings that allowed only one person to enter at a time.'

2. Southern Fujian: the *Yanhai diaobao shuo*, or *A Summary of the Fortifications in the Coastal Areas*, by the Qing dynasty writer Lin Xiechun: 'From the Jiajing reign era (1522-1566) and thereafter, in the rural areas of Quanzhou and Zhangzhou (close to the sea and the mountains), local communities began to build a large number of earthen forts, the borrow pits were usually adapted to be used as entrenchments, on the banks of which thorny plants were widely grown.'

3. Western Fujian: the *Baozhai ji* or *A Biography of Earthen Walls* by the Qing dynasty writer Li Shixiong: 'There had been no such earthen forts at all in the villages of Ninghua county until the late Jiajing reign era (*ca* 1550s to 1560s), with the exception of the site of the foundations of an old fort known as the *Lianfeng zhai* or the Lotus Peak Fort of an unknown date. From the late Jiajing reign of the Ming dynasty, brigands from Guangdong and Liancheng repeatedly came to ravage the village; unfortunately, sometimes they even came three times in a single year. The rich people sought refuge in the better fortified county town. With no such shelter available, the poor had to hide deep in the mountain forests. Without shelter, the refugees were forced to suffer the bad weather in mountain ranges. Many of the poor were finally captured and killed by the bandits. The ones who had luckily survived their knives and swords could also eventually succumb to the atrocious weather, especially the noxious mists in the mountains. The elder brother of Great-grandfather Sanfeng felt deep sympathy for these poor clansmen… Therefore he led the clansmen in search of the foundation site of the old fort at the Lotus Peak. He raised funds to support the restoration work... later, the revolts were put down... As peace was brought to the village, the new fort was renamed the *Taiping zhai* or the Peace Fort. Since the Wanli and Longqing reigns, the local residents had enjoyed a tranquil life for many years … they had no awareness of the need to defend the fort…However, in 1628 (the first year of the Chongzhen reign of the Ming dynasty), the situation in Wuping, Shanghang and Jianning again deteriorated into chaos and violence and, under the leadership of Uncle Chunsu, the clansmen reinforced the Peace Fort… but, there was no such a thing as a small house or cottage inside the walled enclosure, as [it was now] a military facility, people could not live for very long inside the fort. From 1644, the whole Empire became even more deeply embroiled in civil wars (of dynastic succession). Urgent messages came from every county. It was no use hiding in the county seat. The people became aware of the importance of the Peace Fort. Therefore, Uncle Panru began to champion the restoration. My *zong* (lineage) was the first to heed Uncle Panru's call. We constructed cottages inside the fort for our own [use], counting the number of households. Other clansmen followed our example. From 1646 to 1647, more families moved into the fort and built their own cottages

in tight rows, like an epitome of the village.' Some scholars such as Zheng and Chen (1993) believe that this is the earliest evidence of a real residential use of earthen forts. However, it should be emphasized here that this residential permanency was by no means firmly guaranteed. What really matters is that it does prove a likely link between the changes in building function/form and the inexorable heightening of the social pressures. Adaptive use is a common phenomenon, and it does not necessarily mean the fort has been entirely transformed into a permanent residence. This strategy might have been more complicated and more flexible than architectural specialists have considered. The residential use of the fort in the late Ming dynasty should not be overstated. We should be aware of the fact that the temporary adaptive use of an old fort could have had little impact on the settlement pattern and the landscape. These modifications only make sense in their original context; by the late Jiajing reign, village society had been highly stratified. It is very likely that the wealthy people in the village might have owned properties in a town or a county seat. In other words they invested in the urban area on higher administrative levels. The changes in their residential patterns might have resulted in a bleeding of the village wealth and a subsequent lack of financial support that would have enabled the fort to be fully renovated. In the 1620s, their county seat was still possibly the first choice of wealthy people as a place of refuge. About twenty years later, however, when the rich urban areas began to offer a greater inducement to the bandits, they had to change their strategy. This change in their living patterns might have led to the success of these adaptive use in the 1640s. In short, residential strategy was by no means unconditional and unilinear. From 1654, a great change occurred in western Fujian; more brigands, sometimes even the soldiers of the Qing government, began to pour in in great numbers to plunder the village. The fifty-three-year-old local gentleman Li Shixiong, also known as the author of the *Baozhai ji*, advocated the construction of more thick-walled enclosures to protect the clansmen. Li led his clansmen in the building of the construction of the *Quanshang tubao* to the northeast of the village. This is a huge square fort. Each wall measures about 130m long, 7m wide and over 10m high. According to the *Baozhai ji*, more than120 households finally moved into the fort. Outside the huge walls were deep moats. Soon after the establishment of the *Quanshang tubao*, more of these *bao* buildings mushroomed around the village. Among those still extant are the *Haoheng tubao*, the *Yanxiang tubao*, the *Chenjiadi tubao* and the *Tieluokeng tubao*. In short, only from the early Qing dynasty did the local people in Quanshang and Quanxia begin to live more regularly and more frequently inside the earthen enclosures. This pattern diverges sharply from the actual situation from the middle to late Ming dynasty.

4. Western Fujian: the *Chongxiu tuzhai gaoshi* or *Bulletin about Restoring the Earthen Fort* and the *Shenbao tuzhai gaojun wen*, or *Declaration of the Completion of the Earthen Fort Project*, are both extremely important to building up an understanding of the structure and functions of earthen forts in the early years of their use in Liancheng in the western Fujian area. The two documents were both written during the Wanli reign (1573-1620) of the Ming dynasty. As stated in the text, there had not been any earthen fortifications in Liancheng until the Jiajing reign. 'As it commands the strategic passage between the Yangtze River basins and Guangdong, Liancheng has always been a barometer of social security on this trade route… during the Xuande (1426-1435) and Zhengtong (1436-1449) reigns of the Ming dynasty, the notorious bandit leaders Luo Tianlin and Deng Maoqi and their followers exterminated seventy-two families in all among the local communities. During the Jiajing reign, another bandit Li Sannu came from Shanghang…but the local communities still had no fortifications to deter the slaughtering and pillaging; they still lived in their humble thatched residences...finally, for fear of such disasters, the local communities constructed an earthen fort… In the autumn of 1570 (the fourth year of the Longqing reign), the fortification was damaged by a flood…'. From

the statements in the two documents, it seems very likely that the so-called *bao* was indeed a thick-walled enclosure inside which the local villagers could find a place to hide/shelter when social upheavals erupted; unfortunately, it is possible that huge earthen works were viewed by the government with suspicion; certainly, they could be used as a temporary shelter for refugees, but they could also equally provide a lair for brigands and be hotbeds of sedition. The upshot was that the construction of these buildings was strictly controlled by the local government. Cogently, anyone who wanted to construct/restore/reconstruct/re-use the forts would have very likely been required to make an application in writing to the local government, and this is how these two documents came into being. Moreover, from this sort of a simple discourse analysis, we can draw the following conclusions: (1) Peasants were compelled by circumstances to look for a place to seek refuge without moving too far away from their own land and property; (2) the local government did not want the unsophisticated country folk to spend too much time on these military-orientated structures; (3) until the Wanli reign, there is no evidence to support the continued residential use of the earthen forts in Liancheng in the western part of Fujian.

5. Eastern Fujian: the *Mingshenzong shilu, the Wanli sishiyinian*, or *The Chronicles of the Ming Dynasty*, Shenzong Emperor, the forty-first Year of the Wanli Reign (1613): the procurator of Fujian province, Ding Jisi (1545-1623), clearly stated in his memorial to the Throne, 'Anxi, and some other places in Quanzhou county [at least at this point Zhangpu, Pinghe and Yunxiao should be added to the list], have been used to construct fortifications to prepare against [incursions] by sea rovers (since the middle-sixteenth century)...in peacetime, the forts can be adapted for use as storehouses...the central government should make every effort to have this strategy popularized amongst all the counties in Fujian'. This proposal was indeed finally approved by the central government.

6. Southern Fujian: According to the *Quanzhou fuzhi*, or the *Quanzhou Prefecture Gazetteer*, there was also another type of *bao* building in the rural areas of southern Fujian. These constructions were quite different from the forts built inside or near the settlements. 'During the Jiajing reign (1522-1566), in the north-western part of Quanzhou, adjacent to Zhangzhou, Tingzhou and Yanping, forts were built principally by the local peasants and usually occupied advantageous terrain, keeping a look-out on the paths the bandits might take.' Therefore, peasant militiamen could serve the government during emergencies by transforming their forts that controlled the strategic points into the lookout posts on the regional level in order to deter intruders from invading deeper into the county proper.

7. Southern Fujian: the *Zhangzhou fuzhi*, or the *Zhangzhou Prefecture Gazetteer*: in 1505-1506 (the eighteenth year of the Hongzhi reign to the first year of the Zhengde reign, Ming dynasty), 'No walled enclosures had ever been established around Yunxiao county, so people living far and near all relied heavily on the only earthen walled enclosure (*cheng*) to survive the violence in 1507.' This suggests a relatively large space enclosed by reinforced walls/embankments. It sounds just like the strong enclosures recorded in the *Baozhai ji* as mentioned above.

8. Southern Fujian: the *Quanzhou fuzhi*, or the *Quanzhou Prefecture Gazetteer*: during the Jiajing reign (1522-1566), in Anxi county, 'In the past the local residents had been disturbed by the brigands; when the latter pillaged the villages, peasants usually fled into mountains to hide; (during the Jiajing reign) a local gentleman, Lin Chang, raised funds to erect a building complex...placing the major buildings at the center, surrounded by a ring of earthen buildings; granaries, wells, cooking and whatever other facilities were needed for daily life were all prepared inside; males and females lived separately.' This evidence deserves to be paid some attention. It suggests the temporariness of these fort dwellings, and that people would finally go back to their land after the ravages of

the bandits. 'Windows and holes were opened in the walls of the outer buildings that enabled the residents to fire…outside the building complex there was a ring of deep entrenchments.'

9. Southern Fujian: the *Jinjiang xianzhi*, or the *Jinjiang County Gazetteer*: 'In the late Jiajing reign (1522-1566), in Jinjiang county, a local gentleman, Lin Shangxin, advocated fort construction in his hometown.'

10. Southern Fujian: the *Anxi xianzhi*, or the *Anxi County Gazetteer*: during the Jiajing reign (1522-1566), in Anxi county, a local gentleman, Chen Yingchen, '…organized the local people to build the first *zhai* of the village to resist the depredations of the pirates.'

11. Southern Fujian: the *Zhangzhou fuzhi*, or the *Zhangzhou Prefecture Gazetteer*: 'During the Jiajing reign (1522-1566), in Zhao'an county, the incursions of Japanese pirates resulted in serious social chaos…the local gentleman, Zhang Qijie, summoned the people of the whole lineage to search for an appropriate location on which to build a fort in order to survive the Japanese pirates attacks.'

12. Southern Fujian: the *Hegan ji*, or *River Bank Records*: 'During the Jiajing reign (1522-1566), the southern Fujian rural areas were drastically plundered, and in view of this, the local gentlemen began to raise funds and organize the construction work.'

13. Southern Fujian: the *Tong'an xianzhi*, or the *Tong'an County Gazetteer*: 'In 1548 (might be a wrong date, because was no *wusi nian* in the Jiajing reign era), the pirates came from the sea…the county magistrate organized the local people to build an earthen fort to the east of the county proper for reception of refugees from far or near…After the construction was finished the magistrate paid a lot to buy beef and rice wine in local markets to reward the labors.'

14. Southern Fujian: the *Tianxia junguo libing shu*, or *A Statement of the Advantages and Disadvantages of the Administrative Management in Prefectures and Counties of the Chinese Empire*, 'Since the fortieth year of the Jiajing reign (1561), crimes committed by ruffians had been increasing sharply, in response the local peasants began to construct *tuwei* (rammed earthen enclosures) and *tulou* more frequently.' Here by *tulou*, the famous writer and author of this book, Gu Yuanwu, might be referring to the square earthen buildings, like the first *tulou* buildings distributed in the river valleys of Nanjing county.

15. Southern Fujian: the *Wensu lu*, or *Inquiries into Habitudes*: 'In Zhao'an county of Zhangzhou prefecture, since the Jiajing reign of the Ming dynasty… the people living in Sidu have constructed *bao* as if they were building county enclosures…four gates each opening on to one side… whereas the people living in Erdu had no such square enclosures (*cheng*) and they chose to build *weilou* (literally enclosed storied-buildings).' This might also be a reference to the first square *tulou* buildings in southern Fujian. The record here was written by the Qing dynasty writer Chen Shengshao (1775-1861), therefore, what he chose to include in this book is very probably based on the stories he had learned about the fort constructions since the middle Ming dynasty. What he had gleaned reconfirms the purpose of the constructions, namely: they were initially built to resist Japanese pirates, but later they were used in the private wars between different surname clans. However, all such information cannot be used to confirm a continual residential use in the middle Ming dynasty.

16. Southern Fujian: the *Nan'an xianzhi*, or the *Nan'an County Gazetteer*: in 1648 (the fifth year of the Shunzhi reign), 'The pirates continued to rob the villages around Nan'an county … a local gentleman, Dai Yinggun, paid several hundred *jin* to fund the construction of a fort at Getou Mountain… In 1722 (the sixty-first year of the Kangxi reign) once again he paid several thousand *jin* to construct a fort at Fu Mountain for the reception of relatives living far or near…

17. Southern Fujian: the *Fujian tongzhi,* 'In the early years of the Shunzhi reign (the 1650s), in Anxi County, a local gentleman, Zheng Kezan, led

the whole Zheng lineage in a fight against the brigands in the nearby mountains...the lineage built a new *zhai*...the whole township hence remained intact...

18. Southern Fujian: the *Zhangzhou fuzhi*, or the *Zhangzhou Prefecture Gazetteer*: 'From the late Ming onward (this usually refers to from the Wanli reign, the late-sixteenth century to early-seventeenth century), in Longxi county, the intrusions of Japanese pirates disturbed the local society...a local gentleman, Huang Shilei, summoned the villagers to build a fort at the foot of Shigu Mountain to defend the village.' As Chen (2009) has pointed out, 'the Fortification Movement' in Fujian even extended into the early years of the Qing dynasty.

19. Southern Fujian: the *Zhangzhou fuzhi*, or the *Zhangzhou Prefecture Gazetteer*: in the early years of the Kangxi reign [the 1660s], in Changtai county, a local gentleman, Lin Tingyao, gathered together the villagers (neighbors) to construct a fort at Niu Mountain...the new settlers worked on building the defensive system, reaffirmed the regulations and agreements that managed the village and established a self-sufficient economy...the villagers gradually regained their long-lost sense of security.'

20. Western Fujian: According the *Chongxiu qiantai zhi*, or *A Biography of the Reconstruction of the Headquarters for Suppressing the Rebellions* [that haunted the mountain range bordering Yong'an and Liancheng]: 'In 1559 (the thirty-eighth year of the Jiajing reign of the Ming dynasty), the brigands Deng Huiquan, Deng Xingzu and Xie Daji gathered 4,000 people (most probably their clansmen), occupied the key positions with any strategic significance on both the river and land routes, built two *tulou* buildings (here, some scholars, among them Huang Hanmin, regard this as the first appearance of the term '*tulou*' in Chinese historical literature, but, it is most likely that these two so-called '*tulou*' were actually temporary storied fortifications) that were surrounded by moats and road barricades, and fought against the government, conspiring with the Longyan bandit, Liao Xuan,... One of the *tulou* buildings was finally conquered by the government troops, the commander, Wu Changfu, was captured [and]119 bandits were decapitated. Deng Xingzu still resisted in another *tulou*. A troop of 3,400 soldiers were therefore dispatched from nearby Liancheng county. Under the generalship of Liu Zongyin, the troops were initially stationed at Gutian and deployed at night... the *tulou* had not yet been conquered. The *Zhangnan dao* (Zhangnan Road Administration) dispatched 1,000 *Hmong* soldiers with 400 Yongan county militiamen to suppress the riot. A bandit named He Wufu secretly crossed over to the government. He was required by the government to help the troops from the inside... Deng Xingzu and Xie Daji came out of the *tulou* and surrendered to the government...The troops conquered the *tulou* and arrested the wives of the two leaders...burnt down the buildings and withdrew...' This record is fairly important. It briefly outlines the characteristics of what had been called a '*tulou*' in its original context during the Jiajing reign. The first feature of a *tulou* was that it had to be a multi-storied building with a reinforced defensive system. It could be built within a very short period of time and easily managed. The second requirement was that the wooden structures and internal fittings had to be prepared inside for day-to-day use. The third aspect is that the *tulou* in the record were isolated on the outside by moats and barricades. Therefore, it is fairly clear that the term '*tulou*' here refers to a fortification built in haste, that resembled an earthen fort (*bao*) in every aspect. Again, it is very likely that until 1559 in the late Jiajing reign, a *tulou* was in effect viewed by the local people as a temporary military facility. It is conceivable that during this period in the rural areas of Yong'an and Liancheng people were still living in ordinary settlements consisting of cottages, farmhouses, courtyard dwellings and workshops...

Character List

bao	堡
Baosheng dadi	保生大帝
budongchan	不動產
cheng	城
chong xiu	重修
chengshi wenhua kongjian	城市文化空間
chengshi mingpian	城市名片
chuancheng	傳承
citang	祠堂
cunzhang	村長
dan	擔
dazayuan	大雜院
dayizhi	大遺址
Dexin-tang	德馨堂
De shi xiang lü	德式鄉閭
difang wenwu bumen	地方文物部門
fang	房
fenjia	分家
fensi	分祀
fengshui	風水
fengzixing mu	風字形墓
Fulao	福佬
Fu Mei Xiangcun	富美鄉村
gongjia	公家
gongtian	公田
guanshi jianzhu	官式建築
guojia	國家

huanjing zhengzhi	環境整治
huanjing zhili	環境治理
Huaiting	槐庭
Hakka	客家
Hekeng	河坑
heyuan	合院
heng	横
hezu gongji	闔族共祭
jianzhu kongzhi didai	建築控制地帶
jiabao	家堡
jiben nongtian	基本農田
jin	斤
jingji jiti zuzhi	經濟集體組織
Jinshi	進士
jiti	集體
jitian	祭田
kanyu	堪輿
keyan jigou	科研機構
lao fangzi	老房子
liang	兩
li hou	利後
lishi wenhua mingcheng, mingzhen, mingcun	歷史文化名城、名鎮、名村
miao	廟
Minnan	閩南
minxi	民系
minju jianzhu	民居建築
Minzhu gongwang	民主公王
minzu wenhua cunluo	民族文化村落
mu	畝

Nanjing	南靖
nongmin gong	農民工
nongyongdi	農用地
Pinghe	平和
pingzheng tudi	平整土地
qian hai	遷海
Qiaoxia	橋下
Qiyue ban	七月半
Raoping	饒平
quan minzu	全民族
Shanghang	上杭
she	社
shenyi re	申遺熱
shi	世
Shiqiao	石橋
shi qigan	石旗杆
shiye danwei	事業單位
Shiying-tang	世英堂
tan	壇
tang	堂
tang-heng shi jianzhu	堂横式建築
teji	特祭
toujia	頭家
tudi ziyuan	土地資源
tulou	土樓
wenhua chanye	文化產業
wenwu baohu	文物保護
wufeng	五鳳
wufu	五服

wuxing zichan	無形資產
xian	縣
xian guotu ziyuanju	縣國土資源局
xian tudiju	縣土地局
xian wenhuaju	縣文化局
xian zhengfu	縣政府
xiangzhen qiye	鄉鎮企業
Xizhuba	溪竹壩
xindingji	新丁祭
xingzheng cun	行政村
xiu	修
xiu jiu ru jiu	修舊如舊
yangshi	樣式
yaoqianshu	搖錢樹
yewu zhidao	業務指導
yichan baohu guihua	遺產保護規劃
Yuantang	圓塘
yizixing lou	一字形樓
zhai	寨
Zhangzhou	漳州
zhaijidi	宅基地
zhaoshang yinzi	招商引資
zhengfu zhaobiao	政府招標
zhengfu zhudao	政府主導
zhici	支祠
zhugan cuo	竹竿厝
zhuixu	贅婿
ziran cun	自然村
zongci	宗祠

zongti baohu guihua	總體保護規劃
zongzu	宗族
zuchan	祖產
zuo dafu	做大福
zutian	族田
zuwu	祖屋

Bibliography

Agnew, J. A. (1993). Representing space: space, scale and culture in social science. In Duncan and Ley (Eds.) *Place/Culture/Representation*. Routledge. Connerton, P. (1989). *How Societies Remember.* Cambridge University Press.

Anonymous author. *People's Daily* (December, 28th, 2010) P07.

Anyon, R. (1991). Protecting the Past, Protecting the Present: Cultural Resources and American Indians. In Smith and Ehrenhard (Eds.), *Protecting the Past*, CRC Press, Inc., Boca Raton, La.

Appleton Charter for the Protection and Enhancement of the Built Environment. http://www.icomos.org/en/charters-and-texts.

Ashworth, G.J. (1998). The Conserved European City as Cultural Symbol: The Meaning of the Text. In Graham, B. (ed.) *Modern Europe: Place, Culture and Identity*. Hodder Arnold.

Bell, D. (2011). Whose Heritage? Essay commissioned by the Australian Heritage Commission, http://www.environment.gov.au/heritage/strategy/documents.html.

Bao, H. and Peng, Y. (2016). Effect of land expropriation on land-lost farmers' entrepreneurial action: A case study of Zhejiang Province. *Habitat International Journal* 53 (2016) 342—349. Elsevier.

Berdahl, D. (1999). '(N)Ostalgie' for the Present: Memory, Longing, and East German Things. *Ethnos 64*(2): 192–211.

Bloemers, T., Kars, H., Valk, A.van der, and Wijnen, M. (eds.) *The Cultural Landscape & Heritage Paradox: Protection and Development of the Dutch Archaeological-Historical Landscape and its European Dimension*. Amsterdam University Press.

Buchli, V., & Lucas, G. (2001). *Archaeologies of the Contemporary Past*. Routledge.

Burra Charter Article 1.9. http://australia.icomos.org/.

Cai, L. (2007). Kejia fangyan fenlei de yuyan shehuixue kaocha (A sociolinguistic analysis of the divergence of Hakka dialects). In Zhou (Ed.) *Duoxueke Shiye zhong de Kejia Wenhua* (The Hakka Culture in the Perspective of Multidisciplinary Research). The Fujian People's Publishing House.

Chen, C. (2011). Juluo xingtai yu shehui zhuanxing: Ming Qing zhiji Hanjiang liuyu difang dongluan zhi lishi yingxiang (Settlement pattern and social transformation: the Ming to Qing period social upheavals in the Min River reaches). *Shixue Yuekan* (Historiography Monthly) 2011 (2).

Chen, H. and Chen, B. (Qing dynasty). *Qingchu Pubian Xiaocheng* (A Short Biography of the Social Chaos in the Early Days of the Qing Dynasty). In the Chinese Academy of Social Sciences (ed.) *Qingshi ziliao* 1990 (1). Zhonghua Book Company.

Chen, J. (2002). *Shisheng Shisi: Fengshui yu Fujian Shehui Wenhua Bianqian* (Life-friendly or Death-friendly: Fengshui, Cultural and Social Changes in Fujian). Xiamen University. PhD dissertation.

Chen, Q. (2009). *Ming Qing Minnan Zongzu Yishi de Goujian yu Qianghua* (The Construction and Enhancement of Lineage Cohesiveness in the Ming to Qing Period Southern Fujian Area). Xiamen University Press.

Chen, S. (Qing dynasty). (1997). *Wensu lu* (Inquiries into Habitudes). Nantou: Taiwan Wenxian Weiyuanhui.

Chen, S. et al. (Qing dynasty). (1968). *Fujian Tongzhi* (Fujian Gazetteer). Taipei: The tenth year of the Tongzhi reign era of the Qing dynasty, photocopy edition.

Chen, Z. (2005). Cong zupu ziliao kan Kejia ren xiang Minnan Zhangzhou de qianyi lishi (The clan genealogies collected from Zhangzhou area and the origins of the local surname clans). In Chen (Ed.) *Huanan Kejia Zuqun Zhuixun yu Kejia Yinxiang* (In Search for the Hakka Images in Southern China). Huangshan Publishing House.

Chen, Z. (2009). *Fujian Zupu* (Lineage Genealogies in Fujian). The Fujian People's Publishing House.

Chen, Z. (2011). *Jin Wubainianlai de Fujian Jiazu Shehui yu Wenhua* (Clans, Lineages and Cultures of Fujian Province in the Recent 500 Years). Renmin University Press.

Chen, Z., and Xu, H. (2007). *Minnan Quyu Fazhan Shi* (A History of Social Development in Southern Fujian Region). The Fujian People's Publishing House.

China Gazetteer Compilation Committee. (2000). *Pinghe Xianzhi* (The Pinghe County Gazetteer). Shanghai Book Publishing House.

China News reporters. (2014). Zhengxie weiyuan Li Xiaojie: rang gucunluo chengwei yiju jiayuan (CPPCC member Li Xiaojie: making traditional villages livable places of the local people). *China News*, March 12th, 2014. http://www.chinanews.com/cul/2014/03-12/5942154.shtml.

Chinese Tourism Planning Academy. (2008). *Yongding Tulou Lüyou Guihua* (Yongding Tulou Settlements Tourism Design). Unpublished.

Cohen, M. L. (1979). *House United, House Divided.* Columbia University Press.

Dai, X. (1989). *Nanjing Zhangshi Zupu* (The Zhang Surname Genealogies of Nanjing). Published year not clear.

Dai, Z. (2012). Fujian tubao yu Fujian tulou xingtai zhi bianyi (A comparison between the *bao* architecture and the *tulou* architecture). *Zhongguo Mingcheng* (Chinese Famous Cities) 2012 (4).

Dai, Z. (2014). Fujian gucunluo baohu de kunhuo yu sikao (Doubting the protection of Fujian ancient villages). *Nanfang Jianzhu* (South Architectures) 2014 (4).

Demographic Record of the Qujiang Village (including Hekeng). (2011). Unpublished.

Deng, C. (2016). Zhongguo zheng yanjiu wenwu baohu buchang banfa, huanjie wenwu baohu yali (China is now probing a way to compensate the heritage stakeholders and mitigate the pressures on heritage). *CRI online*. April 1st, 2016.

Di Giovine, M. (2009). *The heritage-scape*. Lanham: Lexington Books.

Dong, Y.(2012). Qingdai guangxi gefu liangshi muchan liang chayi kao (A study on the difference of acre yields among the rural areas of the Qing dynasty Guangxi prefectures). *Leshan Shifan Xueyuan Xuebao* (Journal of Leshan Normal University) *27* (1).

Duane, T. P. (1999). *Shaping the Sierra: Nature, Culture, and Conflict in the Changing West.* University of California Press.

Duerken, C. J. (Ed.) (1983). *A Handbook on Historic Preservation Law*. Washington D.C.: Conservation Foundation: National Center for Preservation Law.

Dellios, Paulette (2002). The museumification of the village: cultural subversion in the 21st Century. Culture Mandala: The Bulletin of the Centre for East-West Cultural and Economic Studies: Vol. 5: Iss. 1, Article 4.

Eastern China Area Command of the P.R.C. Army. (1952). The *Investigation of the Rural Areas of Fujian Province* in the Series of Reports on the Rural Economy in Eastern China, restricted data.

Emerick, K. (2003). Use, value and significance in heritage management. In Layton, Stone, Thomas (Eds.): *Destruction and conservation of cultural property*. London.

Fabian, J. (1983). *Time and the Other— How Anthropology Makes Its Object*. Columbia University Press.

Fang, S. (Song dynasty). (1983). *Bozhai bian*. Zhonghua Book Company.

Faure, D. (2005). *China and Capitalism: a History of Business Enterprise in Modern China*. Hong Kong University Press

Fletcher, R. (2007). *The Limit of Settlement Growth*. Cambridge University Press.

Freedman, M. (1966) *Chinese Lineage and Society: Fukien and Kwangtung*. London.

Freedman, M. (1958). *Lineage Organization in Southeastern China*. London.

Fujian People's Congress. (2011). *Fujiansheng di shiyijie Renda changweihui di ershisan ci huiyi jiyao* (The Meeting Notes of the 23rd Conference of the Standing Committee of the Provincial People's Congress, May 2011). Fujian Renda Legal Committee.

Fujian Provincial Government. (2011). *Fujian Tulou Shijie Wenhua Yichan Baohu Tiaoli* (Regulations on the Protection of the Tulou Buildings on the World Heritage List). http://baike.baidu.com/subview/6614408/6735540.htm.

Fujian Tulou Compilation Group. (2007). *Fujian Tulou*. The Encyclopedia Publishing House.

Gathercole, P. (1994). Introduction. In Gathercole, P. and Lowenthal, D. (Eds.) *The Politics of the Past*. Routledge.

Ge, J. (1991). *Zhongguo Renkou Fazhanshi* (A History of Chinese Demographic Development). Fujian Press.

Gobster, P. H. (2007). Unban park restoration and the 'Museumfication' of Nature. *Nature and Culture 2* (2). Autumn 2007: 95-114 © Berghahn Journals doi: 10:3167/nc2007.020201.

Government of Fujian Province. *Fujiansheng Binzang Gaige Shiyiwu Guihua* (The 2001-2005 Plan for Funeral and Internment Reform of Fujian Province), issued in January 2001.

Gu, Y. (Qing dynasty). (2014). Tianxia junguo libing shu (A Statement of the Advantages and Disadvantages of the Administrative Management in Prefectures and Counties of the Chinese Empire). In *The Complete Works of Gu Yanwu*. Shanghai Classics Publishing House.

Graburn, N. (2016). Reconstructing Tradition: Tourism and Modernity in China and Japan (unpublished manuscript).

Guo, X. (2011). *Xi'an Daminggong Guojia Yizhi Gongyuan Yanjiu* (A study on the National Daming Palace Archaeological Site Park in Xi'an). M.A. thesis, Graduate School, China Academy of Social Sciences, unpublished.

Guo, Z. (2007). Kejiaren yu Minnanren shuangyuqu shequn guanxi de lishi kaocha. (The bilingual belt in the contact region between the Hakka and the Minnan). In Zhou (Ed.) *Duoxueke Shiye zhong de Kejia Wenhua* (The Hakka Culture in the Perspective of Multidisciplinary Research). The Fujian People's Publishing House.

Hall, S. (1999). Whose heritage? Un-settling 'the heritage', Re-imagining the Post-nation. http://www.tandfonline.com/doi/abs/10.1080/09528829908576818.

Ho, B. (1959). *Studies on the Population of China, 1368-1953*. Harvard University Press. Hodder, I. (2001). *Reading the Past: Current Approaches to Interpretation in Archaeology*. Cambridge University.

Hobsbawm, E. J. and Ranger, T. O. (1983). *The Invention of Tradition*. Cambridge University Press.

Hong, L. (Qing dynasty). (1995). Yiyan, shengji (Heart stories, subsistence) in *Juanshige Wen Jiaji* (Juanshi Hall Anthology Volume One). Shanghai Classics Publishing House.

Hou, L., et al. (2009). Zhongguo nongcun jiceng zhengfu zhineng de shizheng fenxi (A study on the roles of local governments in rural China). *Jingji Shehui Bijiao Yanjiu* (Comparative Economic & Social Systems), vol. 3.

Hu, C. (2014). Wenhua quanli shiye xia de wenhua yichan quan chutan (A study on cultural heritage rights in the perspective of cultural rights conflicts). *Shenyang Gongye Daxue Xuebao* (Journal of Shenyang Industrial University) (1).

Hu, Z. et al. (Qing dynasty). (1987). *Jinjiang Xianzhi* (Jinjiang County Gazetteer). Quanzhou: Quanzhoushi Lichengqu Difangzhi Bianzuan Weiyuanhui (Gazetteer Compilation Committee of Licheng District, Quanzhou City).

Huadong Junzheng Weiyuanhui Tudi Gaige Weiyuanhui (Land Property Reformation Group of the Military and Political Committee of East China) (Ed.). (1952). *Fujiansheng Nongcun Diaocha* (An Investigation of the Rural Areas of Fujian Province). Unpublished.

Huang Genealogy Compilation Group. (2011). *Huangshi Zupu* (The Genealogy of the Huang Lineage at Shangbanliao). Unpublished.

Huang, H. (1988). Fujian yuanlou kao (A Study on Fujian circular tulou buildings), *Jianzhu Xuebao* (Architectural Journal) 1988 (9).

Huang, H. (2002). Fujian tulou. *Zhongguo Lishi Wenwu* (Chinese History and Cultural Relics). 2002 (7). Huang, H. (2009). *Fujian Tulou*. SDX Joint Publishing Company.

Huang, H. and Chen, L. (2012). *Fujian Tulou Jianzhu* (On Tulou Architecture). Fujian Science and Technologies Press.

Huang, R. (Ming dynasty). *Hegan ji* (River Bank Records). Taipei: The fourth year of the Tianqi reign era of the Ming dynasty, photocopy edition.

Huang, R. (Qing dynasty). (1964). Quanzhou fuzhi, or Quanzhou Prefecture Gazetteer. Tainan: Lai Quanyuan photocopy edition.

Hugh, B. (1979). *Chinese Family and Kinship*. London: Macmillan.

Huxtable, A.L. (1997). *The Unreal America: Architecture and Illusion*. The New Press.

ICCROM (2009). Position paper. In Oliver Martin and Giovanna Piatti (Ed.) World Heritage and *Buffer Zones: International Expert Meeting on World Heritage and Buffer Zones Davos, Switzerland 11– 14 March 2008*. World Heritage Papers 25. World Heritage Committee.

ICCROM. (2016). *Promoting People-Centered Approaches to Conservation: Living Heritage*. http://www.iccrom.org/priority-areas/living-heritage/.

Ingold, T. (2000). *The Perception of the Environment: Essays on Livelihood, Dwelling and Skill*. London: Routledge.

Ingold, T. (2011). Being Alive: *Essays on Movement, Knowledge and Description*. Routledge, London.

Institute of Archaeology CASS and Architecture School of Tsinghua University. (2013). *Qinshihuang's Mausoleum National Archaeological Park Planning*. Approved by the SACH in 2014.

Intellectual Right Research Center of the Chinese Academy of Social Sciences. (2012). *A Study on the Protection of Intangible Heritage*. Intellectual Right Press.

International Expert Workshop on Integrity and Authenticity of World Heritage Cultural Landscapes, 11-12 December 2007, Aranjuez, Spain. http://whc.unesco.org/uploads/events/documents/event-450-1.pdf.

Jiang, T., and Su, J. (2007). Yongding yanye yu tulou (Tobacco business and Yongding tulou buildings). In Zhou (Ed.) *Duoxueke Shiye zhong de Kejia Wenhua* (The Hakka Culture in the Perspective of Multidisciplinary Research). The Fujian People's Publishing House.

Kegan & Paul. Seamon, D. and Sowers, J. (2008). Place and Placelessness, Edward Relph. In Hubbard, P., Kitchen, R. and Vallentine, G. (Eds.) *Key Texts in Human Geography*. London: Sage.

Keesing, R.M. (1976). *Cultural Anthropology: A Contemporary Perspective*. New York: Holt, Rinehart and Winston.

King, T. F. (2013). *A Companion of Cultural Resource Management*. Wiley-Blackwell. King, T.F. (2004). *Cultural Resource: Law and Practice*. New York: Altamira Press.

Kobayashi, H. (2013). Kejia jianzhu yanjiu yu hou xiandai renleixue shijiao (Hakka architecture and anthropological viewpoints). In Hironao, K. (Ed.) *Riben Kejia Yanjiu de Shijiao yu Fangfa* (The Perspective and Methods of Hakka Studies in Japan). Social Sciences Academic Press.

Kolb, D. (2007). *Sprawling Places*. University of Georgia Press.

Kolen, J. (1995). Recreating (in) nature, visiting history. Second thoughts on landscape reserves and their role in the preservation and experience of the historic environment. *Archaeological Dialogues*, 2, pp.127–159.

Kong, Y. (2000). *An Exploration in the Indonesian and Malaysian Cultures*. Hong Kong: South Island Press.

Kuranda, K. M. (2011). Studying and evaluating the built environment. In King, T.F. (ed.) A Companion to Cultural Resource Management. Wiley-Blackwell.

Lagerwey, J. (Lao Gewen) and Faure, D. (Ke Dawei) (2014). *Zhongguo Xiangcun yu Xuzhen Shensheng Kongjian de Jiangou* (Chinese Market Towns and the Construction of Religious Spaces inside Them). Social Sciences Academic Press.

Leng, J. 2007. Luo Xianglin Kejia yuanliu guan de zairenshi (Rethinking on Luo Xianglin's view about the origin of the Hakka people). *Jiaying Xueyuan Xuebao* (Journal of Jiaying University) vol. 25.

Li, C., and Jia, H. (2008). *Zhongguo Gudai Kanyu* (The Chinese Ancient Kanyu), Jiuzhou Publishing House. Li, H. (2013). *Fujian Tulou Jianzhu Yangshi yu Renju Shenghuo Fangshi Eryuan Jiegou Yanjiu* (Building Structures and Lifestyles Represented in Fujian Tulou Buildings). Master dissertation. Hunan Normal University.

Li, Q., Luo, D., He, C. and Chen, Z. (2010). *Fujian Minju* (Fujian Vernacular Buildings), Chinese Vernacular Architectures Series, Tsinghua University Press. Licciardi and Amirtahmasebi (2012). (Eds.) *The Economics of Uniqueness: Investing in Historic City Cores and Cultural Heritage Assets for Sustainable Development*. Urban Development series. World Bank.

Li, S. (Qing dynasty). (2012). *Baozhai ji* (A Biography of Earthen Walls). In Li (Ed.) *Ninghua Xianzhi* (Ninghua Gazetteer). The Fujian People's Publishing House.

Lin, F., and Fan, Z. (2008). *Minnan Wenhua Shulun* (On Southern Fujian Cultures). Beijing: Chinese Social Sciences Press.

Lin, J. (1995). *Tulou yu Zhongguo Chuantong Wenhua* (Tulou and Traditional Chinese Culture). Shanghai People's Press.

Lin, J. (2010). The genealogies collected at Zhangzhou Prefecture and the origin of the local people. In Chen (Ed.) *Huanan Kejia Zuqun Zhuixun yu Kejia Yinxiang* (In Search for the Hakka Images in Southern China). Huangshan Publishing House.

Lin, M. (2006). *Sichou Zhilu Kaogu Shiwujiang* (The Fifteen Seminars on the Silk Roads of China). Peking University Press.

Lin, X. (Qing dynasty). (2011). Yanhai diaobao shuo (A Summary of the Fortifications in the Coastal Areas). In the Compilation Group (Ed.) *Zhongguo Haijiang Shi Wenxian Chubian* (A Preliminary Collection of Official Documents on China's Coastal Defense). Intellectual Right Press.

Lin, X. (Qing dynasty). Bingfang zonglun (An anthology on the principles of military defense). *Zhangzhou Fuzhi* (Zhangzhou Prefecture Gazetteer) vol.7. 1965. Tainan: Zhu Shangyang photocopy edition.

Li, X. and Kuang, M. (2011). Zhongguoshi shenyi beihou de sikao (Several thoughts on the Chinese-style World Heritage nomination). *Journal of Southwest Agricultural University* (Social Sciences Edition), vol. 6.

Lowenthal, D. (1966). The American Way of History. *Columbia University Forum* 9, 27—33.

Luo, Q. et al. (Ming dynasty). (1965). *Zhangzhou Fuzhi* (Zhangzhou Prefecture Gazetteer). Tainan: Zhu Shangyang photocopy edition.

Luo, X. (1992). *Kejia Yanjiu Daolun* (A Preliminary Study on the Hakka). Shanghai Wenyi Publishing House.

Lü, Z. et al. (2006). The Fujian Tulous Protection and Management Plan. Tsinghua University.

Ma, H. (Ming dynasty). (2005). *Yingya Shenglan* (Marvelous Travels to the Corners of the Seas). The Ocean Publishing House.

Marshall, J. (1923). *Conservation Manual*. Superintendent Government Printing, Calcutta, India.

McCannell, D. (1973). Staged Authenticity: Arrangements of Social Space in Tourist Settings. *American Journal of Sociology* 79(3): 589-603.

McClellan, A. (1999). *Inventing the Louvre: Art, Politics and the Origins of the Modern Museum in Eighteenth-Century Paris*. University of California Press.

Meng, Z., 'The Fujian Tulou Buildings Trapped in the Post-inscription Dilemma, the More Well-known, the More Difficult to Protect? ', *Xinhua News*, September 24, 2013.

Meskell, L. (2015). (Ed.) *Global Heritage: A Reader*. Wiley-Blackwell.

Mingshenzong shilu, Wanli sanshinian (Chronicles of the Ming Dynasty, Shenzong Emperor, the Thirty-first Year of the Wanli Reign Era). In Zhao, Q. (Ed.) *Mingshilu Beijing Shiliao*. Beijing Classics Publishing House.

Mingshenzong shilu, Wanli sishinian, (The Chronicles of the Ming Dynasty, Shenzong Emperor, the forty-first Year of the Wanli Reign Era). In Zhao, Q. (Ed.) *Mingshilu Beijing Shiliao*. Beijing Classics Publishing House.

Mürner, J. (2009). Preface. In Oliver Martin and Giovanna Piatti (Ed.) *World Heritage and Buffer Zones: International Expert Meeting on World Heritage and Buffer Zones Davos, Switzerland 11– 14 March 2008*. World Heritage Papers 25. World Heritage Committee.

Nara Document on Authenticity.1994. http://wenku.baidu.com/link?url=vex1yBfJwJO5XpNYiJCWSU5AM1qBzt3TQeOMaONdmrrRXyv_Qr4baGQ8J4M6d-KwIMxgMt36sMlyD6vsbO5O-41bhBzLeBazE4HM48OZBvi.

National Congress (2002). *Zhonghua Renmin Gongheguo Nongcun Tudi Chengbaofa* (Law of Land Contract in Rural Areas of the People's Republic of China). China Laws Publishing House.

National Congress. (2007). *Zhonghua Renmin Gongheguo Chengxiang Guihuafa* (Urban and Rural Planning Law of the People's Republic of China). China Laws Publishing House.

Nanjing County Government. (1984). *Nanjing Xian Diming Lu* (An Atlas of Nanjing County). Unpublished. Nanjing County Government. (2006). *The Regulations on Fujian Tulou Buildings Protection in Preparation for the WHL Application in 2007*. http://www.fjnj.gov.cn/xxgk.asp?id=11.

Nanjing County Government. (2007). *The Notice on the Decision to Establish the Nanjing County Committee for Tulou Buildings Management 2007*. http://www.fjnj.gov.cn/xxgk.asp?id=11.

Nanjing Tulou Guanli Weiyuanhui. 2007. *Hekeng Tulou Dashi Ji* (The Big Events in the History of Hekeng Tulou Buildings). Unpublished.

National People's Congress. (2013). *Zhonghua Renmin Gongheguo Wenwu Baohufa* (The Cultural Heritage Law of the People's Republic of China) *(1982)*. China Laws Publishing House.

National Committee of Development and Reform (Ed.) (2014). *Quanguo ji Gediqu Zhuti Gongnengqu Guihua* (the Primary Plans for National and Provincial Function Zoning). Renmin Publishing House.

Needham, J. (1971). *Science and civilization in China V4*. Cambridge University Press.

Oakes, T. (2012). Heritage as Improvement: Cultural Display and Contested Governance in Rural China. *Modern China* 39 (4) 380– 407.

Operational Guidelines for the Implementation of the World Heritage Convention (WHC. 13/01 July 2013). http://whc.unesco.org/en/guidelines/.

Oxfeld, E. (2010). *Drink Water, but Remember the Source: Moral Discourse in a Chinese Village*. University of California Press.

Paranavitana, S. (1945). *Administrative Report of the Department of Archaeology 1940-45*. Colombo: Government Publication Bureau.

People's Congress. (2013). *Zhonghua Renmin Gongheguo Tudi Guanlifa* (Law on Land Management of the People's Republic of China). China Laws Publishing House.

Philippot, P. (1996). Restoration from the Perspective of Humanities in Historical and Philosophical Issues. In Stanley-Price, Tally and Vaccaro (Eds.), *Reading in the Conservation of Cultural Heritage*: The Getty Conservation Institute, Los Angeles.

Pieke, F. N. (2003). The genealogical mentality in modern China. *The Journal of Asian Studies* 62 (1): 101-128 (2003).

Rapoport, A. (1969). *House Form and Culture*. Prentice Hall.

Rapoport, A. (1990). *The Meaning of the Built Environment: A Nonverbal Communication Approach*. University of Arizona Press.

Relph, E.C. (1976). *Place and Placelessness: Research in Planning & Design*. Routledge.

Ross, M. (1996). *Planning and the Heritage: Policy and Procedures*. Spon Press.

Rowlands, M. and Tilley, C. (2006). Monuments and memorials. In Tilley, C., Keane, W. and Kuechler-Fogden, S. (Eds.) *Handbook of Material Culture*. 500-516. London: Sage.

Roymans, et al. (2009). Landscape biography as research strategy: the case of the South Netherlands Project. In Journal of Landscape Research Group (Ed.), *Landscape Research* 34, No. 3, 337–359.

SACH (2015). *Gujianzhu Baoyang Weihu Caozuo Guicheng* (Conservation of Ancient Architecture, a Guidance). Beijing: SACH.

Sage. O'Brien and Li (2006). *Rightful Resistance in Rural China*. Cambridge University Press.

Several inquiries by the ICOMOS in 2008, date unclear, information collected from the archives of Nanjing County government in July, 2011.

Shen, D. (Qing dynasty). (1965). *Zhangzhou Fuzhi* (Zhangzhou Prefecture Gazetteer). Tainan: Zhu Shangyang photocopy edition.

Shen, L. (2010). *Nanjingxian Shuyangxiang Tianluokeng diaocha baogao* (An investigation of Tianluokeng settlement). *Xiamen University Field Survey Reports in 2010*. Unpublished.

Shepherd, R. J. and Yu, L. (2013), *Heritage, Tourism, and Governance in China, Managing the Past to Serve the Present*. Springer.

Shiqiao Zhang Genealogy Compilation Group. (1994). *Zhang Niansanlang Gong Paixia Zupu* (The Shiqiao Zhang Surname Genealogy). Nanjing County Printing House.

Shuyang Township Government. (2011). The Shuyang Township Government Announcement about the Control on Land-use and Building Forms (2011), Posters.

Silverman and Blumenfield (Eds.) (2013). *Cultural Heritage Politics in China*. New York, Springer.

Skinner, G. W. (1965). Marketing and Social Structure in Rural China. *Journal of Asian Studies*,Vol.24, No.1-3.

Smith, L. (2006). *Uses of Heritage*. London: Routledge.

Szonyi, M. (2002). *Practicing Kinship: Lineage and Descent in Late Imperial China*. Stanford University Press.

State Council and the Ministry of housing and urban-rural development department of China. (2009). *Lishi Wenhua Mingcheng, Mingzhen, Mingcun Baihu Tiaoli* (Regulations on the Preservation of the Famous Cities, Townships and Settlements) (2008). Intellectual Property Publishing House.

State Council. (2012). *Zhonghua Renmin Gongheguo Wuquan fa* (The Property Law of the People's Republic of China) *(2007)*. China Law Publishing House.

State Council. (2011). *Zhonghua Renmin Gongheguo Jicheng fa* (The Inheritance Law of the People's Republic of China) *(1985)*. China Law Publishing House.

State Council and the Ministry of housing and urban-rural development department of China. (2009). *Lishi Wenhua Mingcheng, Mingzhen, Mingcun Baohu Tiaoli Shili* (Regulations on the Preservation of the Famous Cities, Townships and Settlements and Cases). Intellectual Property Publishing House.

Stein, M.(1960). *The Decline of Community: an interpretation of American Studies*. Princeton [N.J.]: Princeton University Press.

Tagami, C. (2013). Ming Qing yihou Kejia zuqun jiangou de lishixue yanjiu (A reconstruction of the formation process of Hakka folk groups since the Ming to Qing period). In Hironao, K. (Ed.) *Riben Kejia Yanjiu de Shijiao yu Fangfa* (The Perspective and Methods of Hakka Studies in Japan). Social Sciences Academic Press.

Tan, J. and Zhang, J. (2010). Fujian tulou ling shiyi zhengshu (Fujian tulou got the World Heritage certificate) . *Zhongguo Jingji Zhoukan* (China Economic Weekly). 2010, vol. 4.

Tan, K. (2008). *Fujian Kejia Tulou de Jianzhu Kongjian Yanjiu* (On the Spatial Characters of the Tulou Buildings in Fujian). Master dissertation. Nanjing Yishu Xueyuan (Nanjing Art College).

Tang, C. (2011). *Fujiansheng Lishi Wenhua Mingzhen Mingcun Baohu yu Fazhan Yanjiu* (Heritage Villages and Towns: Protection and Development). Jilin University Press.

Tang, J. (2013). Qidai shenyi guicheng, gei shenyi re jiangwen (Looking forward to the coming out of World Heritage nomination regulations, temper the enthusiasm of World Heritage application). *Guangming Daily*, September 14, 2013.

Tilley, C. (1994). *A Phenomenology of Landscape: Places, Paths, and Monuments*. Oxford, UK: Berg.

Tilley, C. (2010). *Interpreting Landscapes: Geologies, Topographies, Identities; Explorations in Landscape Phenomenology*. Left Coast Press.

Tongji University. (2006). *The Nanjing Tulou Protection and Management Plan*. Unpublished.

Tsinghua University. (2006). *The Fujian Tulou Protection and Management Plan*. Unpublished.

Tuan, Y. (1977). *Space and Place: The Perspective of Experience*. Minneapolis: University of Minnesota Press.

Turner (2009). Introduction. In Oliver Martin and Giovanna Piatti (Ed.) World Heritage and *Buffer Zones: International Expert Meeting on World Heritage and Buffer Zones Davos, Switzerland 11– 14 March 2008*. World Heritage Papers 25. World Heritage Committee.

Unnamed author. (Early Qing dynasty). Chongxiu tuzhai gaoshi (The Bulletin about Restoring the Earthen Fort) and Shenbao tuzhai gaojun wen (The Declaration of the Completion of the Earthen Fort Project). In Yang, G. and Chen, Z. (1993). *Mingqing Shidai Fujian de Tubao* (The Bao Architectures in Ming to Qing Period Fujian). Taipei: Guoxue Wenxian Guan.

Unnamed author. (Ming dynasty). Chongxiu qiantai zhi (A Biography of the Reconstruction of the Headquarters for Suppressing the Rebellions). In Xie, C. (2009). Tulou zhi gen yu tulou wenhua de jingshen (The roots and basic characters of Fujian tulou architecture). In Fujian Provincial Government (Ed.) *Zhonggong Fujian Shengwei Dangxiao Xuebao* (Academic Journal of the Communist Party School of Fujian). Fujian Provincial Government.

UNESCO Bangkok. (2009). *Aoi An Protocols: for Best Conservation Practice in Asia: Professional Guidelines for Assuring and Preserving the Authenticity of Heritage Sites in the Context of the Cultures of Asia*. Bangkok: UNESCO Bangkok.

Wang, R. (2010). Riben kaogu yizhi guanli kaocha yu sikao, canjia Lianheguo Jiaokewen zuzhi Yatai Diqu Wenhua Yanjiu Zhongxin kaogu yizhi guanli peixunban shouhuo zhaiyao (Japan's Experience in historic preservation, a summary of the ACCU Japan training course). In Institute of Archaeology CASS (Ed.) *Cultural Heritage Studies* vol.1. Science Press Beijing.

Wang, R. (2009). *Dishi Yichan Ziyuan Chuzhi de Jiben Lilun Kuangjia ji Linqiong Dishi Yichan Chuzhi Yuanze Anli Yanjiu* (Land-history Resource Management Framework and Linqong Land-history Resource Management Case Study). CASS Young Researchers Grant Report, unpublished.

Wang, R. (2003). *The Making of Forbidden City in the Republican China*. M.A. thesis, Institute of Archaeology, UCL.

Wang, R. (2010). Woguo dayizhi kaogu yu yizhi guanli zhong de yizhi benwei linian queshi (Who represents the large archaeological sites?). In Institute of Archaeology CASS (Ed.) *Cultural Heritage Studies* vol.1. Science Press Beijing.

Wang, Q. (2003). The UK's Experience in Urban Historic Preservation. M.A. thesis submitted to the Graduate School of Zhejiang University.
Wang, S. (2013). *The Politics of China's Cultural Heritage on Display - Yin Xu Archaeological Park in the Making*. PhD thesis. University College London.

Wang, X. and Wang, R. (2015). *Shierwu Dayizhi Baohu yu Liyong Pinggu* (Assessment of the Archaeological Sites Protection and Use in the Twelfth Five-year Plan Period). Approved by the SACH in 2015, unpublished.

Wang, Y. (2011). Lun wenhua yichan quan (On cultural heritage rights). *Zhongguo Renmin Daxue Xuebao* (Journal of Renmin University of China) 2011(2).

Watson, J. L. (1987). Standardizing the Gods: The Promotion of T'ien Hou (Empress of Heaven) along the South China Coast 960-1960. In Johnson, D., Nathan, A. j. and Rawski, E. S. (Eds.) *Popular Culture in Late Imperial China*. University of California Press.

Weller, R. (2006). *Discovering Nature: Globalization and Environmental Culture in China and Taiwan*. Cambridge University Press. Wolf and Huang (1980). *Marriage and Adoption in China, 1845-1945*. Stanford University Press.

World Archaeological Congress. (2011). *Archaeologies*.7, No.2, Springer.

Wu, F. (2000). Tangmo zhi Beisong de Kejia qianxi (The migrations of the Hakka people from the Tang to Northern Song period). (*Dongnan Xueshu*) Southeast Academics. 2000 (4).

Wu, H. (2006). Zheng He xia Xiyang yu Fujian (Zheng He's Big Travels and Fujian). *Zhangzhou Shifan Daxue Xuebao* (Journal of Zhangzhou Normal University) 2006(59).

Wu, Q. (2008). *Zhongguo Kejia Jianzhu Wenhua* (Chinese Hakka Architecture and Culture). Hubei Education Press.

Wu, R. (2006). Jinshinian lai guonei Kejia yuanliu yanjiu zongshu (A review of the studies on Hakka people's origin in the past decade). *Ganan Shifan Xueyuan Xuebao* (Journal of Gannan Teachers College).

Wu, S. (Ming dynasty). (1963). *Dabu Xianzhi* (The Dabu County Gazetteer). Zhongshan Library.

Xie, C. (2001). Kejia wenhua zhong de Minyue wenhua yinzi (The Minyue cultural elements in the Hakka culture). *A Symposium on Minyue Culture*. Haixia Wenyi Publishing House.

Xie, C. (2007). Tulou de laiyuan yu chengyin (The origins of the tulou buildings of Fujian and Guangdong). *Zhongguo Lishi Wenhua* (Chinese History and Cultural Relics), 2007 (1).

Xie. C. (2011). Guanyu Kejia yimin wenhua rentong de ruogan sikao (Several thoughts on the Hakka migrations and cultural identities). *The Second Symposium on the Hakka Culture, Ganzhou, Jiangxi*.

Xie, Z. (Ming dynasty). (2012). *Wuzazu*. Shanghai Classics Publishing House.

Xu, R. et al. (1967). *Tong'an Xianzhi* (Tong'an County Gazetteer). Taipei: Chongwen Publishing House.

Yan, H. (2014). World Heritage as discourse: knowledge, discipline and dissonance in Fujian tulou sites. *International Journal of Heritage Studies*. Routledge.

Ye, P. (2006). *Jumin, zhengfu he wenhua yichan baohu: Fujian tulou ge'an yanjiu* (Residents, Government, and Cultural Heritage Protection). M.A. thesis. The Chinese University of Hong Kong.

Yongding Tulou compilation group. (1990). *Yongding Tulou*. Fujian People's Press.

Yu, K., Xi, X., Li, D., Li, H., and Liu, K. (2009). Zhongguo guojia xianxing wenhua yichan wangluo goujian (The Designation of the Chinese Linear Cultural Heritage). *Renwen Dili* (Humanistic Geography) 2009 (3), 11–16.

Zhao, L. (2010). Shenyi re beihou de wenhua youlü, jiyu Xingjiaosi shijian de sikao (Worried about the World Heritage passion, the Xingjiao Temple as a case study). *Lilun Guancha* (Theoretic Observation), vol. 111.

Zhao, W. (2013). Local versus National Interests in the Promotion and Management of a Heritage Site: A Case Study from Zhejiang Province, China. In Silverman and Blumenfield (Eds.) (2013). *Cultural Heritage Politics in China*. New York, Springer.

Zhang, F. (2012). Kejia ren de sangzang xisu (The burial practice of the Hakka people). *Shenzhou Minsu* (*The Folklores of China*) 2012(1).

Zhang, H. (1993). Wan Ming Shehui de Jingji yu Renwen (The economic and humanistic conditions of the late Ming dynasty). *Zhongguo Shehui Jingji Shi Yanjiu* (Chinese Social and Economic History Research) 1993 (1).

Zhang, Q. (2007). Tulou kaifa zhong de baohu wenti yanjiu (Protection problems in developing tulou resource). *Fujian Jianzhu* (Fujian Architecture) vol. 4.

Zhang, S. and Li, W. (2014) Yichanre beihou de chanye chongdong yu jingji lunli wenti, yi zhongguo yichan ziyuan weili (The industrial passion and ethical problems behind the World Heritage nomination, to take Chinese heritage resource for example). *Fujian Forum*, vol. 4.

Zhang, X., Hu, H. and Zhang, J. (Eds.) *Blue Book of China's Culture (2008)*. Social Sciences Academic Press.

Zhao, F. (Ming dynasty). Shugao zhubao ji (The Construction of the Earthen Fort at Shugao Mountain). In Yang, G. and Chen, Z. (1993). *The Bao Architectures in the Ming to Qing Period Fujian*. Taipei: Guoxue Wenxian Guan.

Zheng, F. (1994) (recompiled). *Minguo Nanjing Xianzhi* (The Republican Period Nanjing Gazetteer). Nanjing Gazetteer Compilation Committee. Zheng, J. (2012). *Socio-political System and Vernacular Architectural Forms, a Study on Tulou in China (1958-1983)*. PhD dissertation. The Chinese University of Hong Kong.

Zheng, Z. (2009). *Ming Qing Shidai de Xiangzu yu Guojia* (Ming to Qing Period Rural Lineages and the State). Sanlian Chubanshe (SDX Joint Publishing Company).

Zheng, Z. (2012). *Ming Qing Fujian Jiazu Zuzhi yu Shehui Bianqian* (The Family Structure and Social Changes of the Ming and Qing Period Fujian Area). The Renmin University Press.

Zhongguo Guojia Wenwuju (SACH). (2007). *Zhongguo Wenwu Dituji, Fujian juan* (An Atlas of the Chinese Cultural Heritage, Fujian volume). Fujian Ditu Publishing House.

Zhou, L. (Qing dynasty). (1985). *Min Xiaoji* (A Brief Record of Fujian). Fujian People's Publishing House.

Zhou, X. (2007). *Ming Qing Minyue Bian Kejia Diqu de Shehui Jingji Bianqian* (A Socio-economic History of the Hakka Society in Southern and Western Fujian and Northeastern Guangdong). The Fujian People's Publishing House.

Zhou, Z. (1996). Kejia yuanliu yishuo (A different thought on the origin of the Hakka people). *Academic Monthly* 1996 (3).

Zhou, B. (2009). *Daminggong, Zhuorede Dayizhi* (Daming Palace, the Hot Large Site). Renmin Publishing House.

Zhuang, C. et al. (Qing dynasty). (1967). *Anxi Xianzhi* (Anxi County Gazetteer). Taipei: Anxi Tongxianghui.